APRICOT JAM

& other stories

Aleksandr Solzhenitsyn was awarded the Nobel Prize
in Literature in 1970, and his work continues to receive
international acclaim. Through his writings, particularly *The
Gulag Archipelago* and *One Day in the Life of Ivan Denisovich*,
he helped to make the world aware of the Gulag, the Soviet
Union's forced labour camp system. He was expelled from the
Soviet Union in 1974 and returned to Russia in 1994.
He died on 2 August 2008.

These stories have been translated by **Kenneth Lanz**
and **Stephan Solzhenitsyn.**

'Ranking alongside his best work'
Observer

'Explores the impact of a century of turbulence
on the lives of ordinary Russians'
Metro

'In probing the relationship between action and belief during
times of crisis, Solzhenitsyn is unsurpassed'
The Times

'The stories, collected by his son . . . provide a glimpse into
the genius of one of Russia's greatest writers'
Financial Times

Selected works by Aleksandr Solzhenitsyn

FICTION
We Never Make Mistakes: Two Short Novels
For the Good of the Cause
The First Circle
The Cancer Ward
One Day in the Life of Ivan Denisovich
Stories and Prose Poems
August 1914
The Gulag Archipelago
November 1916

PLAYS
Candle in the Wind
Prisoners: a Tragedy
Victory Celebrations: A Comedy in Four Acts
The Love-Girl and the Innocent: A Play

NON-FICTION
The Nobel Lecture on Literature
Letter to Soviet Leaders
Lenin in Zurich: Chapters
Warning to the West
Alexander Solzhenitsyn Speaks to the West
East and West
The Mortal Danger: How Misconceptions about Russia Imperil America
The Oak and the Calf: Sketches of Literary Life in the Soviet Union
Rebuilding Russia: Reflections and Tentative Proposals
Invisible Allies
The Russian Question: At the End of the Twentieth Century

APRICOT JAM

❯& *other stories*❮

ALEKSANDR SOLZHENITSYN

CANONGATE

Edinburgh · London

This edition published in 2012 by Canongate Books

www.canongate.tv

1

First published in Great Britain in 2011 by Canongate Books Ltd, 14 High Street,
Edinburgh EH1 1TE

First published in the USA in 2011 by Counterpoint, 1919 Fifth Street, Berkeley,
CA 94710

British Library Cataloguing-in-Publication Data
A catalogue record for this book is available on
request from the British Library

ISBN 978 0 85786 319 5

Typeset in Goudy by Palimpsest Book Production Ltd,
Falkirk, Stirlingshire

Printed and bound in Great Britain by Clays Ltd, St Ives plc

contents

APRICOT JAM

> & other stories

APRICOT JAM

1

M Y MIND IS all awhirl right now, and if some of the things I say ... don't seem quite right I want you to keep reading, you won't be wasting your time. I've heard that you're a famous writer. I got a little book of your articles out of the library. (I've been to school—the one in our village.) I had no time to read the whole book, but I did read a piece of it. You say that the foundation of happiness is our collectivized agriculture and that now even the most miserable peasant is riding around on his own bicycle. You say also that heroism is becoming a part of our everyday lives and that the purpose and meaning of life is labor in a communist society. To that I reply that there is queer small substance to this heroism and this labor because it comes from driving people like us nigh to we drop. I don't know where you saw all the things you write about. You also say a lot about other countries and how bad things are there and how often you noticed people looking at you with envy: Look, there's the Russian. Well, I'm also a Russian and I recommend me to you. My name is Fedya (Fyodor Ivanovich, if you like), and I want to tell you about myself.

As long as anyone can remember, our family lived in the village of Lebyazhy Usad in Kursk Province. But then they put an end to the way we thought to live. They called us kulaks because we had a house with a galvanized iron roof and four horses, three cows, and a fine orchard by the house. The first thing in the orchard was a spreading apricot tree, and there would be heaps of apricots on it every year. My younger brothers and I would climb all over that tree. Apricots were our most favorite fruit, and I never ever tasted any as good as ours. In the summer kitchen in the yard my mother would make us apricot jam, and my brothers and I just couldn't get enough of that sweet foam. Before they deported us as kulaks, they tried to make us tell them where we had hidden our goods. Otherwise, they said, we'll chop down your apricot tree. And they chopped it down.

They took our whole family and a few others besides to Belgorod in carts. There they shoved us into a church they had confiscated for a prison, and they brought people there from a lot of other villages. There was no room to lie down on the floor, and they didn't give us anything to eat, though a few folks had brought a bit of food with them. At night a train pulled into the station, and there was a deal of heaving and shoving while we were aboarding it, with guards rushing here and there and lanterns flickering. My father told me: "You, at least, can make a run for it." And I did manage to slip away through the huge crowd. The rest of my family went on into the taiga, where they were left to live as best they could, and I never heard from them again.

For me began a life filled with one pain atop the other. Where was I to go now? I couldn't go back to the village, and though this town wasn't small, there was no place for me here, and how could I ever hide out in it? Who would give me shelter in their house and risk grievous troubles? Though I was near to full grown, I did find a sojourning among a band of street kids—orphans and runaways. They had their own secret dwellings in abandoned houses and barns and sewer manholes. The police wouldn't bother with these ragged, barefoot kids because they had nowhere to put them and no means to feed them all. They were all dirty, smudgy-faced, and dressed in tatters. They would go abegging from house to house. But the quicker ones would band together, and the crowd of them would run to the market, tip over the trays, and jostle the sellers so that a few of them could pick up some goods. Another might slit a woman's purse, and another grab someone's wallet right out of his hand and disappear in a flash. Or they might rush into a dining hall, running among the tables and spitting in people's plates. Some of the people didn't manage to cover their plates. Others would stop eating. And that's all these raggedy kids needed—they'd polish off whatever they could grab. They would also rob people at the railway station, and they could warm themselves by the kettles of asphalt when the streets were being paved. But I stood out for being too healthy, not ragged enough, and I wasn't a kid anymore. I could have become the boss of the whole lot, sitting in a cozy spot and sending the others out to bring back some loot, but my heart's too soft for that.

Before long, a task force from the GPU picked me out of the gang and took me to prison. At first I didn't bewray my design—they'd picked me up, and that was that, so I spun them a few stories, but then they threatened to lock me away in a solitary cell and let me rot. I could see it was no good trying to deny it—lying is also an art and one I had not mastered, so I confessed: I was the son of a kulak. They kept me there until the beginning of winter. Then they changed their minds: Maybe they should send me away to my family, but then how could they find that family of mine they'd destroyed? I expect there was a great confusion in their paperwork. And so it was: I was to go to the town of Dergachi near Kharkov and present the local authorities with my certificate of release. The GPU people never asked how I, with ne'er a kopek to my name, was to make my way there, and all they did was make me sign a paper not to say a word to anyone about what I'd seen and heard during these months in a GPU prison, else they would put me back in jail with no investigation and no trial.

I went out of the prison gate without a clue of what to do. Where now could I take my miserable life? How to get to Dergachi? Or should I just flee in all haste, farther away this time? Then two women came up to me from a little street forenenst the prison where they must have been keeping watch: Had the GPU just let me go? They had, I replied. Had I seen such-and-such a man? He wasn't in our cell, I said, though it was more than afull with others. Then the older woman, the mother-in-law, asked if I was hungry. Living ahungered has become a habit, I said. They took me home with them. It was a damp little place in a cellar. The older woman whispered to her daughter-in-law, and she left, while the mother-in-law set about cooking three potatoes for me. I tried to refuse: "They're probably the last ones you've got." "Feeding a prisoner is the right thing to do," she said. She also put a little bottle of hemp oil on the table for me. And I have to say that I fell on those potatoes like a hungry wolf. The older woman said, "We may not have much, but at least we're not in prison, and feeding one like you is God's own command. Someday you may be able to feed one of ours." Then the young woman came back and gave me a ruble bill and two rubles in change. It's for your trip, she said, but it's all we could collect. I didn't want to take it, but the older woman shoved it in my pocket.

When I saw the food at the snack bar in the railway station my whole body ached. The minute I started eating I couldn't stop. And so I spent all the money on food. It was no matter, though—there wasn't enough for the trip anyway. That night I squeezed into the train before they could check for my ticket, but a few stations later, the ticket collector found me. Being without a ticket, I showed him my certificate of release from the GPU. He and the conductor looked at each other, and the conductor took me into his tiny room. "Any lice on you?" "Is there a prisoner who doesn't have lice?" I said. The conductor told me to crawl under a bench and to let him know when to wake me.

Dergachi left me with no good impression, but it was not my lot to live there. I reported to the local soviet, and there they registered me and told me to go immediately to the military enlistment office, though I wasn't yet of draft age. A doctor gave me a quick look-over and then handed me a little cardboard booklet with a gray stamp and the letters "T/O" on it. That meant "Logistical Support Forces." They sent me to another building, and sitting there was a man from the construction office of the Kharkov Locomotive Works. I told him that all our good clothes were taken away when my family was deported. All I had were some castoffs— a worn-out jacket and some homemade pants with the soles of my boots so cracked that I would soon be walking barefoot. He told me that this was no cause for evadement. "When you're serving on logistical support, they'll give you some decent used clothes and boots as well."

I pondered it a time. It seemed easy enough: all I had to do was to prove my age, and then my sufferings would be ended. But now they had me trapped, no one would listen to me and they sent me away. They had put up some barracks for the logistical support troops near the Locomotive Works. The walls were two layers of planks with sawdust between them. The sawdust would drop out from the gaps between the planks or where a knot had fallen out, and the wind blew through the barracks. The mattresses were filled with wood shavings and the little pillows they gave us were stuffed with straw. Each barracks held what they called a platoon of the support forces. Four thousand people or more had been collected here, and that was what they called a regiment. There was ne'er a bathhouse or laundry, and no one was given any uniform. They marched us off to work straightaway. What they told us in the support force for the Locomotive Works was: "You keep going till you drop." We dug foundation pits for three repair shops. For some reason they were built almost entirely underground so that when they were finished you could see naught but the roofs. We carried the earth in barrows, one man at each end, and walked along the whole line like a living conveyor belt. We'd march along the foundation pit, one pair after another, and as we went, each digger would toss on a spadeful of earth. A whole row of diggers would throw so much earth on your barrow that it was too heavy to carry. Still, we had to sweat and strain and learn to live with it. They were digging twenty-four hours a day so that the earth wouldn't freeze overnight, and sometimes they made people work longer shifts. It was like being in the army: reveille, lights-out, form up for work, and they'd blow a bugle just like they did in the army. The mess hall held 600 people, but they served the thousand free employees first and the 4000 in the support force later. There was no breakfast in the morning, and lunchtime didn't come until near to supper. They'd herd off our group for lunch and some other group would be eating, so we'd stand outside the mess hall stamping our feet to keep them from freezing, sometimes in a blizzard, and all this for a bit of lukewarm soup. When you came back from working the cold and into the barracks, the lice would all come right lively and we'd spend some time squashing them. And there was not a scrap of industriosity left in our lives. A fellow who wasn't used to this would fall to pieces very quickly.

Apart from the torment of the work, there were the political officers always harping on how we mustn't slacken off. In the evening, or sometimes on our day off, they'd come to the platoon and start filling our heads with all sorts of ideological gas to make us understand the essence of productive labor so that we would finish the Five-Year Plan in four years. The head of all these political officers was the commissar of the work camp, Mamaev, a fellow who wore a badge with the words "Member of the All-Russian Central Executive Committee" and three bars on his collar tabs.

There were also some sons of NEP-men among the workers. They had arrived with big suitcases and were warmly dressed and well seen with food parcels from home. Then there were some proper criminals, but the court had deprived them of their voting rights. There were also some local folk, and they would be let home on the days off. But most of us were sons of kulaks, almost all of us dressed in rags after we'd worn out our clothes, though the bosses seemed to pay no heed to this. There were holes through the elbows of my shirt and my jacket, one knee had been torn in my pants, and the toes of my boots were so worn that you could see my foot wraps, such was the beggar I was.

Because of that tormenting life I broke out in boils, though the camp doctor just painted them with iodine and sent me back to work. I began to weaken and was already beginning not to care what would happen to me, my own body having become bereft of feelings, as if it belonged to someone else. My hair grew out, I stopped shaving.

Suddenly one evening the bugle called us out to form up. We all formed ranks on the snowy field behind the barracks. The commissar came up with his pistol on his hip, along with a few political officers and a clerk with a paper. The commissar roared out a fearsome speech telling about what was going on in the country and saying that from now on there would be no mercy for those shirking work and there would even be trials and executions. Then he began moving down the ranks pointing at people here and there while the clerk took down the man's name, company, and platoon. He also pointed at me: "This man as well." The clerk wrote it down. Then we were dismissed. That evening the platoon commander came to the barracks: "The commissar has put you down to work on your day off for malingering. I don't know who reported you. I told HQ that no one had come to me about it. No one can countermand the commissar's order. Just go to work tomorrow, and we'll get you the next day off, on the quiet."

This was in February. A powerful blizzard blew in that night, then it rained, but by morning frost had set in. That morning I wrapped some rags around my feet and went to work. Eleven of us were sent to work in the timber yard. There was a stack of long, thin poles there, and we were ordered to shift it to a different spot about forty meters away. "If you finish the job early you can go back to the barracks, if you don't you'll be working into the night." I said not a word because I was well past caring. The others, though, were all sons of NEP-men, city kids, well fed and warmly dressed. They made out that since this was a day off, they weren't going to do any work. A platoon commander, not my own, went off to report this to HQ, but it was some distance away. There was only one path that had been trodden down across the snowy field, and it was no easy job to navigate it.

In my rags and tatters, the icy wind was blowing right through me. "Listen, boys," I said, "you do what you please, but if I don't go to work I'll soon freeze." One smart fellow jumped up and said: "You're a provocateur! You're undermining our solidarity." "You swap me your clothes for mine and I won't work," I told him. Then the others spoke up: "Let him be. Let him work if he likes. When the platoon commander comes back he'll think we've all been working." I picked up a stake and pried up the top layer of the frozen logs. I set them up to make a ramp and began rolling the poles down it. They were frozen and rolled down nicely. I went on working and even got myself warm.

Suddenly I heard a shout and some strong cursing coming from the other end of the yard. It was the commissar, who had sneaked up from behind using a roundabout way; plowing along behind him were the platoon commander and some people from HQ. The lads were expecting them by the path and hadn't seen them coming.

The commissar had drawn his pistol and was waving it around, kicking up a row and cursing: "I'll have you all arrested, you bourgeois scum! Off to the guardhouse! You're going on trial!" And they were herded off. To me he said, "Why are you looking like such a beggar?" "I'm the son of a kulak, Citizen Commissar." He poked at my bare knee with his black leather glove: "What's the matter, don't you have any proper underwear?"

"I do, Citizen Commissar, but only one pair. There's nowhere to wash clothes, and my underwear's dirty. Wearing it all the time makes my whole body ache. My undershirt is as stiff as rubber. So I bury my underwear in the snow by the barracks for a day to disinfect it and then I put it on again for the night." "Have you got a blanket?" "No, Citizen Commissar." "Well, I'm giving you three days' rest."

They issued me a blanket, two pairs of long underwear, some worn, padded pants and new boots with wooden soles that didn't bend—it was hard to walk over icy places in them.

But I'd already suffered so much, and I was covered with boils as well. A few days later, I fell down in a faint at work. When I came to, I was in the city hospital, and I'm writing you from there. The doctor took me to the boss's office: "This man is so exhausted and emaciated that if we can't improve his living conditions, I can guarantee he'll die within two weeks." The boss just said, "You know we have no room for patients like him."

But they still haven't released me. And so I'm explaining my situation to you—who else can I write to? I have no family, no support from anyone, and I've got no way to set myself right on my own. I'm a prisoner here, near hand to dying and trapped in a life that brings one hurt after the other. Would it cost too much for you to send me a food parcel? Please take pity on me . . .

2

VASILY KIPRIANOVICH, A professor of cinema studies, had been invited to advise a famous Writer on types of screenplays and techniques used in writing them. The Writer, evidently, was considering writing something in this genre and wanted to borrow from someone else's experience. The professor was flattered by the invitation, and one sunny day, in an excellent mood, he set off on a Moscow suburban train. He was well prepared to make an impression on the Writer with his knowledge of the latest developments in writing for the screen, and he was curious to see the Writer's well-appointed dacha, a house even equipped for year-round living. (He himself dreamed of having at least a small summer place, but his earnings were still insufficient for that; he had to save his family from Moscow's summer heat by renting a tiny place somewhere as distant as Tarusa, 130 kilometers away. In these times of food shortages everywhere, he would have to take with him suitcases and baskets of sugar, tea, pastries, smoked sausage, and brisket purchased from Yeliseev's.)

In his heart of hearts, Vasily Kiprianovich had little respect for this Writer; he had a huge talent, to be sure, and weighty, meaty turns of phrase, but what a cynic he was! Apart from his novels, tales, and a dozen or more plays—weak things though they were (he also had some silly farces in which abandoned elderly ladies recovered their lost youth)—he managed to keep churning out newspaper articles, each one of them filled with lies. When he spoke in public, as he did quite frequently, he displayed an amazing panache in extemporizing—eloquently and smoothly—the propaganda demanded of him, but always in his own distinctively individual manner. One could imagine that he wrote his newspaper articles in the same way: someone from the Central Committee would phone him, and within half an hour he would be dictating a passionate article over the telephone. It might be an open letter to the workers of America: What lies were spreading there about forced labor in timber cutting in the USSR? Or he would roar like a lion: "Set free our black comrades!" (Eight American Negroes had been condemned to death for murders.) Then there were his fantasies: we will grow apricots under the open sky in Leningrad and Abyssinian wheat in the marshes of Karelia. He was always being allowed to travel in Europe, and he wrote of various abominations in Berlin and Paris, always with convincing details. His trip into industrial London was boldly entitled "Orpheus in the Underworld." (Vasily Kiprianovich could only dream of being allowed a week's trip into any such hell-on-earth.) The Writer might publish an article entitled "I Call Upon You to Hate!" And he often replied to questions from the newspapers with the same obviously insincere intellectual poverty. He wrote on a wealth of literary topics, always treating them in terms of the Marxist view of history, something that was his elixir of life. We writers, he might say, now know less than the upper level of the working intelligentsia. But then he might also say: Until now, only sabotage has prevented our literature from attaining a world-class level, while the American novelists are no better than the pickpockets of an obsolescent culture.

Still, when you think seriously about it, is there anyone today who isn't something of a son of a bitch? All ideology and all art are based on that. Vasily Kiprianovich had made similar comments in his lectures—what else could you do? Particularly if you had even one little dark spot in your background. The Writer, in fact, had a very large dark spot, one known to everyone: he had made a major blunder during the Civil War when he emigrated and published some anti-Soviet things over there, but he came to his senses in time and then worked energetically to earn the right to return to the USSR. Vasily Kiprianovich's own dark spot had almost been rubbed clean, though a little stain remained: he came from the Don region. He was able to cover it up when he filled out some questionnaire, though he had never had any connections with the White Guardists and was even a sincere liberal (and his father, in tsarist times, had also been a liberal, though he was a judge). Still, the very word "Don" was enough to frighten people. And so he could understand the Writer in political terms but not in esthetic terms: How could a man with such talent keep pounding with his sledgehammer and doing it in such inspired language, as if carried away in a rush of sincerity?

The Writer's dacha was surrounded by a tall wooden fence painted dark green, unobtrusive among the natural greenery; the dacha itself, set well back on the property, could not be seen above the fence. Vasily

Kiprianovich rang the bell at the gate. After a time, it was opened by a watchman, a robust old fellow with a magnificent, forked, graying beard who might have stepped from some nineteenth-century painting (wherever could you find someone like that?). He had been informed of the guest and led him along a sandy path past the flowerbeds filled with red, white, and yellow roses. A little farther back was a dense grove of pines with bronze trunks and towering crowns. Deeper into the grounds were some dark spruce with a garden bench beneath them.

The air was scented with pine resin. There was absolute silence. Yes, this is the way to live! (And people say that he also has an intricately decorated old mansion in Tsarskoe Selo.)

The Writer himself descended the staircase from the second floor into the hallway. He was very gracious, and from his first words and gestures he showed cordiality—a particular Russian, expansive cordiality without the least affectation. He was not yet fat but had a very fleshy, broad body with a large face and large ears. The buttonhole of his jacket carried the badge of a member of the Central Executive Committee.

This was a man who, after marking the passing of his fiftieth year with a lavish party, had obviously tasted enough success and fame and behaved with an almost aristocratic simplicity. He led Vasily Kiprianovich up to his spacious, sunlit office. The stove with its large tiles must give off a lot of heat, and it would be cozy here in winter, looking out on the snowy forest. The huge oak desk was not stacked with books and papers; it held a massive writing set—a model of the Kremlin, evidently one of his birthday presents. On a pull-out shelf sat an uncovered typewriter with a sheet of paper in it. (The Writer explained that he always composed his work directly on the typewriter, without any preliminary manuscript. It was odd that given his massive body, his voice was a reedy tenor.)

They sat in armchairs by a small, round table. An open veranda could be seen through the broad glass door. The Writer smoked a pipe filled with expensive, fragrant tobacco. His fair, sleek hair had not yet turned gray, though he had a touch of gray at his temples and a large bald spot. His thick brows seemed to weigh down on his eyes, and the lines of his jowls and chin had lost their sharpness and were beginning to sag.

Their conversation went on in a very friendly though serious manner. The Writer took no notes, and he had a quick grasp of the subject and asked germane and intelligent questions.

Vasily Kiprianovich spoke of the various ways a screenplay could be written: the concise synopsis that allowed the director complete freedom; the emotional, whose main aim was merely to instill a mood in the director and cinematographer; the detailed scenic type in which the writer sets out each scene and even specifies whether the scenes should change using long takes or montage. It was obvious that the Writer was taking this all in and that he particularly liked the idea that a screenplay must always be coordinated with *gesture*.

"Absolutely true!" he agreed, with passion. "That's virtually the most important thing. In fact, I believe that *every* sentence has a gesture to go with it, and sometimes even every word. A person is constantly gesturing— if not physically, then always emotionally. And above all we must find gestures appropriate to whatever social environment we are depicting."

It was already getting on to five o'clock, and the Writer invited the professor to go downstairs for tea. They went back to the ground floor and passed through the living room, filled with antique furniture—a fretwork sofa, some armchairs, a mirror with an intricately modeled frame. There were copies of Serov's *Girl with Peaches* and a Monet landscape with a pink-sailed boat; just as upstairs, there was a huge, white-tiled stove. Obviously they did not spare the firewood in this house.

The Writer led him around the corner from the dining room, not failing to boast artlessly about a remarkable new appliance—an electric refrigerator he had brought from Paris.

At this point—had he known that this was the time for sitting and chatting?—his dacha neighbor, Yefim Martynovich, dropped in. Alongside the massive thoroughbred body of the Writer, he seemed a puny figure, little more than a gnome, yet he behaved with no less importance than the master of the house.

He was about forty, somewhat younger than Vasily Kiprianovich, but what a success he had made of himself! His name was pronounced with awe in Soviet literature, though only until recently and not at the moment. A militant Marxist critic, he was famous for his devastating attacks on some writers and his fulsome praise of others. In all cases he demanded a militant class-based approach from writers, and he was having some success in achieving it. He was everywhere: he taught in the Institute of Red Professors, headed the literary department in the State Publishing House (in other words, it was he who determined which writers would be published and which would not), and he was also the head of the Fine Art Publishing House as well as the editor of two literary journals. In short, he held the reins of the whole of literature in his hands, and it would be dangerous to have him as an enemy. When he was in RAPP, the Russian Association of Proletarian Writers, he was responsible for the rout of Voronsky's group and the school of Pereverzev; and after the recent dissolution of RAPP he had taken up with lightning speed "the consolidation of communist forces on the literary front." All these things he did with such great success that now he too had acquired a fine dacha, right next door and very likely not a bit worse than this one.

Vasily Kiprianovich had heard a great deal about him, of course, and was now seeing him for the first time. He had an unintelligent face, eyes that were very alert, and hair with a touch of red in it. Had you met such a person socially, even one wearing a good suit, you would never have guessed that he was a Servant of the Muses but would take him for a successful manager of a manufactured goods depot or, at best, the chief accountant of a complex of enterprises. Dealing with him, however, was like handling a newly sharpened razor. Their paths had not crossed, though one never knew what the future might hold, and Vasily Kiprianovich found it useful to meet the Critic in the home of the Writer, especially when the latter was looking at him favorably.

The Writer's wife was not at home, but on the ground floor veranda, facing the rays of the late afternoon sun; tea had already been served by an elderly maid with a peasant's face. They sat down in comfortable wicker chairs. Some soft white bread had already been sliced for the butter and cheese, while there were dishes with two types of pastry and two types of jam—cherry and apricot.

There was no breeze. The cap-like crowns of the pine trees towered high above their bronze trunks, and every needle on their branches was motionless. As before, not a sound came from anywhere.

The pleasant aroma of pine resin, the peace, and the silence all accentuated their total isolation from the world outside.

Fresh tea, deep brick red in color, was poured into glasses with filigree holders. The conversation, naturally, turned to literary topics.

"Ah, yes," sighed the Writer, admitting even his imperfections. "How we ought to write! How powerfully we ought to write! We are given the esteem of all the people, we are given the attention of the party, the government, and the particular attention of Comrade Stalin himself . . ."

Was this last little phrase really appropriate for a tea table? But no, it had now become the fashion to speak this way in private gatherings. And the Writer, as everyone could see, was in Stalin's personal favor, to say nothing of his close relationship with Gorky.

"Creating an art of world significance—that is the task of the writer today. The world is waiting for examples, for architectonics from our literature."

His arms, not powerful and even a bit plump but still flexible and free of rheumatism in the hands and fingers, extended to show the scale on which he was prepared to work. (Surely he was not hungry? Yet he had fallen upon the sandwiches almost at once, one after another. People told of how he could give entire lectures, off the cuff, on the kulebyaka or the sturgeon . . .)

The Critic, of course, had to have his say on a topic like this!

"Indeed, they are expecting monumental realism from us. This is an entirely new type and genre of art, the epic of a classless society—literature with a positive hero."

God knows, Vasily Kiprianovich was of two minds. Even though this sounded crude and clumsy, it might well be what was needed. Though this seemed like nonsense, the literature of the past truly could not be brought back. It was a fact that an entirely new epoch was unfolding in a process that was evidently irreversible.

Here on this veranda, at this table, in this warm and peaceful light playing in the vivid colors of the jam, it certainly looked as if everything had now been settled and would go on for centuries. The common life that still lagged behind would be raised up to this level and polished by it. None of life's harshness could penetrate here; there were no days and nights of working to fulfill the Five-Year Plan, one that in fact had now been completed in four years and three months.

In any case, what was wrong with the elevated striving to create epic forms in art?

"Take the tragedy of Anna Karenina, now," said the Writer, making an expansive gesture. "That's no more than an empty spot today; it can't be the basis for anything in our art. The wheel of a locomotive can't resolve the contradictions between romantic passion and social censure."

But the Critic, that guardian who had administered so many public reprimands, now seemed to have much less of the assurance and intransigence he had displayed in his earlier articles. In fact he had none of the bold, persuasive manner of the Writer. He stood up for *How the Steel Was*

Tempered: there was no question about that; it was the high point of the new literature; it was the new epoch.

It was obvious that the Writer did not care for this Critic at all; it was simply that he was a neighbor and he could not tell him what he thought right to his face.

He did not dispute *How the Steel Was Tempered*, though he did parry by saying that not everything new shows us the way forward. Take RAPP itself, for instance: it presented itself as something entirely new, yet it turned out not to be the tribune of the broad masses and in fact was isolated from them behind a wall of dogmatism.

Now that shot hit the mark! And it seemed that it had been carefully aimed at a spot still tender and vulnerable. The Critic shrank like a mushroom near a flame. How this would have infuriated him only a year ago! But as he retreated, he could only say in his high-pitched voice: "Yet RAPP did contribute many valuable things to proletarian culture. It gave it a solidly established center."

"Nothing of the kind! Not a bit of it!" the Writer said, totally sweeping aside the Critic's remarks and almost laughing aloud at the change that had now taken place. "Those who voiced their suspicions that the RAPP leadership was edging into the ranks of the 'wreckers' weren't just making idle chatter."

Indeed! What do you think of that?

"They were trying to find some crafty means of discrediting our literature. They defamed me by calling me reactionary and bourgeois and even claiming that I had scarcely any talent. Yet the critic . . ." he paused, gazing intently at the Critic and, it seemed, considering whether to deliver a final blow. But no, he still had his humor and went on, sounding even inspired: ". . . the critic should be a *friend* to the writer. It is important to know that you have a friend like that when you write. You don't want some Robespierre in a National Convention trying to use his proscriptive gaze to penetrate every convolution of a writer's brain simply to devise a class-based label for him without caring whether you write with a pen or a piece of chalk."

The bit about Robespierre was a shot right to the head. Yes, the epoch had broken in two in quite a disgusting way, and this Writer had managed to shift from being a suspicious Fellow Traveler to someone more reliable. He now had a mysterious aura of independence about him.

Yefim Martynovich blinked his lashless eyes and shrank even more. But was he not a *friend*? He had come, after all, to inquire about the Writer's current work and his plans for things to come. The Writer, with his delightfully expansive nature, no longer bore him any malice, however. He revealed that he was now reworking the second part of his trilogy on the Civil War: "I haven't adequately shown the organizing role of the Party in it. I also have to come up with a courageous and disciplined Bolshevik to include. But how can you go against your heart? Yes, I also love the old Russia. And because of that I was slow to understand all that had happened and didn't come to terms with the October Revolution immediately. That was a serious mistake. And I spent some difficult years there in Europe."

All of this he said easily, in his tremulous tenor voice and with the captivating sincerity of a generous nature. And the strength of his solid position at the center of Soviet literature radiated from him all the more tangibly. (After all, even Gorky had made the same serious mistake by emigrating for a time.)

"And who dares speak of our writers' lack of freedom? When I write, I feel the same free sweep of a mowing peasant from one of Koltsov's poems. My hands are simply itching to get to work!"

What he said had to be believed. It came straight from his heart. Yes, what a fine fellow he was.

Even the bald spot on his venerable head shone honestly and impressively.

But one could never accept that he regarded the upper level of the working intelligentsia as better informed than he.

"Invention in literature is sometimes superior to truth. Literary characters may say things they would never have said in real life, and this can be a greater revelation than the naked truth. It can be a regular festival for art. When I write, I can comprehend my reader through my imagination, and I can see *exactly* what he needs."

He warmed to his topic and said as if addressing only Vasily Kiprianovich, and with fondness: "The *language* of a work of art is simply *everything*! Had Leo Tolstoy been able to think as clearly as Comrade Stalin he would not have tangled himself in long sentences. How can one approach the language of the common people? Even Turgenev, that Frenchman in Russian garb, and the Symbolists are simply seduced by the French syntax. I have to admit that in 1917, when I was still living the bohemian life, with an outrageous haircut though terribly shy, I had a literary crisis. I realized that, in fact, I didn't really know Russian. I didn't have a feeling for what mode of expression to use in a sentence. And do you know what set me on the right path? Studying legal documents from the seventeenth century and earlier. When an accused was being questioned and tortured, the scribes would record precisely and concisely what he said. While someone was being flogged, stretched on the rack, or burned with a hot iron, the most unadorned speech, coming from his very bowels, would burst forth from him. And this is something absolutely new! It's the language Russians have been speaking for a thousand years, but none of our writers have used it. Now this," he said, dripping some of the thick apricot jam from a teaspoon onto a small glass dish, "this very amber transparency, this surprising color and light should be present in the literary language as well."

And, indeed, every single apricot lay like a condensed fragment of sunlight in the crystal bowl. The cherry jam also had its own mysterious color, imperceptibly different from a dark claret, yet it was not the right color and could not be compared with the apricot.

"Now and again these days a letter surfaces from some reader who writes in the primordial language. I had one not long ago from a workman building a factory in Kharkov. His language doesn't follow today's rules, yet it had such compelling combinations and use of grammatical cases! I envy the writer! 'I didn't bewray my design,' 'There was no cause for evadement,' or, 'There's queer small substance to this heroism.' What do you think? Only an ear that hasn't been intimidated by book learning can come up with something like that. And his vocabulary! It makes your mouth water. 'I found myself a sojourning,' 'We sweated and strained and learned to live with it,' 'forenenst the prison,' 'I became entirely bereft of feelings.' Things like that you can't invent, even if you swallow your pen, as Nekrasov said. And if someone offers you such turns of phrase, you absolutely have to pick them up . . ."

"Are you planning to reply in the same fashion?" asked Vasily Kiprianovich.

"What can I say to him? The point isn't in the answer. The point is in discovering a language."

1994

EGO

1

EVEN BEFORE HE reached his thirties, even before the German War, Pavel Vasilyevich Ektov realized that he was a confirmed and perhaps even a natural-born activist in the rural cooperative movement, and so he never took up any of the grandiose, earth-shaking causes of the time. In order to keep true to his beliefs, he had to engage in some bitter debates on how best to remake the life around him and to resist the temptations and withstand the rebukes of the revolutionary democrats: devoting himself to social change by promoting only "small deeds" was something trivial; he was not merely squandering his energy on useless work, he was betraying the whole of humanity for the sake of a few people around him; it was cheap philanthropy that would lead to no great end. Now, they said, we have found the path to the universal salvation of humanity; now we have the actual key to achieving the ideal of happiness for all the people. And what can your petty notions of one person helping another and the simple easing of day-to-day tribulations achieve in comparison with that?

Many activists like Ektov were shamed and wounded by such reproaches and tried to justify themselves by arguing that their work was "also useful" for the general progress of humanity. But Ektov ever more stubbornly maintained that he needed no justification for helping the peasants meet their day-to-day and urgent needs and for easing their destitution by any practicable means, prosaic though such things might seem. His activities, he insisted, had nothing in common with the abstract sermonizing of village priests and the pieties drilled in by the parish schools.

Ektov had experience with all types of cooperatives and was wholeheartedly committed to them. He had spent some time in Siberia and was amazed to find butter-making cooperatives that, without any large plants, managed to feed the whole of Europe on their fragrant and delectable butter. Back in Tambov Province he spent some years energetically working in a cooperative savings bank and continued this work during the war. (At the same time, he took part in the City and Rural Zemstvo system, though he felt squeamish about its partisan politics and the personal exemption from army service that it offered.) He ran the cooperative all through the revolutionary year of 1917, and only in January of 1918, on the eve of what now was the clearly inevitable confiscation of all cooperative funds, did he insist that his credit union secretly return all deposits to the depositors.

For this Ektov would certainly have been *put away* had they made a close check on him, but the energetic Bolsheviks had their hands full. Once they did bring Ektov in to the Kazan Monastery, where the "Extraordinary Commission," the Cheka, had set themselves up, but he got by with just one hasty interrogation and managed to evade their questions. They had plenty of bigger fish to fry. One day, on the main square near this monastery, five age groups being called up to the army had assembled. Suddenly a dashing rider with a Cossack forelock galloped up on a gray horse and shouted: "Comrades! What did Lenin promise? That we wouldn't go to war anymore! So go back to your homes! We've just finished one war. Do you want to be shipped off to another? Go on back to your homes!" And the cry of this young fellow in dark gray peasant clothes was like a spark on tinder: everyone scattered this way and that, some fled the town, some went to the forests to hide as deserters, others rushed through the town to raise the revolt there—and the bosses themselves ran off. They came back a day later with Kikvidze's cavalry.

Ektov lived through the Civil War years utterly bewildered. After the cruel slaughter of some of his countrymen by other countrymen and under the iron heel of the Bolshevik dictatorship, he could find no sense of purpose in Russian life or in his own. Nothing remotely similar had ever happened in his homeland. Human life in general had lost its normal, reasoned flow: it was no longer the activity of reasonable beings; under the Bolsheviks it had become diminished and disfigured, something that moved in mysterious, roundabout ways or by cunning and ingenuity. The staunch democrat Ektov, however, never believed that a White victory and the return of the Cossack whip could be the solution either. And for two days in August 1919, when Mamontov's cavalry broke through to Tambov, he felt no sense of inner liberation or satisfaction—even though the Cheka had fled from the Kazan Monastery. (In any case, it was obvious that Mamontov's horsemen had never planned to stay for long.) Indeed, the whole of the Tambov intelligentsia thought the Bolshevik regime would be short-lived: Give them a few years and they'll collapse; Russia will come back, now as a democratic state. And even the Bolsheviks' most extreme actions stemmed not only from malice or ignorance but from the accumulated problems of three years of foreign war and the Civil War that came in its wake.

Tambov, lying in the middle of a grain-growing province, never experienced real famine in those years, but in the winters it was gripped by critical shortages, shortages that demanded its residents summon up all their bodily strength and resourcefulness in order to survive. The happy and prosperous existence of the Tambov peasantry began to break down under the onslaught of merciless incursions made into it, first by blocking detachments—units stationed here to prevent front-line troops from deserting. They simply confiscated grain and food from peasants taking it to market by road. Then came food requisitioning detachments and more troops sent to hunt down deserters. The coming of one such detachment into an utterly terrified village meant the inevitable execution of a handful of peasants or at least one or two for the edification of all the villagers. (They might also fire off a few random machine gun bursts from the steps of the district administrative office.) These detachments would always indulge in wide-scale robbery. A food requisitioning detachment would be stationed in a village for a time and would first of all demand that it be fed: "Hand over a sheep! Hand over some geese! Eggs, butter, milk, bread!" (And then it was towels, bedsheets, and boots.) The peasants would have been relieved to get off with merely that, but after a day or two of feasting and pillaging, the detachment would force a melancholy train of carts driven by those same villagers to haul away their own grain, meat, butter, honey, and sackcloth—gifts for proletarian power that never shared its salt, soap, or iron with the peasants. (A few village shops would suddenly get a shipment of ladies' silk stockings, kid gloves, or kerosene lamps without burners and without kerosene.) And so they cleaned out the granaries, one after the other, often leaving nothing for food or seed. The peasants called them "The Black Ones," whether because they came from the Devil or because there were many non-Russians among them. The provincial Commissar of Food, Goldin, raged across the whole of Tambov Province, neither sparing human lives nor caring for human misery and women's tears, things that shook even the food requisitioning detachments. The Borisoglebsk County Food Commissar, Alperovich, was not much gentler than he. (The Bolsheviks themselves chose some appropriate titles for their own: there was even the *Nachpogub* Veydner, and it took even Ektov a long time to comprehend what this word meant: Head of the Provincial Political Section, or *Nachalnik politicheskogo otdela gubernii*.)

At first the peasants couldn't believe it: What on earth was going on? Soldiers returning from the German front, from reserve regiments, or from prisoner of war camps (where they'd been given a good dose of Bolshevik propaganda) came to their villages with the news that now, at last, the time of peasant rule had come and a revolution had been made for the sake of the peasants: peasants would now be masters over the land. But what happened? The city folk sent out mobs of heathens to abuse the working peasants. They didn't sow any of their own grain, so they hanker after ours? Yet Lenin said, he who does not plow or sow, neither shall he eat!

There was another rumor that ran through the villages: They've betrayed us! They've slipped a false Lenin into the Kremlin!

For his whole life, Pavel Vasilyevich's heart had been at one with the peasants and their troubles, with their sense of life and their well-reasoned thrift (boots for going to church, bast shoes for the village, and bare feet for plowing), and now that heart ached over the devastation of the countryside: the Bolsheviks were stripping the villages bare (and every featherbrained inspector or instructor who stopped by made sure to scoop up whatever he could as well). There was a time when one could watch the leisurely return of a fine herd of several hundred cows to the village in the evening. Here and there, children with switches are separating their own cattle; a steady cloud of translucent dust, glowing in the rays of the setting sun, hangs over them; the well sweeps groan, heralding the watering that will come before the abundant milking. Such scenes of the prosperous and peaceful life in the villages were nowhere to be seen now, however. These days there were no brightly lit windows in the peasants' huts: kerosene lamps stood dark, and within there was only the faint glow from the mutton fat burning in saucers.

Meanwhile, the Civil War had ended, and the opportunity for the Tambov peasants to join the Whites had passed. Now, however, their patience had reached its limit and they were seething. In the autumn of

1919, the peasants killed the chairman of the provincial executive committee, Chichkanov, while he was making a trip around the province. The authorities responded by sending in a powerful punishment detachment (Hungarians, Latvians, Finns, Chinese—you could find all sorts in the punishment detachments); and again there were many executions.

Peasant anger continued to mount and accumulate through that winter of pillaging. In the spring, as the snow was melting, Pavel Ektov made a trip in the wagon of a peasant friend to lay in some supplies: he went from Karavaynovo to a spot he knew well, where the Mokraya Panda and the Sukhaya Panda join and then go on to flow into the Vorona. He knew the villages in that region: Grushevka, Gvozdyovka, Treskino, Kurgan, Kalugino. Grushevka, with its lush hayfields that lay right outside the village and filled it each June with the aromas of meadow grass, brome, and clover; Treskino and its peculiar church, a three-story cube, and the grand church in Nikitino, faced in bluish brown tiles and a roof of fish-scale pattern shingles; Kurgan, where there was a burial mound from Tatar times; and Kalugino, laid out in a curved line with its disorderly row of huts scattered along the bare gully of the Sukhaya Panda. And the bottomland along the winding Mokraya Panda, covered in lush grass, with the quails singing their hearts out. This was a glorious spot for village kids, for fishermen, geese and ducks—the children would play in the water, only as deep as their waists, though the cows would climb out of the same river for their daily milking. Beyond Grushevka and Gvozdyovka was a large forest, and near Nikitino, with its many orchards, there were a few wooded gullies.

That spring the peasants waited and worried, and many didn't even want to begin seeding: It's all for naught, they'll just come and take it. But how can we get by with nothing to eat? They began gathering in gangs in the woods and ravines, talking of how they might defend themselves.

It was no easy matter, though, for peasants from different villages to agree to join forces, make the decision, and then to find the right moment to cross the line into full-scale war.

Meanwhile, Goldin's food detachments kept up their pillaging of the villages, and they continued their lavish feasting when they took up quarters. (There were instances when they ordered a certain number of women be sent to them for the night, and the village would comply—what else could they do? It was better than being shot.) The detachments hunting down deserters would still make examples of those they caught by executing them. (They had called up three age groups at once, the eighteen- to twenty-year-olds. But if you joined the party, you were exempted.)

In August 1920 there was a spontaneous uprising in Kamenka, in Tambov Region: the peasants massacred the food detachment that had arrived and seized their weapons. About the same time, something similar happened in Treskino: a food detachment had called together a group of local communists outside the district administration office when suddenly a band of peasants armed with pitchforks, spades, and axes came running down the street. The detachment fired at them, but the peasants rushed over them like a wave and cut down two dozen along with some communist wives. (They also killed a small boy from the crowd. He recognized one of the rebels: "Uncle Petya, remember me?" And the man killed him so that the boy would not later give him up.) And in Grushevka they were so enraged by all the pillaging that they knocked down one of the men in the detachment and sawed through his neck as if it were a log.

It's a long and difficult task to get the Russian peasant to move, but once the pressure from the people's ferment bursts forth, it cannot be contained by the limits of reason. A crowd in bast shoes, armed with axes, oven forks, and pitchforks and driven by a righteous quest for justice, set off from Knyazhe-Bogoroditskoe in Tambov Region to "take Tambov." They were "men with pitchforks" such as had risen up in the time of the Tatars. They marched to the sound of church bells in the villages along the way, their numbers growing as they went. They advanced toward the provincial capital until, at Kuzmina Gat, the helpless crowd was cut down by machine gun fire from the outposts guarding the town. The survivors scattered.

Like fire along a line of thatched roofs, the rebellion immediately spread across the whole district; the Kirsanov and Borisoglebsk districts were ignited as well. Local communists were massacred everywhere (and the women attacked them with sickles), village soviets were destroyed, state farms and communes were broken up. Those communists and activists who survived fled into Tambov itself.

The communists from outside—well, you could understand where they came from. But how did we come to have our own homegrown ones? Pavel Vasilych had figured this out from things he picked up in the villages, and there were other facts he had known already. In the first regional and local soviet elections, the peasants still didn't realize the all-embracing power this new system would have. They imagined it would be a small thing, since now that everybody had got their freedom, what mattered was taking over the landowners' land, not the elections. And what proper peasant would drop all his farmwork to take up some elected post? So the ones who got these posts were peasants only by birth, not by the work they did. They were the troublemakers, the reckless, the lazy, the beggars, and the ones who had moved from one unskilled job to another in towns and on building sites, managing to pick up a few revolutionary slogans along the way. And then there were all those who had deserted from the army in 1917, the ones who were quick to take up pillaging. Such were the people who became village communists and activists, the ones who held the power.

All of Pavel Ektov's education and the humanitarian tradition he came from made him absolutely opposed to bloodshed. But now, particularly after this righteous march of the people at Kuzmina Gat, the relationship between those who were powerless but right and those who relentlessly wielded brute force was as obvious as the naked truth itself: the peasants could do nothing other than take up arms. (And there were still many rifles, cartridges, sabers, and grenades available, brought home from the German War or left behind after Mamontov's breakthrough. Some had been hidden, some buried.)

As a Russian populist and lover of the people, Ektov saw no alternative but to join them and do as they were doing. Still: The great Civil War had ended, and what chances were there now for a peasant uprising? There was no doubt, though, that the peasants would have few competent leaders who could guide their movement. Granted, he was just a worker for the co-op and no soldier, but he was competent and clever. He could be very useful to them in some capacity.

But then there was his wife, Polina, an inseparable part of his heart. And Marina, the little five-year-old with cornflower eyes. How could he abandon them? What trials and dangers would they face? He might well be leaving them to starve. Yes, indeed, family was the greatest worry—the source of our happiness and our weakness.

Polina was deeply alarmed, but she forced herself to be strong and blessed him on his decision: You're right . . . Yes, right . . . Go.

He left her and their daughter in their city apartment with a small supply of food and firewood for the coming winter; and she, a teacher, was earning something.

Pavel Vasilych left Tambov and set off to find what he supposed was the headquarters of the uprising.

And he found it, a small, mobile group around Aleksandr Stepanovich Antonov. He was a Kirsanov townsman by origin and, in 1905, had been an "expropriator" (meaning he robbed banks) for the SR party. (You couldn't close your eyes to that: So now you're mixed up with criminals?) He'd come back from Siberian exile in 1917, and before the Bolshevik coup was the head of the Kirsanov militia that later collected a large stock of weapons during the disarming of the Czech Legions passing through Kirsanov. In the summer of 1919, with a small body of troops, he was raiding and destroying local communist cells here and there at a time when the SRs themselves could not resolve to stand up to the Bolsheviks for fear of aiding the Whites. Now Antonov was not acting for the SRs, he was acting on his own. The provincial Cheka searched for him all through the winter of 1919—20, but they couldn't catch him. Antonov had no education to speak of and hadn't even finished the district school, but he was bold, decisive, and sharp.

In the headquarters that Antonov was forming—which could hardly be called a headquarters—there wasn't a single officer with staff experience. There was a local fellow with a good deal of natural talent, Pyotr Mikhailovich Tokmakov, from the peasant village of Inokovka-1. He had been an NCO in the tsarist army, and on the German front had risen to the rank of warrant officer and then to second lieutenant. He was a first-class soldier, but had no more than three years of parish school. There was also a wild, combative warrant officer, another former NCO, bursting with energy: this was Terenty Chernega, who had joined the Bolsheviks in 1917 and served with them for two years, even in their special forces; but after he had seen the things that were happening he went back to the side of the peasants. Another NCO and artillery man, Arseny Blagodaryov, came from the same village of Kamenka where it had all begun; he was one of the people who had begun the revolt. Later, each of these three took command of a partisan regiment. Tokmakov would eventually command a brigade of four regiments, but not one of them was even close to being able to do staff work. Antonov's adjutant wasn't a soldier at all but a teacher named Starykh who came from Kalugino on the Sukhaya Panda.

When Ektov reported to Antonov, it turned out that he was just the man to be his "chief of staff," if only because he was a competent and smart fellow who could also read a topographical map. Antonov asked his name. Strangely enough, Ektov didn't reveal himself. He began saying "Ek . . ." and then caught himself: he mustn't give his name! What came from his throat was only, "a . . . ga . . ."

Antonov heard it as "Egov."

Why not? It wasn't bad as a pseudonym. He answered clearly: "Ego. Let's keep it at that."

Well, so be it. Antonov didn't ask any more questions.

And soon everyone knew him as "Ego," and also as Pavel, only it was Pavel Timofeevich. Before long they accepted his authority as "chief of staff" (he himself was amazed), but he was barely able to establish some communications and coordinate their joint actions, while Antonov himself and his partisan leaders more often ran their detachments by their own sudden impulses, asking no one's approval and responding to the sudden changes in circumstances.

Tambov Region was not well suited for a partisan war. Like much of the province, it had little forest; it was a plain with some low hills, though there were a lot of deep gullies and ravines (*yarugi*, as called locally) that gave cover for cavalry. There was a network of dirt roads rutted by cart tracks, but the cavalry could move at speed across the plain.

And what a cavalry it was! Stirrups made of rope, saddles most often just pillows (feathers would drift out from beneath the rider as he trotted along). Some had military uniforms, some kept their peasant dress (they wore red ribbons across their hats: they were for revolution and were Reds, too, and called each other "comrade" when they didn't use their village nicknames). On the other hand, the rebels always had fresh horses since they could easily change them in the villages (though not without a lot of grumbling from the peasants: *Our* lads may be ours, but that horse is *mine* . . .) They collected Berdanka rifles here and there, along with shotguns, sawn-off rifles (they were easier to hide and almost as accurate at close range), and some Mannlicher and Gras rifles brought back from the war. At the beginning they had no more than five cartridges per rifle, but then they captured some ammunition from the food detachments and special forces and even captured a few entire arms depots. Once Antonov carried out a daring operation: he seized a whole trainload of military supplies from the Reds and hastily carried them off in wagons to the villages well back from the railway, which couldn't be secured for long.

Because there were so many rebels, however, they were still very short of weapons, even sabers, and when an alarm was given, they still came running from the villages with pitchforks. (The rebels would signal the arrival of a Bolshevik detachment by stopping the arms of the village windmill or by sending a messenger galloping out from the far end of the village to warn the neighbors.)

The joy of successful raids, and of successful withdrawals as well, amazed Ektov and greatly raised his spirits: How could they manage to do these things? They had begun with nothing, after all!

And so they lived—first for weeks, then for months: by day they would work like peasants; by night, or when the alarm was given, they would mount their horses and go off on a raid. Rebel and Soviet detachments pursued one another through the deep gullies. When the rebels were routed, they would disperse and hide their weapons—not in their own yards but in some gully.

. . . And after a battle a dead man lies, his head in the water of a brook. For hours his horse stands sadly next to its dead master . . . A wagtail bird flutters over the grasses . . .

A favorite refuge of the Antonov cavalry was the lowland along the Vorona River. There was a broad circle of clearings among the oaks, elms, aspens, and willows that seemed to have been carefully arranged there. The exhausted riders would drop from their horses to lie in the clearings grown over with meadow grass and horse sorrel; the horses would nip at the grass as they slowly wandered nearby. Only a few abandoned tracks led to the place, and beyond it lay dense and impassable woodland—low thickets of entangled bushes and dry grass in which lurked five-foot-long vipers with darkly hatchmarked backs. (One of the most inaccessible spots was in fact called Snake Bog.)

In September the rebellion broke out in Pakhotny Ugol as well, a place well north of Tambov, toward Morshansk. The year before, the communists had cobbled together a "model commune" there, but now the commune people had come to their senses and become a separate but powerful ally of the rebels.

The numbers of rebels were multiplying and, emboldened, at the beginning of October they launched an attack from the south on Kamenka to free it from the Red garrison quartered there. The Reds replied with artillery, and in their counterattack they sent in infantry along with their cavalry. The rebels dismounted and—for the first and only time—dug trenches, something that had become second nature in the German War. But this was their mistake: they could not sustain a two-day, pitched battle. They abandoned their trenches and withdrew to Tugolukovo, where there was a plentiful supply of horses. Many peasants from Tugolukovo mounted their horses and, leading another horse behind them, went off with the *partisans*.

The area of rebellion was dangerously restricted within a triangle of the rail lines between Tambov, Balashov, and Rtishchevo, and troops were garrisoned at the major stations. These rail lines had to be sabotaged at every opportunity. Antonov's forces did dash in several times to cut the lines and then use their horses to bend the rails into a bow.

The mass of the railway workers, particularly the telephone and telegraph operators, sympathized with the rebels, and some of them would hold up the transmission of instructions to the Reds, or they would lose or garble them and even pass them on to the partisans, so that the Bolsheviks

could not fully rely on their lines of communication. The railway workers in Rtishchevo District even elected a delegation to go to the rebels and
show their support, but the Chekists managed to arrest the delegates and
declared a state of emergency for the whole area.

The rebel forces continued to grow, and new partisan regiments of
1500 or 2000 men were formed one after another. There were now more
than ten regiments, and they had their own banners and Maxim and Lewis
machine guns. Former sergeants and warrant officers, veterans of the
German War, assumed command; there were also some simple peasants
who came straight from the plow. And they were good commanders.

In November, Antonov's main force advanced on Tambov itself, creating great confusion among the authorities there (they felled ancient oak
trees to block the roads into the city and sited machine guns in church bell
towers). Ektov couldn't believe it: Was it possible that he could dash into
Tambov to rescue his family? (He would take them to Serdobsk, where
Polina had a cousin. They would be safe with her.)

But no, twenty *versts* from Tambov, at Podoskley-Rozhdestvensky,
the rebels had to withdraw after a major battle.

A new Vendée? But there was one obvious difference: our Orthodox
clergy, living in some other world, did not join forces with the rebels; they
did nothing to inspire them, as the militant Catholic clergy of France had
done, but remained cautiously in their parishes and in their houses, though
they surely knew that when the Reds came they would be slaughtered just
the same. (As happened in Kamenka, where the priest Mikhail Molchanov
was shot just like that, while sitting on the steps of his own home.)

A Vendée? A forced one, at times. A Red Army soldier would come
home to his village on leave, and his fellow villagers would destroy all his
documents—and now what could he do? All that was left were the partisans. And there was no way he could desert from a partisan detachment,
even though he might want to: his own folk wouldn't let him live in the

village with his family. Or people found out that some old woman had let slip to the Reds something about the movements of the rebels; and in the square in front of the church, she was given a public whipping across her bare backside.

The peaceful peasants of Tambov were now catching it from all sides: if you did something wrong, it might be the Reds who punished you later or it might be the rebels. They were even afraid to talk to their neighbors in case they might say the wrong thing. Once one of the "men with pitch-forks" joined a band of others in raiding some nearby spot and was cap-tured; though he was released, in the eyes of the authorities he remained guilty for the rest of his life.

A knock comes at the door: "Who's there?" "Friends." Just in case, so as not to fall into a trap: "The whole lot of you are no better than devils. You may be friends, but you make our life a misery."

The Reds questioned one woman about the whereabouts of her son. "I don't have a son!" she told them. And then when they captured him, he said he was the son of so-and-so. So they shot him: he must have been lying.

Pavel Vasilych often put himself in the position of the peasants. The family: man's eternal joy, and his eternal weak spot! Who could have a heart so ironclad that it would not agonize over the fate of his dear ones who might be torn to pieces at any moment by someone's devilish claws?

Things like this also happened: A requisitioning detachment had been badly mauled in one village, but two of its members, a Chinese and a Finn, managed to hide themselves behind some old peasant's house. The Chinese was found and executed, but the old peasant felt sorry for the Finn and, risking his own neck, hid him in a haystack. He let him go at night, and the Finn took to his heels, back to his garrison in Chokino. (Ready for the next expedition . . . ?)

A Vendée? The SRs of Tambov Province couldn't make up their minds: they couldn't support a rebellion against the revolution, and they had missed the chance to head it; no one would follow them now. And yet, now that the Civil War was over, how could they not take advantage of the people's resistance to the communists? They joined with the Unions of Working Peasantry that were now springing up and wrote some leaflets claiming the whole rebellion for the SR Party.

The rebels, in any case, had their own slogans: "Down with the Soviets!" (that certainly wasn't from the SRs—they supported the Soviets); "We will not pay the assessments!"; "Long live the deserters from the Red Army!"

Ektov had a typewriter that had been taken from a central executive committee office, so he himself wrote and painstakingly printed some proclamations: "To those conscripted into the Red Army! We are not bandits! We are the same peasants as you. But we have been forced to stop our peaceful work and rise up against our brothers. Are your families not in the same situation as ours? Everything has been crushed by the Soviets; at every step the communists are running wild, taking away the last of the grain and executing innocent people. They smash our heads like clay pots and break our bones—is this how they promise to build a new world? Throw off the communist yoke and go home with your rifle in your hands! Long live the Constituent Assembly! Long live the Unions of the Working Peasantry!"

The partisans themselves, those who were able, would write proclamations on scraps of paper they came across: "Pay no more heed to these brazen communists, parasites on the backs of the working people!"; "We have come to cry out to you that the power of the wrongdoers and bandits must be ended!" And for those who had not yet made up their minds: "Peasants! They steal your bread and your livestock! Will you not awaken?"

The communists replied with a mass of printed leaflets reflecting their usual narrow-minded class viewpoint or satirical cartoons: Antonov wearing a bloodstained cap, carrying a bloody knife, and on his chest, looking like medals, were drawings of Wrangel and Kerensky. "We, Antonov the First, Incendiary and Destroyer of Tambov, Autocrat of all Thieves and Bandits . . ."

This had been put together by Eidman, head of propaganda in the province, someone no one here in Tambov had heard of before. And the ominous series of directives being issued were more often signed by the provincial committee secretaries, Pinson, Meshcheryakov, Rayvid, and Meyer; the chairmen of the provincial executive committee, Zaguzov or Shlikhter; the chairman of the provincial Cheka, Traskovich; and the head of the political section, Galuzo. These names were also completely unknown in Tambov and also belonged to people sent here from elsewhere. There were others among the staff of the provincial administration who did not sign ominous orders but made all the decisions jointly: Smolensky, Zarin, Nemtsov, Lopato, and even some women—Kollegaeva, Shestakova . . . Ektov had never heard of them either, but there was one among them who truly was local, the vicious and unrestrained Bolshevik Vasilyev, a man known to everyone from his crude behavior in the city in 1917, when he had stamped his feet and whistled down speakers at formal meetings in the Naryshkin Reading Room. Ektov had never heard of any of the others, and yet this whole pack must have come from the same intelligentsia opposition that he had. And if they had met somewhere just a few years earlier, before the revolution, would he not have shaken their hands . . . ?

But propaganda is only propaganda, and the Bolsheviks had to call in reinforcements. Antonov's intelligence determined that a Cheka special forces regiment had arrived from Moscow along with another squadron from the Tula Cheka, 250 more cavalry from Kazan, and about a hundred from Saratov. From Kozlov had come a "communist detachment," and two more of them had been mobilized in Tambov. Even the "Sverdlov

Mechanized Detachment" appeared among them, as well as a separate railway battalion. (The risky business of intelligence was carried out by a faithful peasant woman who went about with a milk pot, and by a reliable peasant who hauled firewood into the city. It was through such a woman that Pavel once sent an oral message to Polina and got a reply that she and their daughter were unharmed and still undiscovered by the Cheka; they had little to live on, but their hopes were high . . .)

No longer fearing for the safety of Tambov city, the Red leaders began stationing their expanded forces through the three rebellious districts, in particular the Tambov District, aiming at systematically occupying it. (In a large village of some 10,000 inhabitants, they took eighty hostages and announced to the residents that if they did not turn in all their firearms by noon the next day, all eighty would be shot. The threat seemed far too extreme to be true, and the village did not believe it. No one turned in any weapons, and at noon the next day, before the villagers, all eighty were shot.)

Bolshevik airplanes (some painted in boastful red) began making flights to observe and sometimes even drop bombs, terrifying the villagers.

In the autumn, to avoid the growing pressure from these new forces, Antonov began temporarily withdrawing his main forces to neighboring Saratov or Penza Province. (The Saratov peasants, in revenge for the horses that were requisitioned or exchanged, began capturing the Tambov rebels and dealing out their own crude reprisals. Such is the fate of peasant uprisings . . .)

Ego took part in these raids along with the rest of the staff. He had grown accustomed to a life on horseback, always on the move and with no roof over his head, often cold and often terrified as he fled before pursuers. Did be become a soldier? No, that he could not do. He found it too difficult and had never been trained for it. It was a matter of simply enduring. He shared the pain of the peasants, and that filled the empty places in his soul: he was where he should be. (And had he not come here, he would be sitting and trembling in some little hideaway in Tambov, despising himself.)

Still the rebellious land refused to be pacified! Though it became much more difficult in late autumn and early winter to find cover and bivouacs for the night, the ranks of the partisans continued to swell. The requisitions made by the Red detachments, their brazen robberies in which they divided up the peasants' belongings right before the eyes of their owners, their vicious beatings of old men, and the villages like Afanasyevka and Babino that they burned to the ground, driving the old and the young out into the snow—all this gave new impetus to the partisan resistance. (But the partisans also had to feed themselves. Formerly, they had taken food from the families of the militant Reds, then from the families of Red Army soldiers; but eventually, this was not enough, and they had to take from the peasants. Some gave willingly, others became bitterly resentful.)

By midwinter, two partisan armies had been formed, each having ten regiments. The first army was commanded by Tokmakov, the second by Antonov. Now there were some genuine soldiers among the staff and they set things in order, beginning with uniforms: private soldiers were to wear a red patch above the elbow on their left sleeve; commanders also wore a ribbon and a triangular patch, top down or up; brigade commanders wore a diamond patch. Commanders were elected at regimental meetings (they also chose political commissars and even members of the regimental tribunal). Clear orders were issued: there was a complete ban on entering villages to confiscate clothes and goods and search for food; partisans were instructed to exchange horses with the peasants as rarely as possible and only with permission of their medical assistant, and they were to take better care of their horses. The partisans were granted leave just as in the regular army, but they also had their own militia in the villages to check each partisan's pass.

That winter the hatred of each side for the other grew even more bitter. Red detachments would execute their proven and their suspected enemies, shooting them without trial and without consequences. Within these punitive detachments were people who had become so accustomed to executions that they would raise their weapons unthinkingly, as if to wave off a fly, and their pistols seemed to fire themselves. The partisans had to ration their ammunition and more often hacked their prisoners to pieces or smashed their heads with some heavy object. Commissars were hanged.

On both sides the fury for revenge grew to the point that they would put out a captive's eyes before killing him.

Children from devastated villages would go out with sleds to get horse-meat from the dead animals. Many wolves, grown very bold, appeared that winter. Dogs also ate the corpses scattered across the steppe and in the gullies and dug up bodies from shallow graves.

A tribunal from the provincial Cheka made a circuit through the occupied villages. Its members, Ramoshat, Rakuts, and Sharov, issued a stream of death sentences and began sending those suspected but never proved to be rebels to "concentration camps." In January the Antonov staff learned of a secret letter: the central camp administration of the Russian republic had given the Tambov Provincial Cheka an additional 5000 places in camps for those it had arrested. The guards in the nearby camps amused themselves with the women and girls sent there or simply raped them; rumors spread across the land.

The villages grew barren. Even in the once prosperous Kamenka there remained only about two dozen horses. People fastened wooden soles to worn-out boots; peasant women went about without stockings in the freezing cold. More voices could be heard complaining: "When we lived under the tsar you could go to the market and buy whatever you wanted: boots, calico, pretzels." One thing that could be found was paper for rolling cigarettes—from the books of former landowners and from the "Red Corners" in village reading rooms.

Once Ektov was speaking to an aged peasant from Semyonovsky Hamlet about the general breakdown of everything around them. Life, it seemed, was reaching the point where it could get no worse, and what would be left of it after all this?

"Never mind," said the silver-haired old fellow, "the grass lives on beneath the scythe."

A few Tambov peasants, though, did manage to get to the Kremlin. In mid-February there were announcements that grain assessments in Tambov Province were being ended. No one believed it. Then the newspapers reported that Lenin had suddenly "received a delegation of Tambov peasants." (Could that be true? Later, Antonov's staff found out that a few peasants working with the Tambov Cheka had indeed been hauled off, terrified, to the Moscow Kremlin.)

The Bolsheviks, obviously, were rushing to put down the rebellion by spring so that a new crop could be planted (and confiscated again in the autumn).

The fury of the battles did not subside, however. In March two regiments of the Antonov army made a lightning attack on the factory town of Rasskazovo, very close to Tambov. They routed the garrison and took a whole Soviet battalion prisoner. Half of them willingly joined the partisans.

Since autumn, Pavel Vasilych had lost hope of escaping the many perils that lay ahead and surviving the winter. But now, here he was: it was March and he was still alive. Now his military expertise was recognized by his appointment as assistant to the regimental commander of the special forces regiment attached to the staff of the first army.

He also read the two orders issued in March by the brutal head of the Bolshevik punishment detachment: "Every inhabitant of every village is bound by the same surety: if anyone in a village provides assistance in any form to the bandits, *all* inhabitants of the village will be regarded as responsible," while "bandits are to be hunted down and exterminated like beasts of prey." And the harshest measure of all: "The entire healthy male population between seventeen and fifty years of age is to be arrested and confined in concentration camps!" And one addressed directly to the rebels: "Keep in mind that your muster rolls are, for the most part, in the hands of the Cheka. If you report to us voluntarily with your weapons, you will be pardoned."

But the rebels, hotly pursued through the frozen, snowed-in gullies and copses, paid no heed to attempts at persuasion or brutal threats. Spring was beckoning, and then they'll never take us!

It was then, in March, that Ektov, having survived the winter, caught a severe chill; he fell ill and had to remain behind his regiment, bedridden in the warmth of a village.

On his second night a neighbor woman betrayed him to the Cheka.

He was arrested.

But he was not shot on the spot, though they knew his role in Tokmakov's staff.

Instead they took him to Tambov.

The city looked like a military camp. Many houses had been boarded up, and the sidewalks were covered with dirty snow. (He could not see his house, which lay on a side street.)

They took him through Tambov and put him in a railway car with barred windows, bound for Moscow.

Though he was not going to a meeting with Lenin.

2

HE WAS IN the Cheka's Lubyanka Prison, alone in a cell in a semi-basement, with one tiny window at the level of the prison yard.

From the very first, he saw his greatest challenge would be to ensure that he not reveal his identity. It was the same challenge faced by every second Tambov peasant, and with the same options: If you tell them who you are, you're finished. And if you don't tell them, you're still finished, though by some other means.

He invented a biography for himself: he would still be a worker in the cooperative, but from the Trans-Baikal area, one of the places he knew well. Given the conditions these days, it would be difficult for them to check.

The interrogations took place three stories above, always in the same office with two large, high windows, filled with the old, expensive furniture of the Rossiya Insurance Company once housed here and with a shoddy paper portrait of Lenin set in an expensive frame on the wall above the interrogator's desk. But there were three interrogators working in shifts.

One, Maragaev, looked Caucasian and worked only at night and so gave Ektov no chance to sleep. His interrogation technique had little subtlety: he shouted and raged, striking Ektov's face and body and leaving blue bruises.

Another, Oboyansky, had a gentle manner that betrayed his blue blood. He did not interrogate as much as try to instill a feeling of hopelessness in the prisoner, even seeming to sympathize with him on one point: *Those people* were going to win in any case, and in fact they already had won everywhere. Tambov Province was the last. No one could stand up to *them*, either in Russia or anywhere else in the world; they were a force that humanity had not yet reckoned with, and the most sensible thing to do was to give in before they passed sentence. Then, perhaps, they might lighten his punishment.

The third, the fat-cheeked, black-haired Libin, cheerful and lively, never laid a finger on the prisoner and never shouted. He always spoke with cheerful and exultant confidence, and it was obvious that this was quite genuine. He tried to awaken the prisoner's democratic conscience: How could he betray the glorious ideals of the intelligentsia? How could a democrat turn his back on the inexorable march of History, marred as it might be by cruelty and violence?

Ektov could say a good deal more about cruelty and violence than his interrogator imagined. He could, but he did not dare. And his interrogator had picked the wrong approach: in this area Ektov felt on solid ground. He was a democrat, a populist whose heart had been moved by the tribulations of the peasantry, and there was not a trace of the White Guard in anything he had done. (In fact, this was quite true.)

Libin, as if taking up this same cause of liberating the peasants, met him head on: "In days to come, school textbooks will tell of more than one episode of the heroism of the Red forces and communists in putting down this kulak rebellion. The battle against the kulaks will have a place of honor in Soviet history."

It was hopeless to argue with him. And what was the point? The main thing was whether they would find out just who he was. It was good they had taken him to Moscow. In Tambov they could bring in witnesses to identify him. Yet there was one dark premonition that kept nagging at him: he had been photographed head on and in profile. They could make copies of the photo and sent them to Tambov, Kirsanov, and Borisoglebsk. On the other hand, after six months of campaigning, Ektov's appearance had greatly altered: he now looked severe and tough; his skin had darkened from sun and wind; he scarcely recognized the man he had seen in the mirror of some peasant hut, though the mirrors there were rather shoddy.

So long as they did not find out who he was, his family was safe. As for himself, well, they could go ahead and shoot him: over these months of merciless war, Ektov had learned to live with the idea of death, and he had been a mere hair's breadth away from it many times.

Indeed, they could simply have shot him when he was captured. He did not understand why they found it necessary to identify him. Why take him to Moscow? Why waste so much time trying to change his convictions?

The weeks passed—in hunger, with only a bit of watery soup and a scrap of bread. His body itched; there was no change of underwear, and he tried to wash as best he could on the rare trips to the bath.

He was moved from his solitary cell to another, first with just one cell-mate, then with several. Now, with neighbors, there was no avoiding the questions: Who are you? How did you get mixed up in the rebellion? And what did you do? It was impossible to answer these questions, but equally impossible not to answer. Both his cellmates were shady characters, and his heart told him to take care. He concocted some stories for them.

April passed, and they still hadn't identified him! But they did take more pictures.

The pincers were closing.

Then he was back in a single cell in the basement.

May also passed.

The days dragged on, but the nights were even more painful: at night, flat on his back, a man weakens along with his vital force of resistance. A little more of this, it seemed, and he would be unable to summon the strength to go on.

Oboyansky would nod with a pained smile: "No one can resist. A powerful new breed of people whose like we've never seen has now arrived. Remember that."

Libin told vivid tales of the Reds' military victories: the number of troops run to ground in Tambov Province and—it was no secret here, in *this* place—even the numbers of their regiments. Cadets from several military academies had been stationed in the villages across the province to reinforce the occupation.

Yes, Antonov's forces were finished! They were finished, and now there were only a few remnants to be mopped up. Hordes of them are coming to the Red headquarters and turning in their weapons. They're also helping to locate and disarm the rest. In fact, a whole regiment of bandits came over to the Reds.

"Which one?" Ektov couldn't help but ask.

Libin had a ready and precise answer: "The Fourteenth Arkhangel Regiment from the Fifth Tokay Brigade."

Ektov knew them well. But believing Libin—that was another matter . . .

Libin even brought in some Tambov newspapers to back up his statement. Judging by them, the Bolsheviks really had been victorious.

But then, how could it have ended otherwise? Even when he joined the rebellion he realized how hopeless it was.

Then there was Order No. 130: the families of the rebels are to be arrested (and Libin emphasized the word *families* when he read it aloud), their property confiscated, and they are to be moved to concentration camps and then exiled to some distant region.

Then Order No. 171, also on punishing families.

There was no surprise here; Ektov knew it would happen.

Libin assured him that these orders were having a huge effect. So as not to fall victim to these measures, peasants were coming in and revealing who was in hiding and where.

This might well be so. The Bolsheviks were applying a huge lever by taking families hostage.

Who could hold out against this? Who does not love his children more than his own self?

"And now," Libin assured him, "there's a *great purge* beginning in the villages. We're picking people up one by one, and no one can hide from us."

More than a few peasants knew Pavel Vasilych Ektov from peacetime and might betray him.

Ektov, however, was in his third month of prison and was still concocting stories and telling lies. But now—had they seen through them?

Meanwhile, Libin carried on with his happy smile, even seeming well disposed toward this hopeless democrat and populist—though he had seated him under a much more powerful light. His moist, rapacious mouth formed a smile: "So, Pavel Vasylich, we didn't finish our conversation last time . . ."

And then everything came crashing down.

It was all over.

He was already slipping down the steep slope, clinging to a few shreds of hope with his fingernails: Surely this didn't mean they had his family as well? Polina and his little girl might have taken precautions, found a different place to live, moved away somewhere . . . ?

But Libin, his black eyes gleaming with the enjoyment of watching his distraught prisoner making pointless denials, now tightened the noose around his neck: "Polina Mikhailovna doesn't approve of your stubbornness. Now that she knows the facts, she's amazed that you still haven't broken ranks with the bandits."

Ektov sat on the stool for a few minutes, utterly stunned. His thoughts danced away in every direction, then slowed their whirl and became frozen.

Libin continued to look at him. But he was silent and did not urge him on.

That was something Polina would never have thought and never have said.

But could she have reached the end of her rope?

Yet, this might also be his chance: Let me meet with her! Let me talk to her myself!

Libin gave a hesitant "No": "You have to earn a meeting, first of all by your repentance."

Two or three days passed in this way, Ektov insisting on a meeting, Libin insisting first on complete repentance.

But Ektov could not trample into the mud all the things he had seen with his own eyes and absolutely knew to be true. And he was incapable of pretending.

Libin, however, was also unwilling to give an inch. (And his stubbornness proved that what he had said about Polina was untrue! That was not *her* at all!)

Then Libin abruptly ended the duel, and in a way that took Ektov's breath away: To hell with you, don't repent! To hell with you, you can keep your brainless populism! But if you don't cooperate with us, I'll hand over your Polina to the Hungarians in the special forces and make you watch. And we'll put your little brat in an orphanage. And after you've seen the show, you'll get a bullet in the back of the neck. That's less than you deserve, and we should have done it sooner.

Icy fingers seemed to grip his chest. These people certainly were capable of doing all that Libin had said. Such things had happened more than once. Their power rested on such things, in fact.

Polina . . . !

They gave Ektov a day and then another day *to think*.

And how could one *think* inside this torture chamber where you're surrounded by threats and have no way out? His thoughts simply passed through his head, disconnected, as if he were only half awake.

How could he do it—sacrifice his wife and Marinka and simply step over them? Was there anyone else on earth, anything else on earth, to which he felt more responsible? Everything that made his life meaningful lay in these two people.

And was he to be the one to give them up? What kind of person could do such a thing . . . ? And afterwards they would shoot Polina. And they wouldn't spare Marinka either. He knew *these people*.

What if he could save some peasants by doing that? But the rebels had already lost, that was clear. They've lost in any case.

As for his *cooperation*, what did that mean these days? How could it tip the scales of an uprising that has already been put down? The only question was the sacrifice of his family. Nothing else could be changed.

How he hated that swarthy face of Libin with its insolent, triumphant expression and those eyes with their predatory gleam! Giving up would bring a kind of relief. It was probably the same feeling a woman has when she ceases to struggle. All right, you're stronger than I am. I'll throw myself on your mercy. It's a way to make dying a little easier.

What use could he now be to the Reds, though?

He gave in. But there was a condition: he wanted a meeting with Polina.

Libin confidently accepted his surrender. As for the meeting with his wife, that will only happen when you carry out our assignment. Then, of course—we'll simply let you go back to your family.

What else could he do?

You would have to have an incredibly stony heart to trample in the mud all that was dearest to you. And now, for what cause?

Oboyansky's melodious incantations also left their trace on him. He was right, they were a powerful generation! The new Huns, but armed with a socialist ideology. A strange mixture . . .

And perhaps it was also true that we, the old school intelligentsia, had failed to understand something. The paths to the future don't easily reveal themselves to the human eye.

EKTOV'S ASSIGNMENT WAS this: He was to be a guide for the cavalry brigade of the famous Grigory Kotovsky, the Civil War hero. (The brigade had just moved through the rebellious Pakhotny Ugol and slaughtered 500 rebels.) Ektov was not to invent any new identity for himself, he was to go as the famous Ego from Antonov's staff. (Antonov's forces had been utterly routed and his army had ceased to exist. He had fled and was still in hiding. But Antonov was not their concern.)

And what was his job to be?

That would be explained on the way.

(Still, somehow, he might be able to wriggle out of it.)

It was a short trip from Tambov to Kobylinka, a place that bordered on one of the areas the partisans favored.

They went on horseback. (And the Chekists, in civilian clothes, rode beside him, never leaving him for a minute. They had half a squadron of Red Army troops with them.)

Once again he was in the open air, under the open sky. It was early June, and the lindens were in blossom. Just fill your lungs with that air!

So many of our poets and writers had told us the same thing: How beautiful the world is, and how people debase and poison it with their endless antagonisms. Will this strife never end? Will people ever be able to create a life freed from such afflictions, a splendid, sensible life of abundance? That was the dream of generations.

A few *versts* before Kobylinka, they met Kotovsky himself. He was a huge, powerful man with a shaven head and the savage face of a convict. Kotovsky's squadron was in peasant garb, not Red Army uniforms, though they all wore riding boots and sheepskin hats or astrakhans. A few of them had the red Cossack stripe on their trousers. Were they supposed to be Cossacks?

Indeed, they were. They had been told to call each other "neighbor," in Cossack fashion, and not "comrade."

The senior Chekist accompanying Ektov now explained his task: This night they were to meet with the representative of a band of some 500 rebels. Ego was to confirm that *we* were Cossacks from the Kuban and

Don insurgent army and had broken through Voronezh Province to link up with Antonov.

As night fell, Ego was given an unloaded Nagan pistol to strap on his hip and a puny nag to ride. (The four Chekists in civilian clothes stuck close to him, playing the role of the new staff he had collected after the defeat of Antonov's forces. Their Nagans were fully loaded, and it was clear they would shoot him at his first wrong move.)

Kotovsky and his squadron had arranged the meeting in a forester's cabin on the edge of a clearing. Misha Matyukhin, brother of Ivan Matyukhin, the commander of a rebel detachment that was still active, was coming from the other direction with a few dozen horsemen. (Several brothers would often join the Tambov rebels. Aleksandr Antonov's younger brother Mitka, a village poet, always went into battle by his side. The two of them had also escaped together.)

The riders stopped at the clearing. The main negotiators entered the forester's hut, where two candles burned on the table. Their faces could just be made out.

Misha Matyukhin had never seen Ego's face, but his brother Ivan had. "He'll vouch for me," said Ektov, who could barely recognize his own voice and believe that he was serving such brazen falsehood to the peasants. But once he had taken his first steps across this shaky little bridge, there was no stopping. Looking at Kotovsky, he said: "Here's the head of their detachment, Lieutenant Colonel Frolov." (So as not to overdo it, Kotovsky had not donned a Cossack colonel's insignia, though he could easily have done so.)

Matyukhin insisted that Ego come with him to a place a few *versts* away to meet his elder brother, who could confirm his identity. This was no problem for the Chekists, and they never hesitated; they had good cavalry horses and a stock of ammunition for their Nagans.

They rode first along a cutting through the forest, then across a field, under a starry sky. In the darkness and moving at a brisk trot, no one wondered why Ego's horse was so wretched in comparison with those of his aides.

As he jolted along in his saddle, Pavel Vasilyevich kept thinking, desperately thinking, that soon he would tell Matyukhin the truth; he would be killed, but these four Chekists would be slaughtered along with him! And Matyukhin's 500 troops would be saved. They were an elite force!

But still—and how many times he had gone through this, forming logical arguments in his head, while his heart overflowed with pain. Not pain for himself, of course—there was none of that. But they would take it out on Polina, as they had threatened, and perhaps on his little daughter as well. For a long time now he had known what the Chekists were capable of, and after those months in the Lubyanka and those days traveling here, he knew it even better. So how could he save his family? How could he do it *himself*, with only his own hands?

Antonov's military campaign had failed, after all. If you took a broader view and put it in a larger context, the whole province might be better off if peace at last did come. The merciless requisitions of food had now been stopped and would be replaced by a fair tax on food. Perhaps it would be better, then, to end the fighting as soon as possible. The wounds would heal gradually. It would simply take time. And life, an entirely new way of life, would somehow come to rights, would it not?

We've been through enough pain, every one of us.

They came to a new hut, much better lit up.

Ivan Matyukhin, a sturdy, powerful man with a thick moustache the color of ripe wheat, a tireless warrior, strode up to meet them, recognized Ego, and swung his arm forward to clasp his hand.

Ektov felt the ache of a Judas in his hand! Who could understand his pain unless he himself had experienced it? But he had to carry on, confidently and without hesitation, looking like a commander.

The honest and straightforward Matyukhin, with plump, rosy cheeks and a thick, fair forelock slanting across his forehead, had a powerful grip—a warrior from head to toe.

He trusted Ektov, and he was overjoyed: Our ranks have filled out! A new chance to thrash the Bolsheviks! He grinned like a man who knew his strength.

They talked of their plans. Tomorrow evening both detachments would assemble in one of the large villages, and the next day they would begin an offensive.

Now was the moment! Like a lightning flash, Ektov thought: No! *I tell you, no!* Shoot me, torture my family, but I can't betray these honest men!

But at the same moment, his throat seized as if it had been scalded.

As he swallowed, someone interrupted to put in his word. And then someone else. (The Chekists were playing their roles well, and each one of them had his own story about why no one had seen him in the uprising before. All of them had the bearing of soldiers or sailors.)

And now this moment of decisiveness had flown past and dissolved into impotence.

At this, the two groups parted.

THEN HE SPENT an endless and agonizing day with Kotovsky's detachment.

He despised himself. His treachery had plunged him into a nightmare of darkness. One could not go on living in such darkness, one could no longer be a man. (The Chekists were watching every movement of his brows and every blink of his eyes.) Once I've done what they've asked, most likely they'll just shoot me. (And then they'll leave Polina alone!)

Toward evening the whole cavalry brigade mounted their horses. Many of them were dressed as Cossacks.

They moved off in formation. Ego was there with his retinue of Chekists. Kotovsky's feral gaze could be seen from under his shaggy Kuban *papakha*.

Was it Kotovsky or Katovsky (from the word *kat*, executioner)? He'd been in prison for murder, and not just one murder. He was a horrifying man, and just looking at him was enough to turn your stomach to jelly.

At twilight the detachments entered the village where they had agreed to meet from opposite directions; the troops dispersed among the huts. (Kotovsky's men, though, left their horses saddled, ready for the slaughter that would begin in another hour or two. Matyukhin's men settled in and made themselves at home.)

They met in a large house of a prosperous family that stood in the middle of the village, near the church and where the lines of houses met. The imposing woman of the house, not yet old, and her daughters and daughters-in-law had set up a row of tables to seat twenty. There was mutton, roast chickens, new cucumbers, and potatoes. Bottles of home-brewed vodka were set along the tables, together with some cut-glass tumblers. There were kerosene lamps on the tables and on the walls.

The Matyukhin men were mostly on one side of the table, Kotovsky's on the other. Ego, presiding over the dinner, had been seated at the end where he could be seen by both sides.

What vital strength emanated from these rebel commanders! So many of them had gone through the German War as NCOs or private soldiers, but now they were serving as commanders.

They were Tambov types, with high cheekbones, rough and hardened faces, and thick lips; a few had bulbous noses, others long and drooping ones. Some had forelocks as fair as flax, others as black as coal; and there was one man who looked like a gypsy, with a face so reddish black that it set off the whiteness of his teeth.

Kotovsky's men, to pass themselves off as Kuban peasants, were to speak in the dialect of that province and some of them in Ukrainian. There was not a single man from the Don region among them, but they counted on the Tambov people not recognizing the Don dialect.

One of the Matyukhin men had a prominent chin and the suspicious face of a backwoodsman. He had bags under his eyes and a drooping moustache; clearly, he was exhausted. But another was a dashing and slender fellow with a twisted moustache and eyes darting about, alert but cheery. He sat at the corner where there was more room, turned sideways with one leg crossed over the other. He seemed not to be expecting any surprises, but was ready for them and for anything else.

Ego could not refrain from nudging him with his foot, twice. But the fellow didn't seem to understand.

Glasses of vodka were poured, raising the mood and the fellowship of the meeting. Mutton and ham were sliced with long knives; smoke from the bracing homegrown tobacco rose here and there and spread across the ceiling. The hostess floated about the room while the younger women fussed, served, and cleared away the dishes.

What if some miracle suddenly took place and saved everything? What if the Matyukhin men realized what was going on and saved themselves?

The "Cossack" second lieutenant, "Borisov" (a commissar and Chekist), rose and began reading a fabricated "Resolution of the All-Russian Conference of Partisan Detachments" (that now must be convened). Soviets, but without communists! Soviets of the working peasants and Cossacks! Hands off the peasant harvest!

One of the Matyukhin men, a younger fellow with a round, flowing beard, a fluffy moustache, and a face well tested by life, looked at the speaker with calm, intelligent eyes. His neighbor, who might have been cast from iron, cocked his head and squinted a bit.

What fine fellows they are! And how unbearable this is!

But now it's too late to save anything, even if you shout out loud.

Matyukhin, showing his support of the second lieutenant, pounded the table with his fist: "We'll destroy their bloody communes!"

From the far end of the table, a young fellow with a broad forehead and flaxen hair that looked as if it had been freshly curled, a village dandy, shouted out: "Hang the bastards!"

Kotovsky returned to the business at hand: Where was Antonov? Without him we're not likely to make it.

"We still haven't found him," Matyukhin said. "I've heard he got shell shock in the last fight and is getting treatment. But we can raise all the Tambov people again on our own."

His next plan: attack the concentration camp near Rasskazovo where they put the families of the rebels and are killing them off. That's our first job.

Kotovsky agreed.

Now—was that a signal from Kotovsky . . . ?

All the Kotovsky men, in unison, whipped out their weapons—some of them huge Mausers, others Nagans—and began firing across the table at their "allies."

A thunderous roar filled the hut; there was smoke, fumes, and the desperate cries of the women. The Matyukhin men fell, one after the other, onto the table with their chests in the food, onto their neighbors, backwards off the bench.

The lamp fell on the table, and a burning stream of kerosene ran along the oilcloth.

The dashing, sharp-eyed fellow in the corner managed to fire back twice and drop two Kotovsky men. Then a saber cut off that head with the twisted moustache, and it tumbled onto the floor; a crimson stream of blood spurted from the neck to the floor, forming a pool around his body.

Ektov did not move; he was frozen. If only they would finish him off quickly—a Nagan, a saber, it made no difference.

Kotovsky's men ran out of the hut to seize the confused Matyukhin guards who still did not realize what was happening.

Kotovsky's horsemen were already rushing in from the other side of the village, shooting and cutting down the Matyukhin men in the yards, in the huts, and in beds, not letting them mount their horses.

The few who were still able galloped toward the dark forest.

1994

THE NEW GENERATION

1

THEY WERE WRITING the strength of materials exam.

Anatoly Pavlovich Vozdvizhensky, an engineer and associate professor in the Faculty of Civil Engineering, could see that his student Konoplyov's face was very flushed. He had broken into a sweat and had missed his turn to come up to the examiner's desk. Then, with a heavy gait, he approached and quietly asked for a different set of questions. Anatoly Pavlovich gazed at the sweaty face beneath a low forehead and met the desperate, imploring look in his bright eyes—and he gave him some new questions.

Another ninety minutes passed, a few more students had already submitted their answers and the last four in the class were already sitting before him ready to present their results, but Konoplyov, who had been sitting among them and who now seemed even more flushed, was still not ready.

He sat there until all the others had left. The two were now alone in the lecture hall.

"All right, Konoplyov, your time's up," said Vozdvizhensky, firmly but not crossly. By now it was clear enough that this fellow didn't have a clue about anything. The few scribbles on his paper bore little resemblance to formulas and his diagrams bore little resemblance to engineering drawings.

The broad-shouldered Konoplyov rose, his face covered with sweat. He did not go to the blackboard to write his answers but plodded over to the nearest desk, settled himself behind it, and in the most artless and open-hearted way said: "Anatoly Palych, this stuff's so complicated it's buggered up my whole brain."

"Then you have to apply yourself methodically to your work."

"Methodically, Anatoly Palych? That's what they tell us in all the courses, and there ain't a day passes when they don't. I never fool around and I'm at the books every night, but the stuff still won't get through my thick skull. Maybe if they didn't throw so much at us and took it a little easier. But it just won't sink in—I'm not cut out for this sort of thing."

His eyes looked out earnestly and his voice was sincere; he wasn't lying, and he didn't look like a loafer.

"You came here from the Workers' Faculty?"

"Uh-huh."

"How long were you there?"

"I took a two-year intensive course."

"And what did you do before that?"

"I was at the Red Aksai Factory. A tinsmith."

His nose was large and broad, his face large-boned, his lips thick.

This was not the first time Vozdvizhensky had wondered why they put fellows like him through such torment. He'd be better off making pots and pans in Aksai.

"I sympathize, but there's nothing I can do. I have to fail you."

But Konoplyov would not accept this and did not pull out his student record book. He pressed both his paw-like hands to his chest.

"Anatoly Palych, this just can't be. It's bad enough they'll take away part of my scholarship. And the Komsomol will give me a real blast. But no matter what they do, I ain't never gonna make it through strength of materials. What'll I do now? My life's been dragged upside and down, and I'm out of place here."

Well, that was obvious enough.

There were a good many of these fellows from the Workers' Faculty whose lives had been "dragged upside and down." What on earth were the authorities thinking when they pushed them into universities? They must have anticipated cases like this. The administration had given unambiguous instructions to make allowances for people from the Workers' Faculties. It was part of their policy of mass education.

Make allowances—but how far could you go? Some of the Workers' Faculty people had taken exams today, and Vozdvizhensky had been fairly tolerant with them. But not to the point of absurdity! How could he give a pass to this fellow when he didn't know a thing? Everything I've tried to teach him has gone right over his head. As soon as he begins engineering it'll be obvious that he hasn't a clue about strength of materials.

He said, "I can't do it." And he said it again.

Yet Konoplyov kept begging, almost in tears—a rare thing to see in a roughneck like him.

And Anatoly Pavlovich thought: If the authorities have such a strict policy and are fully aware of the absurdities it creates, then why should I care more than they do?

He gave Konoplyov a little lecture, advising him how to change his study habits, how to read aloud to help himself absorb the material, and what he should do to get his thoughts organized.

He took his student record. He heaved a deep sigh. Slowly and deliberately he wrote in "pass" and signed.

Konoplyov, radiant, jumped to his feet: "I'll never forget this, Anatoly Palych! Maybe I'll squeak through my other subjects, but that strength of materials is queer stuff for sure."

The Institute of Railways and Highways was on the outskirts of Rostov, and Anatoly Pavlovich had a long journey home. Riding in the streetcar, he could see how shabby and nondescript his fellow passengers had become over the past years. Anatoly Pavlovich dressed in a modest and well-worn suit but still kept his white collar and tie. But now there were some professors in the institute who made a point of going about in a simple shirt, belted and worn outside their trousers. In spring, one of them would wear sandals on his bare feet. This no longer astonished anyone and was completely in keeping with the spirit of the times. This was how the times were changing, and everyone was put out when they saw the wives of the NEP-men decked out in fancy dresses.

Anatoly Pavlovich arrived home just at the dinner hour. His exuberant wife Nadya, the light of his life, was now in Vladikavkaz with their elder son, newly married and a railway engineer like his father. A cook fixed the meals in Vozdvizhensky's apartment three times a week, though today was not one of her days. But Lyolka bustled about energetically to make sure her father was properly fed. Their square oak table was already set and had a sprig of lilac at its center. She brought in a pitcher of vodka from the icebox for his invariable daily drink, taken from a small silver goblet. She heated and then served him soup with pastries.

She was making wonderful progress in the eighth grade at her school, taking physics, chemistry, and math. She excelled at drawing and had her heart set on entering the same institute where her father taught. But four years ago, a decree of 1922 had made it mandatory to filter the applicants and strictly limit the number of those of non-proletarian origin. Entrants not recommended by the party or the Komsomol had to present proof of their political reliability. (His son had managed to enroll the year before the decree.)

The way he had stretched the truth in Konoplyov's record book today continued to weigh heavily on his conscience.

He asked Lyolka about her school. The whole nine-year school (the Zinoviev School, though the name had now been erased from the sign) had been shaken by a recent suicide: a few months before the end of the school year a grade-nine student, Misha Derevyanko, had hanged himself. There was a hasty funeral, and immediately thereafter all the grades held meetings for criticism and tongue-lashings: this event had been a product of bourgeois individualism and a symptom of the moral decay of everyday life; Derevyanko was nothing more than a spot of rust that everyone must scrape away. Lyolka and her two friends, though, were sure that Misha had been badgered by the school's Komsomol cell.

Today she was worried and mentioned something that was no longer a rumor but a certain fact: the school principal, Malevich—a man everyone adored, an old teacher from a pre-revolutionary *gimnaziya* who had somehow held on for all these years and who kept the whole school running like a well-regulated machine through his cheerful discipline— Malevich was being *removed*.

Lyolka ran off to the primus stove for the beef Stroganoff, and then they had tea and pastries.

The father gazed at his daughter with tenderness. How proudly she tossed back her head with its curls of chestnut hair (she had no interest in the fashion for keeping hair short), and how intelligent she looked as she crinkled her forehead and spoke her mind so precisely and simply.

As is often the case with girls, her face expressed the wonderful riddle of her future. But as her father gazed at it, this riddle had become a nagging ache: How could he determine what would become of her in this future that no one could predict? Would these many years of growth, education, and concern for her reach a triumphant conclusion, or would they do her damage?

"Just the same, Lyolyenka, you can't avoid joining the Komsomol. You've only one year more, and you can't take the risk. Otherwise they won't accept you anywhere, and I won't be able to help you get into my institute either."

"I don't want to!" She tossed her head, setting her hair awry. "The Komsomol is disgusting."

Anatoly Pavlovich sighed once more.

"You know," he suggested gently and, indeed, he truly believed it himself, "this new generation of young people really does have something, some truth that we can't fully understand. They certainly must have something."

Three generations of the intelligentsia could not have been mistaken about how to give the people access to culture and liberate their energies. Of course, not everyone has what it takes to cope with this surge ahead, this leap forward. The mental effort is simply too much, and they don't always have the strength of character—it's no easy thing to educate oneself outside the framework of years of inherited tradition. But we absolutely must help them scale the heights and patiently put up with their sometimes clumsy escapades.

"Yet you must agree that they have amazing optimism and a powerful faith in their cause that we can only envy. And you simply can't avoid swimming along in this stream, my dear, or you might well let the whole epoch slip past, as they say. What's being created—and granted, it's being created stupidly, clumsily and by fits and starts—is something majestic. The whole world is watching and holding its breath, all the intelligentsia of the West. People in Europe aren't fools, after all."

AFTER SUCCESSFULLY RIDDING himself of his strength of materials course, Lyoshka Konoplyov was happy to join his comrades who were going to the Lenin Regional Soviet House of Culture that evening. The gathering was not only for Komsomol members; some of the new generation's non-party young folks had also come. A fellow from Moscow was giving a talk—"On the Tasks of Today's Youth."

The hall held about 600, and it was crammed full, some even standing. There was a whole lot of red to be seen: at the back of the platform were two red banners embroidered with gold, spread out and leaning toward each other; in front of them, high as your chest, was a bronze-colored Lenin on a post. The girls had red kerchiefs round their necks, and a few had bands of red calico round their heads; the Young Pioneer leaders all wore red pioneer neck scarves and some had brought a few of the older pioneers, who were sitting with their leaders.

So here we are, a united crowd, all us young people close friends, even though we don't know each other: this is what we are, we're all *our people*, all of us like one. Builders of the New World, as they say. And knowing that gives each one of us the strength of three.

Then three buglers marched out to the front of the platform, also with red cloths dangling from their bugles. They formed up in a row and blew the call to muster. The call of those buglers came like the crack of a whip and brought the whole crowd to life. There was something in this grand ceremony of coming together that just seemed to draw you in—the red banners by the corner, the bronze Lenin, the gleaming silver of the bugles, the proud bearing of the buglers, and the piercing sounds they made. It hit you like some great battle cry, like making a solemn promise under oath.

The buglers stepped off smartly in line. Then out marched the speaker, a short, fat little fellow who couldn't keep his arms still. He took his place behind the rostrum and started to talk—quickly, confidently, forcefully—and he didn't read it from a paper, it was all from his head.

First he talked about how living through the great but stormy times of Revolution and Civil War had disrupted the lives of young people, but at the same time it had forced them to turn away from the pettiness and dullness of everyday reality.

"This transition has been hard for you, this new generation. The emotions brought on by the events of revolution are felt particularly keenly by young people like you who are at the age of transition. A few of you might think that it would be much more fun to begin a real revolution all over again: you would know at once what you had to do and where you had to go. Hurry up—press on, blow up something, shake up something, otherwise what was the point of October? Take China, now—they need a revolution, and why isn't one starting? What a fine thing it would be to live and fight for World Revolution, but here we are, forced to study some rubbish like theorems in geometry, and what's the point of that?"

Or strength of materials. He's right, there's a better use for idle arms and legs, and a better place for strong backs.

"But no," the speaker urged them, and he came out from behind his rostrum and trotted across the stage, getting really carried away by his own speech.

"You have to understand the present moment correctly and master it. Our young people are the most fortunate in the entire history of humanity. They are ready for battle, ready to take a productive place in life. Their qualities are, first, godlessness, a sense of complete freedom from all that is unscientific. The huge store of confidence and thirst for life that the old beliefs once held in check have now been unleashed. The second quality of our new generation is avant-gardism and planetism, the need to be at the forefront of our epoch. Our friends and our enemies are watching us."

And he turned his little head to gaze around the hall, as if seeking out those friends—and particularly those enemies—from all the distant lands across the seas.

"No more do we base our lives only on what we can see from our own doorstep. Now our young folks examine every detail of life but do so exclusively from a universal point of view. Then there is the third quality: a scrupulous class consciousness, a necessary though temporary rejection of 'the sense of humanity in general.' And then comes optimism!"

He approached the very edge of the platform and, showing no concern about tumbling off, he leaned toward the crowd as far as he could: "You must realize! You are the most exuberant young people in the world! What staunchness and determination this joyous energy gives you!"

He trotted across the stage again, never stopping the flow of his speech: "And then you have the thirst for knowledge. And the scientific organization of your labor. And you want to rationalize your biological processes as well. You have a militant passion—and what a passion it is! You also want to become leaders. And your organic, class brotherhood has given you a sense of collectivism, one that has been so ingrained that the collective even involves itself in the intimate lives of its members. And that is just as it should be!"

Even though the speaker was acting a bit like a clown, no one was laughing. They weren't whispering to one another; they were all ears. The speaker was helping these young people understand themselves, and that was a useful thing. As he grew more heated he would raise one short arm and then both, as if calling out to them, as if to convince them completely.

"Look also at the young women of this new generation, and how they have become aware of the power of the socialism we are creating . . . In only a few short years women have acquired personal freedom in their intimate lives—sexual liberation. And woman demands that a man reexamine relationships, otherwise she herself will break down the backward, slave-owning attitudes of the male as she brings a revolutionary freshness into sexual morality. And so the revolutionary resultant force is being sought and is being found in the realm of love as well: we switch our bioenergy onto socially creative rails."

He finished. But he didn't seem tired. He must be used to this. He headed back behind the rostrum. "Are there any questions?"

They began asking questions, right from their seats or in notes that were passed to him.

Most of the questions were about sexual liberation. One comment hit home for Konoplyov: "It's easy to say, 'Achieve a whole decade of development in two years,' but working at that pace might well kill you."

Then even the young pioneers felt bold enough to ask some questions:

"Can a pioneer girl wear ribbons in her hair?"

"Can she wear a bit of makeup?"

"And who should listen to whom: a good pioneer to a bad father, or a bad father to a good pioneer?"

2

As EARLY AS 1928, the Shakhty Affair, so close to Rostov, had thrown a huge scare into the city's engineering fraternity. And here, too, people had begun to *disappear*.

It took some time to grow accustomed to this. Before the Revolution, an arrested person continued living, behind bars or in exile, keeping in touch with his family and friends. But now? He simply dropped into oblivion . . .

In the past September of 1930, there was an ominous rumbling across the land: forty-eight people—"wreckers in the food supply chain"—were sentenced to be shot. "Responses from workers" appeared in the newspapers: "Wreckers must be wiped from the face of the earth!" The front page of *Izvestia* proclaimed: "Crush the serpent beneath your heel!" and the proletariat demanded that the OGPU be awarded the Order of Lenin.

In November they published the indictment in the case of "The Industrial Party," and that meant a direct attack on the engineers. Once more the chilling phrases appeared in the newspapers: "Agents of the

French interventionists and White émigrés" and "Sweep away these traitors with an iron broom!"

Such things tore at your heart, but you were helpless. Not everyone could even express their fears, and those who did could only speak to someone they knew well, as well as Anatoly Pavlovich had known Friedrich Albertovich these past ten years.

There was a four-hour demonstration in Rostov on the day the Industrial Party trial began, with the demonstrators demanding that all the accused be shot! It was unbearably vile. (Vozdvizhensky had managed to wriggle out of it and did not attend.)

Living day after day, feeling the tension and the darkness within, the sense of doom grew ever stronger. But why would they come for him? He had worked as if inspired all through Soviet times; he was resourceful, he believed in what he was doing, and it was only the stupidity and shoddy practices of the party bosses that hindered him at every step.

One night, less than two months after the trial, they *came* for Vozdvizhensky.

THEN BEGAN AN incomprehensible, nightmarish time of delirium, and it went on for many days and nights. It began with being stripped naked, having all the buttons of your clothes cut off and the soles of your shoes pierced with an awl; it continued in a stifling underground chamber with no ventilation, breathing air already breathed by many people. There was not a single window and never the light of day, but set in the ceiling were squares of bottle glass you couldn't see through. In this cell without beds you slept on the floor, on concrete that had been covered with loose planks. Everyone was stupefied from nighttime interrogations, some beaten until they were covered with bruises, others with hands burned by cigarette butts, some sitting in silence, others telling half-insane stories. Vozdvizhensky had never once been called out or touched by anyone, but his mind had already been shaken from its foundations and could no longer grasp what was happening or even connect itself with his former life—now, alas, gone forever. His poor health meant that he hadn't been called up for the German War; no one had bothered him during the Civil War that had run violently through Rostov-Novocherkassk. He had spent a quarter century at deliberate intellectual labor, and now he could only tremble each time the door opened, by day or by night: Had they come for him? There was no way he was prepared to stand up under torture!

He wasn't called out, however. Everyone in the cell in this underground warehouse was amazed. (Only later did they realize it actually was a warehouse, and the thick glass apertures in the ceiling were set into the sidewalk on the city's main street, along which carefree pedestrians constantly passed, people who had not yet been doomed to end here; and they could feel the walls tremble as streetcars passed above.)

They didn't call him out. Everyone was amazed: These newcomers usually get dragged out straightaway.

So maybe it really was a mistake? Maybe they would let him go?

But on one of those days—he had lost count which one—he was called out. "Hands behind your back," and a warder with jet-black hair led him out and then up a flight of stairs—to ground level?—and then higher and higher, several stories, the whole while clucking his tongue like some mysterious bird.

An interrogator in a GPU uniform sat at a desk in a shadowy room. You could barely make out his features, only that he was young and broad-faced. He silently pointed to a tiny table that stood in the opposite corner, diagonally from his desk. Vozdvizhensky found himself sitting on a narrow chair, facing a gloomy window some distance away. The lamp had not been turned on.

He waited with sinking heart. The interrogator continued to write in silence.

Then he said, severely: "Tell me about your wrecking activities."

Vozdvizhensky was more astonished than frightened. "There was never anything of the sort, I assure you!" He wanted to add a perfectly reasonable thought: How can *an engineer* spoil anything?

But after the Industrial Party affair?

"Never mind that, just tell me."

"There was nothing, it could never happen!"

The interrogator went on writing but still didn't switch on the lamp. Then, without getting to his feet, he said in a firm voice: "You've had a good look at your cell? But you haven't seen everything yet. We can have you sleep on concrete without any planks. Or in some damp pit. Or keep you under a thousand-watt light that'll blind you."

Vozdvizhensky could barely prop up his head in his hands. They really could do any of these things. And how would he ever endure it?

At this point the interrogator switched on his desk lamp, rose, switched on the overhead light, and moved to the middle of the room to look at the person he was interrogating.

Though he wore a Chekist's uniform, his face looked utterly simple and naïve. Broad-boned, a short, wide nose, and thick lips.

Then, in a milder voice: "Anatoly Palych, I know very well that you weren't involved in wrecking. But even you have to understand that *from here* no one leaves with an acquittal. It's either a bullet in the back of the neck or a term in the camps."

It was not the harsh language, it was the kindly voice that amazed Vozdvizhensky. He stared fixedly at the interrogator's face, and saw something familiar in it. It was such a simple face. Had he seen it before?

The interrogator went on standing in the middle of the room, under the light. He said not a word.

Vozdvizhensky knew he'd seen him before. But he couldn't recall where.

"You don't remember Konoplyov?" he asked.

Konoplyov! Of course! The fellow who didn't know his strength of materials. And who then disappeared from the faculty.

"Yes, I didn't finish at the institute. On orders of the Komsomol they took me into the GPU. I've been here three years."

So what now?

They chatted a bit, quite easily, a normal human conversation. Just as if it were happening in *that* life, before the nightmare.

Konoplyov said: "Anatoly Palych, the GPU doesn't make mistakes. No one ever gets out of here just like that. And though I'd like to help you, I don't know how I can. So think about it. You have to make up something."

Vozdvizhensky returned to the cellar with new hope.

But also with a fog whirling about in his mind. He wouldn't be able to *make up* anything.

But then to go to a camp? To Solovki?

He was struck and encouraged by Konoplyov's sympathy. Inside *these* walls? In a place like this?

He thought about these people from the Workers' Faculties who were now rising through the ranks. What he had seen of them until now was something different: a crude, conceited fellow had been Vozdvizhenky's boss when he worked as an engineer. And in the school that Lyolka had finished, some dimwit had been assigned to replace the gifted Malevich.

And, to be sure, poets long before the Revolution had foreseen it and predicted the coming of these new *Huns* . . .

After three more days in the cellar under the street, beneath the steps of unsuspecting passersby, Konoplyov summoned him again.

Vozdvizhensky still hadn't thought of anything to make up.

"But you must," Konoplyov insisted. "There's nothing else you can do. Please, Anatoly Palych, don't make me resort to *measures*. Or have them give you a new interrogator. Then you've had it for sure."

Meanwhile, he was moved to a better cell—less damp and with bunks to sleep in. They gave him some tobacco and allowed him to receive a parcel from home. The joy over the parcel came not because of the food and clean underwear it contained, it came because his family now knew he was *here*! And alive. (His wife would get his signature on the receipt for the parcel.)

Konoplyov summoned him again and again tried to persuade him. But how could he dishonor his twenty years of diligent, absorbing work? Simply—how could he dishonor himself, his very soul?

As for Konoplyov, he would now pass on the investigation—*inconclusive*—to someone else.

Another day Konoplyov told him: "I've thought of something and made the arrangements. There's a way you can be let out: just sign a promise to supply us with the information we need."

Vozdvizhensky recoiled: "How can that be . . . ? How . . . ? What . . . ? And what information can I give you?"

"About the mood among the engineers. About some of your acquaintances, Friedrich Werner, for instance. And there's others on the list."

Vozdvizhensky squeezed his head in his hands: "That I can *never* do!"

Konoplyov shook his head. He simply couldn't believe it.

"So—is it the camps? Just keep in mind: your daughter will also get kicked out of her last year as a class alien. And maybe your possessions and your apartment will be confiscated. I'm doing you a big favor."

Anatoly Pavlovich sat there, unable to feel the chair beneath him and scarcely able to see Konoplyov right before him.

He dropped his head on the little table—and broke into sobs.

A WEEK LATER he was set free.

1993

NASTENKA

1

NASTENKA'S PARENTS DIED young, and her grandfather, Father Filaret, who by then had also lost his wife, raised her from the age of five. The girl lived in his house in the village of Milostayki until she was twelve, through the years of the German War and the revolution. Her grandfather took the place of her own father—and of her parents, in fact—and, with his gray head and bright, penetrating eyes (eyes that filled with tenderness when they fell on her), he became the dominant and unfailing figure in her childhood. Other figures, and her two aunts as well, came later. She learned her first prayers from her grandfather, along with moral precepts to guide her through life. She loved going to church. On sunny mornings, on her knees, she would lose herself in contemplating the rays of sunlight shining through the tiny windows of the cupola, in which she saw the solemn yet compassionate descent of the Almighty from the dome above. When she was eleven, at St. Nicholas in the Spring, Nastenka walked alone some twenty-five *versts* through the fields to the monastery. At confession, she would search her conscience for something to tell and then complain that she could find no sins. Father Filaret, speaking through his stole he had placed over her, would say: "Now you, my girl, must repent for what is to come. Repent for what is to come, for there will be sins, many sins."

The times were quickly changing. The fifteen *desyatins* of church land Father Filaret and his parishioners had been allotted were confiscated and he was given four hectares, in accordance with the mouths he had to feed, which included the two aunts. But then, to ensure that all of them would work with their own hands, even those were taken away. At school they began looking askance at Nastenka, and her schoolmates would taunt her as "the priest's granddaughter." The school in Milostayki, in any case, was soon closed. If she hoped to get any more schooling, she would have to leave her home and her grandfather.

Nastenka moved the ten *versts* to Cherenchitsy, where four of the girls had taken a room. The boys in that school were bullies: they would line each side of the narrow corridor and let none of the girls through until each boy had felt her all over. Nastya made a quick exit to the school-yard, broke off a branch of prickly acacia, then boldly walked back and whipped any boy who reached for her. They left her alone after that. And in fact she was red-haired, freckled, and not considered pretty. (And if one of the other girls read a passage about love from some book, she would feel vaguely troubled.)

Like all priests' daughters, her two aunts—Auntie Hanna and Auntie Frosya—could see no future for themselves. Just as Uncle Lyoka had ear-lier bought himself a certificate stating that he was the son of an impov-erished peasant and then disappeared in some distant province, so now Auntie Frosya went off the Poltava in hopes of "changing her social ori-gins." Auntie Hanna, on the other hand, had a fiancé back in Milostayki, and would have stayed on there, but she happened to find out in the town hospital that a woman friend of hers had aborted a child fathered by her fiancé. Auntie Hanna came home, scarcely able to breathe, and within a week, out of spite, married a Red Army soldier, a communist, one of the troops then billeted in their house. And what kind of a wedding could they have? They simply went to the registry office, and she moved to Kharkov with him. Father Filaret, shattered, damned his daughter from the pulpit for not having her marriage sanctified by the church. Now he was entirely alone in the house.

Another winter passed, and Nastenka finished her seven-year school. What should she do now, and where should she go? Auntie Hanna, meanwhile, was doing rather well: she was the head of an orphanage on the outskirts of Kharkov, but she and her husband could not get on together and divorced, though he held an important post. She invited her niece to live with her. Nastenka spent a final summer with her grandfather. At his bidding she took with her a little paper icon of the Savior, "Persevere and Pray." She hid it in an envelope and then put it inside a notebook: it was a bad idea to let anyone see it there. And when autumn came, she went off to her aunt.

Auntie had already figured out which way the wind was blowing: "So now what can you do? Work at the brick factory? Or scrub floors? You've got no choice, you have to join the Komsomol. Then you can come and work for me." For the time being, she took her on as a teacher's assistant to play around with the kids. Nastenka liked that a lot, though it was just a temporary job. But she already knew what she had to do: to tell the children *what was right* and not lead them astray, while she prepared herself to join the Komsomol. There already was a Komsomol girl, Pava, who was the leader of the Young Pioneers and carried around a red volume of Marx and Engels from which she never parted. Even worse were the really nasty books she had, one of them a novel about a Catholic nunnery in Canada and how they prepared the girls for consecration. Just before this was to happen, they would take the girl to spend a night in a cell where a beefy young monk would pull her into his bed. And then he would console her:

"This is only for your instruction. The body will perish whatever you do. It's not the body that needs salvation, it's the soul."

This could not be, it was a lie! Or maybe . . . somewhere across the ocean? But Pava kept insisting it was so, claiming that she knew the Russian nunneries were nothing more than lies and hypocrisy.

It was just sickening to think about going into the Komsomol: Would they sneer at things in the same way? Would they all be like Pava?

But Auntie Hanna kept insisting and trying to impress on her: "You've got to understand that the Komsomol's your only choice. Otherwise, you might as well hang yourself."

Yes, her path in life was becoming more and more narrow and constricted . . . Was it really leading her to the Komsomol?

Late one evening when no one was watching, Nastya took out the little icon of Christ and gave it one final and penitent kiss. Then she tore it into tiny pieces so that no one could tell what it had been.

January 21 was the first anniversary of Lenin's death. The Council of People's Commissars of Ukraine was in charge of their orphanage, and Vlas Chubar himself came to the commemorative ceremony. The stage was draped in red and black, and before a huge portrait of Lenin, the little Mishkas and Mashkas entering the Young Pioneers were being renamed Kim, Vladlen, Marxina, and Oktyabrina. The kids beamed with joy to have their names changed and kept repeating their new ones.

As for Nastya, she took the Komsomol oath.

She stayed at the orphanage until spring had passed, but there was still no job open for her there. So Auntie Hanna managed to find her a place running a tiny reading room in the village of Okhochye. Nastya, who was not yet sixteen, took the little bundle containing all her possessions and went there in a cart, jolting all the way, via the regional town of Taranovka.

She found her "library" was a single, dirty room in a hut shared with the Okhochye Village Soviet. She tucked up her skirt and set to washing the floor. She had to wipe down or wash everything and hang the portrait of Lenin—along with a rifle with no bolt that for some reason belonged in the room—on the wall. (It was just at this point that the chairman of the regional executive committee, the tall Arandarenko with jet-black hair, popped in and oohed and aahed, praising her for the way she had cleaned up the room.) The little reading room carried a few pamphlets and the newspaper *The Village Poor*. A couple of peasants might drop by to have a look at the paper (and, at the same time, how could they keep from carrying it off to roll cigarettes?), but no one ever picked up any of the pamphlets.

So now, where was she supposed to live? The chairman of the village soviet, Roman Korzun, told her: "It's not safe for you to go off too far, someone might take a shot at you." He found a spot for her in part of a house requisitioned from a deacon, quite near the village soviet.

It took a while for Nastya to understand why it was dangerous: now she was a dyed-in-the-wool part of Soviet power. Then came St. John's Day, the festival of the church in Okhochye; there was to be a fair, and a lot of visitors were expected. Their Komsomol cell had rehearsed an anti-religious play for the holiday, and they put it on in a large shed. They also sang a little ditty:

> *French kisses only make me bored,*
> *I'm not the Virgin Mary.*
> *I won't give birth to Christ the Lord,*
> *So let us both be merry.*
> *This wrung her heart. It was a humiliation, a disgrace.*

Even more: the whole family from the deacon's house was now looking at Nastya with hostility, and she didn't dare explain things and be honest with them. That, maybe, would make things even worse. She went quietly past the house to her own entryway. But Roman lived here as well, and though he was over thirty, he was a bachelor or perhaps divorced. He told her that he was taking the first room; it led into a second, where Nastya would live.

The problem was that there was no proper door between the rooms, just a curtain.

Yet Nastya felt quite safe. Roman Korzun was a grown-up and he was her boss, so she would go to her room, lie down on the bed, and read a book by the kerosene lamp. But only a day went by before he was grumbling: "I don't like these city bitches. Every one of them acts like she's still got her cherry." On the third evening she was again lying on her bed reading. Korzun silently came up to the doorway, tore back the curtain, and rushed at her. He immediately pinned back both her arms and stopped her from crying out by covering her mouth with his burning lips.

She couldn't move. Even more, she was utterly stunned. He was damp with sweat, disgusting. So, is this how it happens?

Roman saw the blood and was amazed: from a Komsomol girl? And he asked her forgiveness.

Now she had to wash it all off in the basin so the deacon's family wouldn't see.

But that same night he came back to enjoy himself once more, and then again, covering her with kisses.

Nastya felt as if someone had struck her over the head, and she had no strength to resist.

After that he no longer came to her; he would call her to his room every evening, and somehow she would meekly obey. He would keep her there for a long time, smoking a cigarette in the intervals.

It was during those same days that she heard something that made her blood run cold: syphilis was raging in Okhochye.

What if he had it?

But she dared not ask him directly.

How long could this go on, anyway? Korzun was masterful and insatiable. Early one morning when it was already light, while he slept and she was awake, she caught sight of the hateful little secretary of the village soviet looking in the window. He had probably come to summon Korzun for some emergency, but he had already seen what was going on—and seen that she saw him—and he only smirked in a vile and filthy way. He even stood there for a time to have a good look and then went away without knocking.

The secretary's fiendish grin pierced and cut through all the stupor and numbness in which Nastya had spent these weeks. It wasn't just that he would now spill this story all through the village, his grin alone was a disgrace!

She kept fidgeting, but Roman wouldn't wake up. She stealthily gathered her few things into the same small bundle she had brought here and quietly went out. The village was still asleep. She went to the road to the region's main town, Taranovka.

The morning was still and mild. The cattle were being driven out to pasture. She could hear the crack of the herdsman's whip, but not a single carriage was yet rumbling along the road, and there was nothing to raise the dust that lay like velvet beneath her feet. (It reminded her of that morning a few years back when she had made her trip to the monastery.)

She didn't know where she was going and why. She knew only that she couldn't stay in the village.

But she did know someone: Shura, the unmarried girl who carried messages for the regional executive committee. She went to Shura's tiny room, burst into sobs, and told her everything.

Shura hugged her and wiped away her tears. Nastya thought: I'll go straight to Arandarenko and tell him the whole thing.

Arandarenko didn't even call her in, but he remembered her. He gave orders to have her taken to someone's desk in the executive committee office, and she was given some papers and paid her wages.

Her surprise at his kindness didn't last long. People in the office told her that he was a regular outlaw where women were concerned. This was how he worked: He would take one of the nurses from the hospital or a young teacher for a ride—in summer in a carriage with springs, in winter in a sleigh. His driver would race the horses into the steppe to someplace where there wasn't a soul to be seen and then, while they raced along at full gallop, he'd spread the girl's legs. That was how he liked it.

Nastya, too, didn't have to wait long for her turn. (Anyway, how could she fight him off? And where else could she go with her little bundle?) Smolyanoy, the driver, called her in, gave her a pat on the shoulder, and gestured for her to follow him. And off they galloped! Lord, those horses flew like demons, and it seemed for certain they'd be thrown out of the carriage. The vicious Arandarenko with the forelock threw her on her back and twisted her arms over her head. Past his dangling forelock she could see the driver's broad back—he never turned around once—and the clouds in the sky above.

A few days later Roman Korzun came to Taranovka, begging her to come back to him and promising to marry her. Nastya felt a wave of anger at him and scornfully turned him down. Then he threatened to kill himself. "What, a party member like you? No, you won't do that." Then he submitted an official paper demanding that the librarian return to the village—she was a deserter! The central executive committee refused his request. Korzun even called a meeting of the villagers and made them vote: Return our librarian! Nastya was very afraid they would send her back to Okhochye. (Thank God she hadn't come down with the disease there.) But Arandarenko said no.

He ordered Nastya to pack her things and go to Kharkov for a two-month librarian's course. He went along. He reserved a room with a cot for her for a few days.

And he would come to her. To this point she had only been unhappy, but now some new feelings were stirring inside her and she began to sense what might happen to her. Arandarenko had compliments for her: "You're turning into a proper young tart. Your eyes sparkle, you're lovely."

Then Arandarenko went back to Taranovka, and Nastya's courses continued. She came back to Taranovka as a regular librarian. She was expecting Arandarenko to come to her, but he didn't see her even once and seemed to have forgotten about her.

There was a drama society in the Komsomol club, and Nastya began attending in the evenings. They were putting on the Ukrainian play *Till the Sun Rises* and a new play about the class struggle, showing how the children of kulaks try to make children of poor peasants fall in love with them so as to "sneak their way into socialism." One of the people in their drama society was Sashko Poguda—broad-shouldered and slim, with curly blond hair, and he could sing the Ukrainian song, "Something Fills Me with Sadness Today" so beautifully.

Nastenka began to like him more and more, in the real way, from her heart. Spring came, this one her seventeenth. Nastenka was happy to go out walking with him along the railway or across the fields. He began talking of marrying her, without asking his parents. And they became lovers. They wandered into the cemetery and there, on the fresh grass of April, just beside the church . . . Anyway, what did she have left to preserve, and why? She conceived from their very first time. She told Sashko, and all he said was: "How do I know who else you've been running around with?"

She wept. She made a point of lifting heavy loads and moving heavy furniture, but nothing helped. And Sashko began dodging meetings with her. His parents wanted to marry him to the medical assistant's daughter, who would bring a good dowry.

She tried to drown herself in a well, but one of her friends managed to stop her. Word leaked out. And the Komsomol cell forced Sashko to marry her. They went to the registry office. (As the popular taunt at the time had it, "Civil marriage—that's just doggy-style in the barn.") His parents didn't want Nastya to show her face in their home.

They rented a wretched little apartment. Sashko never shared what he earned but spent it carousing. In January, in a very cold snap, Nastya gave birth on the sleeping platform atop a Russian brick stove. They couldn't get her to move from that spot to go to the hospital. Her little girl burned her foot on a hot brick and carried the scar for the rest of her life.

And her daughter—was she to go unbaptized? But these days, where could she have it done? If word got out, they'd kick her out of the Komsomol, and then she'd have nothing.

Poguda was drinking even more. He'd basically abandoned her and didn't care at all about their daughter. Nastya decided to leave him. Divorce was simple enough: you paid your three rubles and they sent you a postcard from the registry office: divorced. The Komsomol helped her get a librarian's job on the outskirts of Kharkov, in Kachanovka, a settlement attached to a slaughterhouse and a sausage factory. She found a nice childless couple who agreed to take in little Yulka, now weaned, for six months or a year and Nastya could visit. There was no choice if she wanted to find a place to live, and she rented a little corner of a room from a widow who was alone.

But swearing off men didn't last. The warm weather set in again. One of the people in their Komsomol cell was Teryosha Repko, a quiet, sweet, pale fellow. Once, after a long evening meeting (that year they were battling with the Trotskyite opposition) he offered to see her home: the settlement was notorious for its number of robberies, and they had to go past a rubbish dump on a piece of waste ground where dead bodies would even turn up. When they came to her house, they kissed with a tenderness that Nastya had never experienced. He went on walking her home from the library—a second time, then a third. Each of them had a powerful longing for the other, but they had nowhere to go. She couldn't take him back to the widow's; she went to bed early, and there was just one room. But there was a glassed-in veranda, and they tiptoed into it and reveled in each other right on the floor.

She loved him, she wanted to cling to him, to hold him in her arms, to keep caressing him. She wanted to marry him. Late that fall she became pregnant. And then suddenly Teryosha's landlady, a woman of forty, burst into the library: "I came to have a look at you and see for myself just what you are!" Nastya froze while the woman shouted abuse at her. Only later did she find out that the landlady was supporting Teryosha and in exchange he was living with her and couldn't leave.

But why on earth didn't he tell her that before? She was lost in black despair. She had an abortion—it was only a month, after all.

Her life now was utterly empty. And she had to collect Yulka.

It was the icehouse manager, Kobytchenko, who took notice of her and found her a room. She took Yulka back. Kobytchenko kept her well fed all through the winter. This time she missed the first signs of her pregnancy and had to go to a private hospital. They took out a three-month fetus, and the doctor cursed her; they could already tell that it was a boy: his body was tossed into the waste bucket.

Kobytchenko either lost his job or was transferred, but he vanished. And Nastya developed pneumonia. She knew that Sashko Poguda was now in the central committee of the trade union, so she went to ask him for a voucher for a sanatorium in the Crimea. He promised, but while he was arranging it her pneumonia passed. She went away just the same, without Yulka.

The sanatorium was in the former St. George's Monastery, not far from Sevastopol. It was the year after the huge Crimean earthquake, and not many people wanted to come here so there was no shortage of rooms. And just think: right around the corner was a detachment of sailors. A few women and girls from the sanatorium would go over for a visit and spend an hour or two under the bushes. And Nastya couldn't fight off her constant cravings. She had become something of a charmer and never lowered her eyes. She, too, found herself a sailor, and then another.

She came back to Kachanovka, and the elderly bookkeeper from the factory told her he had to make a business trip to some far-off town. She could bring Yulka as well. It took a few days to get there, traveling in a private compartment on the train. They spent a few more days there and then came back. He was nice to her in a lot of ways. She had her nineteenth birthday there in the train, and they celebrated it with a bottle of wine. But after the trip, the bookkeeper never visited her again. He had a family.

Somehow, she had to get herself back on her feet. Thank heavens the club manager sent her on some preparatory courses for an institute. It was like a workers' faculty, but just for six months. The stipend was thirty rubles, just enough for some thin soup and porridge. Things were getting a lot more expensive. The dormitory was in a former church, vast and cold. The courses had already started, and all the double bunks were taken. So she wouldn't have to sleep on the concrete floor, she and Yulka made a bed on the table where they had once laid the shroud or rested the coffin at funerals. Then, since she was a mother with a child, they moved her into an unused bathroom in another dormitory, a place without a window. She would leave Yulka at the nursery school from seven in the morning until seven at night. Here, too, a "visitor" turned up—Shcherbina, a well-fed, strong, heavy fellow. He was married and claimed he got on well with his wife, but would drop himself on Nastya like an eager stallion. Given the hunger and barrenness of her life, Nastya welcomed his visits and was always ready for him. Shcherbina would bring something for her whenever he came—a pair of silky cotton stockings, some perfume, sometimes just money. And what could she do? She accepted it all. Maybe it was because of her last, difficult abortion, but she never got pregnant again.

In September of the next year, Nastya was accepted into a three-year course in the Institute of Social Education. She moved to a proper dormitory—one room for three mothers—and put Yulka in nursery school.

That winter Auntie Hanna, who had disappeared for a long time, showed up in Kharkov again. Nastya rushed to see her. It turned out that Granddad Filaret had been exiled to Solovki.

She felt cold shivers all over. She could see his considerate, kind face framed in gray hair, and she could even hear his warm voice that gave so much good advice. Solovki! The most terrible word in the language after "GPU."

And so for fear of showing our connection with him, we had all abandoned him. We betrayed him.

But how could we help him?

We couldn't. Auntie Frosya from Poltava, it seems, had been writing to him while he was still in Milostayki, and so they found out she was a priest's daughter and kicked her out of the accounts office and wouldn't let her get a decent job. And through Auntie Frosya, Auntie Hanna was also found out and lost everything. But she had a friend in the GPU and he set up a job for her: she was to get herself a good apartment in Kharkov and seduce whomever they told her to. Even though she was past thirty, she still had her looks and now dressed very well; and her apartment had all you could ask for, three rooms and it was warm. (Warm! These days, not everyone had such luck.)

After they had met a few times, Auntie Hanna asked: "Do you know what Athenian evenings are?" Nastya didn't know. "All the women have to walk around undressed, and the men make their choice. Next time I don't have enough women, I'll give you a call on the telephone, OK?"

Well, it was OK, of course. In fact, Nastenka even went eagerly, so hungry had she become for loving. Auntie Hanna had a skintight dress made for Nastya and then one as transparent as muslin. It was all carefree fun. The life all around her had become so barren—just ration cards, and little enough you could get on them—but here her cup was overflowing.

And so two winters passed, and the summer between them. Yulka had already turned four, then five, and Nastenka was twenty-two. Then, suddenly, a couple of agents picked up Auntie Hanna, and she disappeared without a trace. And all that life was over.

In her final year, Nastya worked all the harder to get good marks. Now all the general schools were full of "socialist education"; it was pedagogy and pedology everywhere. The graduates were supposed to bring socialist thinking into mass education.

At the same time, deathly famine hung over the whole province and over Kharkov itself. Your ration card would get you 200 grams of bread. Starving peasants would slip past the guard posts to get into the city where they could beg for food. Mothers abandoned their dying children at strangers' doorways. Dying people lay here and there on the streets.

A letter came from Auntie Frosya saying that Father Filaret had died. (The letter couldn't say plainly where, but it was clear enough that it had happened *out there*.)

And yet, somehow, there wasn't much grieving.

Could that really be?

It was the past. All of it, every trace, had vanished somewhere.

In January '32 the students were sent out on teaching practice. But a lot of the village schools stood empty because of the collectivization and the famine—there weren't any school kids left. Nastya's assignment was to the Tsyurupa Children's Village on the former estate of General

Brusilov. The children were from Kharkov, but since it was easy for the local peasants to get here, they brought in their starving children and then went back home to die. (In fact, there were even cases of cannibalism in some villages.) Many of the little boys in the orphanage were so emaciated they had become "wetters"—they couldn't hold their urine. They were fed barely enough to stay alive, and they fought over every scrap of food and clothing they were given. In the spring, the kids from the city, not knowing any better, would pick the wrong sort of grasses to eat and poison themselves on henbane. An ex-soldier ran the Children's Village, and he would go around in a service jacket and breeches, strict, straight-backed, always insisting on good order everywhere and in everything. (He had a pretty wife who would come out from the city, yet he began paying visits to Nastya. There was something about her that drew in the men.)

In May they returned to Kharkov for their final exams. Nastya had a classmate, Emma, who was already married and came from a well-off family. She could have easily gone to the very best institute, but for some reason she had come to this one. One day in May—Nastya knew nothing about this and only later figured it out—the Civil War hero, Viktor Nikolaevich Zadorozhny, came from Moscow to Kharkov on business. He knew Emma from somewhere and sent her a note to arrange a meeting— "I'm waiting to hear from you." The messenger thoughtlessly delivered it when her husband was there, and Emma had to read it aloud. But, laughing, she read out that Zadorozhny was looking for her classmate but didn't know her address. While her husband watched, she wrote down where and when to find Nastya. But then she had no chance to slip away from her husband in time to warn Nastya. Zadorozhny got the note and was surprised, but went to Nastya's at once and invited her out to the boulevard and sat with her beneath a fragrant acacia.

Zadorozhny was tall and slim, also in a service jacket and breeches, but he had only one arm: the Cossacks had cut off his other one at the elbow during the Civil War. (It was as if they knew who he was. He loved to tell the story of the times before the revolution when he and the strikers, expecting the Cossacks to come and run them off, would put a harrow, teeth upwards, on the road. The galloping Cossacks would fall and be injured along with their horses.) He had been a party member since 1917 and was now studying at the Industrial Academy of the Central Committee.

Barely able to pull herself together from the surprise of it all and still unaware of what had brought about this meeting, Nastya, in a simple white blouse with greenish stripes, suddenly decided that he was in her power and she was not going to let him go.

Fortune was smiling on him: they chatted for half an hour, and then he invited her to come to his hotel that same evening. And she went, of course, knowing that after that he wouldn't abandon her.

And, sure enough, in the morning he told her that he was taking her back to Moscow. (The next day he tried to pass it off to Emma as a joke, but she was furious at Nastya.)

He spent a few more days in Kharkov. Nastya didn't tell him about Yulka at once, but he accepted the child as well and would take her along. She still had her final exams, but they had already promised to send her for advanced study at the Institute for Shevchenko Studies. Viktor only laughed: he was Ukrainian himself, but he didn't think much of the Ukrainian language.

Getting out to Moscow—or anywhere else—was impossible: no one could buy a ticket without a lot of papers with official stamps and approvals. But within a month, Zadorozhny arrived with all the necessary papers, and he took Nastya and Yulka out of the starving, almost dying city. Luck was with them.

And in one of the first shop windows in Moscow Nastya caught sight of some white rolls! For only ten kopecks! A mirage . . . Her head whirled and she felt sick to her stomach. This was a different country entirely.

But the students' residence of the Industrial Academy turned out to be even more amazing: no more "shared" rooms with cots for four, six, or ten people. Each door from the corridor led into a tiny anteroom with two doors leading to different rooms. A married couple lived in the room next door, while Zadorozhny himself had a large room, and now he'd come back with his trophies. A little cot had already been set up for Yulka.

Viktor told her that Stalin's wife was also studying at the Industrial Academy. The Academy cafeteria was a good one. And there was a clean kindergarten with good food.

There was one more mysterious object in the room: a small electrical apparatus that cooled the things inside. You could keep your fresh food in it—sausage, ham, butter.

And you could eat whenever you felt like it!

2

NASTENKA HAD SPENT her childhood in Moscow—the old Moscow, on a little street near the Pure Ponds. The German War had not yet begun when she had already learned to read, and then Papa gave her permission to borrow any books she wished from his shelves. The colorful spines of the books were like a flower garden! The writers' names themselves were a flower garden, and their verses, poems, and stories were like a flower garden. In a few years she had begun to tackle novels as well. Tatyana Larina and Lisa Kalitina and Vasily Shibanov and Gerasim and Anton the Wretched and the little boy, Vlas, hauling a cartload of brushwood—all of them stood before her as if alive, right next to her; she could see them in the flesh and hear their voices. She was also taking German lessons with Madame and already reading "The Tale of the Nibelungs," Schiller's poetry, the sufferings of young Werther, and they, too, were also clear and vivid, though still some distance away, while the heroes of the Russian books were right beside her, her dear friends or her enemies. Gripped by this second life of hers, she was unaware of the hungry years in Moscow.

Just before the revolution, Nastenka entered a classical high school, one of the best in Moscow. By some miracle this school remained open not only through the revolution but even for a few years in Soviet times. It was still called a *gimnaziya* as before, and the previous instructors were still there, one of them being the ashen-haired Maria Feofanovna, who taught literature. She opened the world of literature to all her students, but Nastenka went much farther than anyone else. She learned to look at books in a new way—not just to live with the characters but to live constantly with the author: What was he feeling when he wrote that? How did he regard his characters? Was he the sole master of their lives, or were they independent of him? How did he organize this scene or that one, and what words and phrases did he choose in doing so?

Nastenka fell in love with Maria Feofanovna and dreamed of becoming like her: when she grew up, this was just how she would teach and explain Russian literature to children, making sure that they learned to love memorizing poetry, that they read the plays aloud in class and performed excerpts on the school stage on special evenings. (Maria Feofanovna herself gave Nastenka a good deal of attention and encouraged her enthusiasm.) Nastenka had not yet developed a crush on any boy, but how she loved everything that was literature! It was an entire, enormous, organic world, more vivid than the reality that flowed around her.

When she finished school, she hoped to enter Moscow University, in what remained of the former Faculty of History and Philology. Her father, Dmitry Ivanych, an epidemiologist and a great lover of Chekhov, also encouraged her in her choice.

But then came the misfortune: he was transferred to work in Rostov Oblast and they had to leave Moscow at a time when Nastenka, at sixteen, had only one year of school remaining. (True, Maria Feofanovna was no longer allowed to teach, being regarded as ideologically outmoded.)

Moscow! There could be no city more beautiful than Moscow, a place that had been formed not by the lifeless plan of some architect but by the active lives of many thousands over the course of centuries. Its boulevards and its two ring roads, its noisy, colorful streets, and its crookedly wandering lanes and grassy courtyards in which people lived their separate lives, its sky filled with the many voices of bells ringing in every pitch and timbre. Moscow, with its Kremlin, its Rumiantsev Library, its famous university, and its Conservatory.

It was true that they received quite a decent apartment in Rostov and, by the standards of the day, even a very good one. It was on the second floor, with large windows overlooking quiet Pushkin Street that also had a boulevard running along its middle. Yet the city itself seemed utterly foreign, not Russian, because of its multiracial population and, in particular, because of its corrupted language: the sounds of the local speech were distorted, and the stresses on words were not right. She made no friends at school, and the whole atmosphere there was also harsh and foreign. Another horrid thing was that she had to join the Komsomol to have any chance of getting into a university or institute. Awake and asleep, Nastenka was haunted by pictures of Moscow. She was quite prepared to live in a student residence, so long as it was at Moscow University.

On the wall of the Rostov apartment, just as in her Moscow one, Nastenka had assembled about two dozen portraits of Russian writers. From them she sought to fortify that truth in which she had grown up and which had become somehow obscured and thrust aside in the new, chaotic reality around her. The portrait of Nekrasov dying in his bed particularly tore her heart. She loved him fiercely for his unfailing response to the tribulations of the people.

And now—was there some sinister resemblance to Nekrasov here?—her father had come down with a severe cold after a trip along the Don in foul autumn weather. He developed pneumonia, and that developed into tuberculosis. The very word was terrifying (as were the terrible posters about tuberculosis in the clinic waiting rooms). How many lives had it already carried away? Even Chekhov's. There were no medicines to treat it. Now he needed a better climate. Should they move once more? But he hadn't the money or the strength to do it. This accursed city! The whole move here had been disastrous. Icy northeast winds blew through Rostov even into April. It was so painful to look into her father's eyes: Did he *know* even better than she did? And was he *preparing himself* within?

How could she now go to Moscow University? To make matters worse, doctors had forbidden him to take up any private practice. Her father's strength was failing in any case. And so she had to enroll here in Rostov, in a Faculty of Literature, but one in a pedagogical institute (that was soon renamed the Industrial-Pedagogical Institute).

But did Russian literature still remain the center of Nastenka's life? Well, not really. Somehow she couldn't recognize the literature of the past in what was now being laid out before her in the lectures. Though they did acknowledge, in passing, the musicality of Pushkin's poetry (but never mentioned the transparent clarity of his perception of the world), they insistently pointed out that he expressed the mindset and ideology of the mid-level landowners during the incipient crisis of Russian feudalism: this meant the portrayal of well-being on the feudal estate and the fear of peasant revolution, as vividly depicted in *The Captain's Daughter*.

It seemed more like some form of algebra than literature, and wherever had poor Pushkin vanished?

Her class was filled mostly with girls, some of them not at all stupid. And she could see that this or that one was troubled to learn that poets and writers did not create their works guided by free inspiration: though the writers themselves might have been unaware of it, unwittingly but objectively they were fulfilling someone else's social command. One had to have a sharp eye here to perceive what lay beneath the surface. Yet the institute girls never openly expressed any disagreement with the lectures to one another: either this was simply not the common practice or—more likely—it was something quite risky.

And how boring it all was! How could one live on this? Where were those radiant faces she had known?

Nastenka now had to cram into her head that Ostrovsky also reflected the process of decay of the feudal, serf-owning system and its displacement by developing industrial capitalism, and that his identification with that system had cast him back to the camp of reactionary Slavophilism. And this whole dark kingdom had best been penetrated by Dobroliubov's *ray of light*.

The bit about Dobroliubov—well, that was gospel.

The boys in the class were basically stumblebums who appeared to have entered this faculty simply by accident. But then there was Shurik Gen—impulsive, quick-witted, a bundle of energy with jet-black hair and eyes full of expression. Now, he was in his proper place here! A natural leader who excelled in his studies, he immediately became the Komsomol organizer. And in discussions outside of class, which were now becoming frequent, he brought in a vital stream of literature that they had not yet taken up in their program. This was the literature of today, turbulent and filled with furious struggle among various literary groupings. How can anyone turn his back on the contemporary world? (And, indeed, why should one try to avoid it?) As it turned out, there were many groups that had already burned themselves out or grown shallow over these years— but the Smithy, Vagranka, Lef, October—"These are all on our side of the literary trenches."

"But," his voice rang out, "our ideological antipodes aren't simply sleeping. Take the Fellow Travelers: these writers are our enemies of yesterday and the corpses of tomorrow. They are reactionaries at the core, and they slanderously distort the revolution. And they're all the more dangerous the more skillfully they do it. Literature, though, isn't some object of enjoyment, it's a battlefield. All these Pilnyaks and Akhmatovas and their kin, all these Serapion Brothers and wretched little Scorpios must either be forced to fall into line with proletarian literature or be swept aside with an iron broom; there's no room for compromise. We mustn't let the trenches of our literary position be overgrown with thistles! And we, the youth—all we Children of October—must also help establish a single communist line in literature. Despite the way some of these melancholic scribblers have tried to frighten us, the basic spirit of our new beginnings is vigor, not despair!"

Shurik always spoke out with such passion and heat that no one could match him. His classmates were left speechless. He simply drew everyone along in his wake. To say that these discussions were interesting wasn't enough; they provided a connection with living life; whole new currents, previously unknown, flowed from them. Nastenka was one of the most dedicated listeners among his audience, and she spent more and more time asking him questions after the others had gone.

And it was true: one couldn't live only on the literature of the past, one had to hearken to what was happening today. Real life was flowing around them in a vigorous stream, and they had to enter into it.

How did Shurik know all these things? When had he found the time to soak it all up? As it emerged, he had wasted no time even in the last years of his high school. While there, he had even made his way through the yellow-, green- and crimson-colored anthologies of the Futurists, then through LEF ("Lef or bluff?"), then through Komfut (communist futurism), and the Litfront (all of them searing his heart) and had already become a dedicated On Guardist while at his school desk. (And in fact the journal *On Literary Guard* was right there in the institute's library, but no one bothered to peer into it or take a deep breath of its heady spirit.)

"None of these Fellow Travelers should even be allowed to exist," Shurik would shoot back. "You're either an ally or an enemy! Just look at what they most value: the subtlety of their emotions. But what is decisive is not the writer's heart, it's his outlook on life. And we value a writer not because of what and how he experiences life but by his role in our proletarian movement. Psychologism only gets in the way of our triumphant movement forward. But what they call 'reincarnation into a character' only deadens one's class consciousness. One can say that the revolution in literature hasn't yet truly begun. After the revolution we need not just new words but even new letters for them! Even the periods and commas of the past become repulsive."

This was positively staggering! It made your head spin. Yet how transported he became by all this fervor, this unyielding conviction.

As for the lectures, they moved along the clearly specified paths laid out by the stolid textbooks of Kogan and Friche. They wrote in similar fashion: Shakespeare was a poet of kings and lords; do we have any use for him? And all these Onegins and Bolkonskys, are they not our total class aliens?

That may be so, yet they certainly knew how to love in those days!

There was no way to maintain a sustained argument against Kogan, however: he couldn't have constructed all these many things on utter nonsense. Surely there was a genuine historical and social basis for them?

Month by month, it seemed, her father's eyes occupied more and more space on his face and expressed more and more meaning. So much depth and suffering and wisdom had accumulated in them! He seemed to acquire a profound understanding as he detached himself from life. Yet she didn't dare say it aloud: Was this part of his *passing over*? Had he already crossed some sort of threshold? His face had yellowed, he had grown utterly gaunt, and his gray moustache had lost its resilience and now drooped as if it had been pasted on.

How terribly he coughed, and for such a long time, tearing away not only at his own breast but those of his wife and his daughter as well. The sense of grief now never left their home; it had become permanent. But when she came to the institute, her mind was filled with other thoughts. Since childhood Nastenka had been closer to her father than her mother, and she always loved to tell him everything; and now everything that absorbed her outside the home was so new and so disconcerting.

He would listen to her. He showed no surprise but only looked, looked at her through those eyes that had become so large and which, month by month, ever more clearly expressed the inevitability of *loss*—that was their dominant expression.

He would stroke her head (now he was always in bed, propped up on thick pillows). Sometimes, using his ebbing strength to breathe and speak, he would reply that the acquisition of any form of knowledge is a long and far from straightforward process and that which his daughter had now learned would also pass; she would still look at things in ever new ways, and there was no limit to the depths of human life.

She was growing ever closer to Shurik, and nothing and no one other than he could bring Nastya the very breath of the Era, as hot as Rostov's torrid summer wind. He felt it so strongly, and he conveyed it with such vital power! He had already published things in the regional newspaper *The Hammer*; he never missed an opportunity to speak in class or at institute gatherings or rallies and literary debates; between classes he gladly shared his ideas with his friends and, most of all, with Nastenka, whom he had begun to walk home. (He came from a good family, the son of an important lawyer, and never treated girls with the coarse boorishness that was becoming the norm.)

Now he admitted that the On Guardists had been in error when they took the side of Trotsky during a party debate, but they had admitted their mistake and corrected themselves. And even before the Shakhty Affair, he boldly declared: "We are proud to be labeled literary Chekists, proud that our enemies call us informers!" Now he was entirely consumed with the struggle against Polonsky-ism, against Voronsky-ism, against the literary group Pereval that had descended to the point of neo-Slavophilism, of kulak humanism, of "love for man in general," of "the beauty of the universal man." At last the Literary Section of the Communist Academy sentenced Voronsky-ism to liquidation. But the enemies multiplied: simultaneously, there was a struggle against Pereverzevism. Those people—though they were correct in understanding that the author's personality, biography, and literary predecessors had no significance whatsoever in his work and that his system of imagery stemmed from the system of production—still overdid it in arguing that every author was a writer only of his own class, and that a proletarian writer could not describe a bourgeois. And this was certainly a leftist deviation.

After the walk home he and Nastenka kissed in the semidarkness—and sometimes under a full moon—on Pushkin Boulevard, about twenty paces across from the window behind which her father lay, coughing his life away.

But Shurik was now insisting, more and more assertively, on taking their relationship right to its final point. She put him off, imploring him. She yielded as much as she could, but still, there was a limit!

In fact, did *marriage* really exist these days? It might as well have been abolished. When people came to an arrangement, they went to the registry office, and many of them never bothered with that and simply got together and then separated without bothering to register.

But Shurik demanded: Either, or! Either that or a breakup.

She was wounded by his stubborn refusal to be swayed. She wept in his arms and begged him to wait.

Absolutely not!

But she was not yet prepared to let him have his way about *this*.

On one of these intensely painful evenings, he brusquely and emphatically broke up with her.

In class in the days that followed he made a point of showing his indifference and avoided her.

How her heart ached!

She loved him and she revered him. But still, she couldn't . . .

How long would her suffering have gone on? And how far would it have gone? But at this point her father began living out his final days.

Now each day and each week before the numbing cold of parting were numbered; soon the final thread that linked the consciousness and the purpose of the three of you would slip from your caring fingers, and you and Mama would be left here, while he, forever, would . . .

The full sense of emptiness set in after the funeral (her mother was a believer, but there was not a single church or a single priest left in the city of four million; a religious funeral was a very risky thing in any case). Her mother grew wrinkled; she weakened and lost all her vitality. It happened so quickly that Nastenka felt somehow older and more responsible. Mama now could offer her no guidance.

As for Shurik, once he had broken with her, he made no move to restore their previous relations. He had a will of iron.

At the end of winter the graduates were being given their job assignments, and now Nastenka held out for a place in Rostov. She had nowhere else to go. And she got her place.

That last summer, nervous about her coming encounter with the forty-odd young minds that would be entrusted to her, Nastenka spent a lot of time in the library. She worked through the *Encyclopedia of Literature* that was just now being published, the methodological journal of the Directorate of Education of the Russian Republic, and various other journals filled with critical essays. She filled in the gaps in what she had learned earlier from Shurik, and all those things, to be sure, were being published everywhere. You needed only the time to read and summarize them.

As for Shurik, he went to Moscow for good. He'd been given a job in some publishing house. Back to that beautiful Moscow that she'd left behind and now would never recover . . .

Yet it was better that he had gone.

You could reach the library by taking the narrow Nikolaevsky Lane that dropped down through the ravine that was there in those days, or you could go more directly through the city park. The park had many things to offer. There was a straight and level central pathway from which the ground sloped downward on both sides to little squares with flowerbeds and fountains. A band shell where there were free classical music concerts in summer stood on the hills on one side, and on the other side was a summer restaurant where a tiny variety band played irritating music.

Nastenka's face was rather broad, and her figure was nothing special, but her eyes were filled with an amazing radiance and she had a smile that simply captured people's hearts, as she was often told and was well aware.

During her years at the institute there would be parties with the kids from other faculties, and if they could get some gramophone records they would dance the foxtrot and the tango (and though older people generally denounced such things, the dances were something that was *ours*!). Now she and the one or two girlfriends she had left in Rostov would go to the city park in the evenings; the young people who knew each other would pair off and slip away along the dark pathways to find some privacy. (Once you've become a teacher, though, there'll be no more of such foolery.) The surprising thing was that every single boy behaved crudely, with a complete lack of sensitivity. None of them could understand the slow, gradual development of feelings. All of the boys had accepted the notorious and opportunistic slogan, "Forget about the cherry blossoms." People said with conviction that love was nothing more than "some bourgeois gimmick." One of the characters in some new play expressed it like this: "I need a woman, so why can't you do me this favor, as a comrade and a Komsomol girl?"

No, Shurik wasn't like that.

But all that was over.

Time rushed on. (There was even a new novel entitled *Forward, Time!*) The Five-Year Plan in Four Years extended itself and rumbled over them. Back in the Pedagogical Institute they had all been instilled with the idea that Soviet literature—and therefore, teachers of literature—must not lag behind the demands of the Period of Reconstruction. The very same month Nastya was preparing to teach her first lessons, the Russian Association of Proletarian Writers published its resolution calling for positive heroes in literary works and for shock-worker projects in literature; workers themselves should become writers and thus ensure that art did not lag behind the demands of the working class. Some were even setting forth the idea that only the newspaper or the propaganda poster could be the literature of our time—certainly not the novel.

Well, this was all so rash and impetuous that it took your breath away. What did they mean—no novels? What would happen to the novel?

Now you have to go and meet the children, at a time when the Education Directorate is saying that teaching Krylov's fables within the walls of the Soviet school poses a definite pedagogical risk.

Nastenka (now she was addressed as Anastasia Dmitrievna) was given three parallel fifth-grade classes—twelve-year-olds—and was the homeroom teacher for Five A.

Her first lesson! But it was the first for the children as well: in this second level they were no longer little kids, and how proud they were of that!

September 1 was a joyful, sunny day. A few of the parents brought flowers to class. Anastasia Dmitrievna wore a bright shantung dress; the girls were all in white frocks, and many of the boys wore white shirts. Their funny little faces and brightly shining eyes were full of exultation. At long last her dream had come true, and she could do all that Maria Feofanovna had done . . . (And even more: in this present age, when everything had become coarse and crude, she could make sure that these little boys became decent men, not like the ones today.) Now, in lesson after lesson, she could pour into their heads all the things she had preserved from this great and good literature.

But somehow it wasn't happening that way. She could not yet see a way to break through the rigidly determined teaching program:

The building cranes crash
By the foundation pit . . .

And the regional inspector might drop in on any of her classes to check on her. She had to begin with the Turkestan-Siberian Railway that was now being completed and see that the children memorized how the trains passed through the desert:

. . . past all they fly
Scaring people and flocks,
Not letting them by
On the caravan tracks.

And then she had to take up Magnitogorsk, and then the Dnieper Dam and Bezymensky's poem ridiculing a doomed professor-suicide from the dying class. And then there was the poem about an Indian boy who had heard something about Lenin, the inspiring leader of all the oppressed in the world, and who had made his way to him in Moscow on foot all the way from India.

Next, they saddled her with the slogan "To Demyanize Literature": to instill it with the militant spirit of Demyan Bedny.

Anastasia Dmitrievna, completely perplexed, saw no way to resist these things. And how could she take the responsibility for shutting off these little children from the era in which they were living?

It was good, though, that they were still in the junior grades. Today's harsh conditions will pass, and with a few years' more study they'll get to the cherished classics. And even today not all of Pushkin has been written off:

> Here all bear heavy yokes unto the grave,
> Afraid to cherish hope or private dream;
> A maiden blossoms to become a slave
> And victim of her heartless master's scheme.

She read it aloud in class, striving to convey to the children the poet's pain, but alongside the crashing of the cranes, the lines of his verse seemed to be coming from another world, one that was far, far away.

Inspiration came only in her Russian language classes: this was a straightforward, unshakeable, and eternal subject. But it, too, had been shaken! Look at what they were doing with the new orthography! And the rules were changing so quickly, she couldn't keep up with them herself.

Still, Nastenka taught all these production and Five-Year Plan works with the same dedication that she felt to her own sacred cause of literature; she taught so that the kids loved her, surrounded her during recess and looked at her with gratitude, reflecting the constant radiance in her own eyes.

Meanwhile, the stores in the city stood empty, and all the private shops had been closed. There were the first mentions of "difficulties in the meat supply," and then "difficulties in the sugar supply." Soon there was nothing left to buy, and food ration cards were introduced. (Teachers were considered civil servants, and this entitled them to 400 grams of bread, while her ever-weakening mother went to work in a tobacco factory so as to get a "worker's" ration card for 600 grams.) A hungry time set in, and no one had wages high enough for the private market. In fact, the militia were driving off the market sellers.

Even the old week, with each day measured off, had ended. Now there was an "unbroken five-day week." Members of a family would have free days at different times, and the common Sunday was done away with . . . "*Forward, Time!*" Time rushed along so quickly that it lost its very dignity and seemed to stop simply *being*.

Life grew ever harsher. One day you might get 200 grams of bread on your ration card, the next day 300, and the amounts would alternate. You always went around feeling hungry. Rumor had it that people were dying of hunger in the villages across the whole region. You would come across the bodies of people who had made their way from the countryside and dropped dead on the streets of the city. Nastenka herself never stumbled on a corpse, but once a peasant woman from the Kuban, emaciated beyond belief and barely able to stand on her feet, knocked at her door. They fed her some of their own thin soup and she, no longer able to weep, told of how she had buried her three little children and set off across the steppe haphazardly in hope of saving herself. The whole of the Kuban had been cordoned off by soldiers, and they would catch anyone trying to flee and turn them back. This woman had somehow managed to slip through the cordon by night, but boarding a train was impossible: they could pick her out near a station or inside the train, and then it was back behind the line of doom or to prison.

Should they let her stay with them?

She left, stumbling at every step.

Mama said: "I feel like dying myself. Where will all this end?"

Nastenka tried to raise her spirits: "We'll break through to a better world, Mama! Communism, after all, is based on the same ideals as Christianity; it just takes a different path to reach them."

Student notebooks had disappeared from the stationery stores. There were a few lucky children who still had some from their previous stock, but a regular two-hundred-page notebook bound in oilcloth was now a real treasure. Then notebooks were reduced in width and made with rough paper that caught at the pen nibs. They began distributing notebooks through the schools, each pupil getting two of them for a quarter of the school year, and they had to be used for all the subjects together. Somehow the kids had to divide these skinny little notebooks among their different subjects and write smaller—so much for penmanship. What remained was the blackboard and more rote memorization. A few parents were able to get old bookkeeping forms or warehouse timesheets, and their children wrote on the backs of them.

But children of that age could cope with absolutely everything. They still laughed and ran around at recess. But what about you? How were you to get through this painful year? How were you to lead the children toward a better time while preserving unspoiled their sense of the Pure and the Beautiful? And how were you to teach them to discern the rightness and the inevitability of the New Era through all the jumbled ugliness of the life around them? Nastenka vividly recalled Shurik's enthusiasm. Even now she was still infected by him: there was someone who possessed a true vision! As the poet said:

> They'll bear it all, and build themselves a road
> With muscle and bone . . .

Was Russian literature not continuing even today? Was the present love for the people not the direct product of the sacred precepts of Nekrasov, Belinsky, Dobroliubov, and Chernyshevsky? All those dry commentaries of Kogan and Friche, or the passionate monologues of Shurik—surely they weren't built on thin air?

When one considered it carefully, Dobroliubov's ray of light had never stopped shining! It had penetrated into our time as well, but now was it not a ray of burning scarlet? One simply had to be able to pick it out in today's conditions.

But then she went to read the latest instructional guidelines from the Education Directorate, the articles of Osip Martynovich Beskin in particular, and her heart sank: she read that an artist could not rely on intuition in his work; he was obliged to take control of his perception through class consciousness. And furthermore: this so-called literature with a heart was nothing more than a slogan soiled by the greasy fingers of Russophiles, and it had been raised in Russia over a foundation laid by a patriarchal cabal.

Literature with a heart! That was what she longed for most of all!

The program for next year included the "iron foundation" of Soviet literature: Fadeev's *Rout*; Panfyorov's *Bruski*, about collectivization; Gladkov's *Cement* (a horrid thing because it presented thirteen-year-old children with violent scenes of erotic conquest). Yet it was true that Serafimovich's *Iron Flood* showed in remarkably laconic fashion the actions by a mass of people as a whole—something, it seems, that our literature had never done before. Libedinsky's *The Week* aroused sympathy for Robeyko as he forced his tubercular throat to call out the inhabitants to cut down the monastery forest for firewood so that the peasants could buy seed grain. (Still, that must mean that every tiny bit of last year's seed grain had been confiscated.)

Forty pairs of childish eyes were fixed on Anastasia Dmitrievna every day, and how could she betray their trust? Yes, children, sacrifices are inevitable, and the whole of Russian literature has called out to us to make sacrifices. Yes, there has been "wrecking" going on here and there, but the unprecedented scale of our industrialization will bring us all a happiness we've never known before. And when you grow up, you'll have a chance to take part in it. You have to examine every event carefully, even the dark ones, as the poet said so aptly:

> Only he can rise to glory,
> Only he can join our rush
> Who finds, 'neath petty facts, the story
> Of Revolution's forward push.

But then they took back the textbooks they had just given out for the year: they had been found incorrect and lagging behind reality. They began publishing "loose" textbooks—ones that dealt with contemporary issues and were to be used only for the current half of the year, because by the next year they would already be outdated. A newspaper published Gorky's article "To the Humanists," in which he denounced and damned those humanists—and this was immediately included in the next loose textbook: "It is entirely natural that workers' and peasants' power is crushing its enemies like lice."

It all left you terrified, scarcely able to catch your breath, and utterly confused. How could you possibly present that to the children? And *why*?

But Gorky was a great writer, a Russian classic, and an authority respected across the globe, so how could your wretched little mind dare challenge him? And here, right alongside, he writes about those who have lost contact with reality and live lives of ease: "What is it that this class of degenerates wants? . . . a well-fed, colorless, licentious, and irresponsible life." And then you remember Nekrasov's lines, "From the exultant, idle chatterers . . ." And didn't Chekhov call for a little man with a hammer to trouble the sleeping conscience each day?

So she decided to organize a literary circle. A dozen of her most responsive, favorite students from Six A signed up, and after class Anastasia Dmitrievna would take them through the best of the nineteenth century, things that weren't included in the syllabus. But there was no way she could hide her circle from the principal (a caustic woman who taught social science). From her it went up to the Region, and an instructor from the methodology office came and sat down like a toad at one of the meetings of the literary circle. Anastasia Dmitrievna cut out all of the enthusiasm, all the sense, all the inspiration, and could scarcely recognize what remained as her own. The verdict of the toad was: Enough harping on the classics! The fact is that it distracts students from life.

"Fact" had become a byword in these years. The word rang out as something incontestable, deadly as a pistol shot. (And the toad-like instructor could have reached a far more brutal verdict: "This was *sneak attack*!")

There was another possibility—outings to the theater. The five-day week had now changed to six days, and every date divisible by six was a common rest day, similar to the former Sunday. On these free days the theater put on cheap matinees for schoolchildren. Children, accompanied by their teachers, would come from all across the city. The enchantment of the lights dimming in the hall, the curtains drawing back, the actors moving under the bright spotlights, their vivid appearance in makeup, their ringing voices—how these things could capture the heart of a child, and what a shining path to literature they offered.

It was true that the plays were what you could expect, requisites of the Five-Year Plan: Trenyov's *Lyubov Yarovaya*, in which the wife of a White officer shoots her husband out of ideological commitment; and quite a lot of Kirshon—*The Rails Are Humming*, about the subversive activities of engineers; and *Bread*, about the vicious resistance of the kulaks and the ardor of the poor peasantry. (After all, you couldn't deny the class struggle and its role in history.) She did manage to bring her students to Schiller's *Kabale und Liebe*. And so, taking up the children's enthusiasm, Anastasia Dmitrievna arranged a reading in which students in group Seven A took the various roles in the play. A star student, a skinny boy with disheveled hair that would never stay in place, read in an unnatural voice dripping with tragedy and aping his favorite actor: "Louisa, did you love the marshal? This candle will not burn out before you die . . ." (This same boy was the class deputy on the school pedagogical council, as was the practice.) Schiller's play was considered compatible with revolutionary times and attending it would not bring a reprimand. But if they were thinking of reading anything by Ostrovsky they had to choose very, very carefully.

Rostov-on-the-Don was declared "a city of hundred-percent literacy" (though there were still more than plenty illiterates). In the schools, they were using the "brigade-laboratory method": the instructor did not present the lesson and did not assign individual grades. The class was split into brigades of four or five, and the desks were rearranged accordingly; one of the students in each brigade would read aloud, in a low voice, from the "loose" textbook. Then the instructor would ask for one student to answer for the whole brigade. And if the answer was "satisfactory" or "very satisfactory," then each member of the brigade would receive a "sat." or a "v. sat."

Then there was a school quarter when none of the usual loose textbooks arrived and no required curriculum was assigned. Without them, even the city education authorities were lost: Did this mean some major shift in the party line? They decided that for the time being each teacher would carry on however they chose and take responsibility for what they did.

It was then that their social science teacher and principal began teaching bits from Marx's *Capital* to the fifth, sixth, and seventh grades at once. Did that mean Anastasia Dmitrievna could now teach some of the Russian classics? But how could she make the right choice and not fall into error? Dostoevsky, of course, was ruled out, and in any case the students were not yet ready to be exposed to him. And Leskov—no, even he was ruled out. Nor could she take Aleksei Tolstoy's *Death of Ivan the Terrible* or

Tsar Fyodor. As for Pushkin—well, not everything. And Lermontov—not everything. (And if any of the young lads asked about Esenin she would change the subject and not answer—he was strictly forbidden.)

In fact, she had grown unaccustomed to such freedom. She herself could no longer even express what she had once felt. After all that Nastenka had read, discovered, and had been taught to see over these past years, even the former unshakeable integrity of Russian literature now seemed to have been shaken. Now she was frightened to talk about an author or a book without providing some class basis for them. She paged through Kogan and found the phrase, "the types of ideas with which this work falls into line."

Meanwhile, new issues of Soviet literary journals were coming out, and the newspapers were heaping praises on some new works. She lost heart: she could not allow these young adolescents to lag behind. They were the ones, after all, who would have to live in this world, and she must help them find their way into it.

And so she sought out these new poems and stories that had been hailed in the press and brought them to her students. Here, children, is the highest degree of selflessness for the sake of the common cause:

> *I'll gladly give up both my name and rank*
> *For a number, a letter, a tag!*

This did not go over well. Young hearts must be set aflame with something that soars, something romantic. And then there was:

> *Cavalry horses*
> *Carried us there!*
> *The enemy forces*
> *Advanced 'cross the square!*
> *But, dripping hot blood,*

We rose up once again
And our unseeing eyes
We opened again!
. . . So that this harsh nation
Would flow with our blood,
So a new generation
Would stand where we stood.

And her students' glowing, inspired little eyes were Anastasia Dmitrievna's best reward.

A reward for a whole life that, till now, had been a failure.

1993; 1995

ADLIG SCHWENKITTEN

A TALE OF TWENTY-FOUR HOURS

Dedicated to the Memory of
Major Pavel Afanasyevich Boyev and
Major Vladimir Kondratyevich Baluev

1

O N THE NIGHT of January 25–26, the army artillery staff informed the staff of our artillery brigade that our forward tank corps had broken through to the Baltic coast! East Prussia, therefore, had been cut off from Germany.

It had been cut off, but for the moment only by this long, thin wedge that was still far in advance of all its supporting troops. But the days when we retreated were over. Prussia had been cut off! Surrounded!

And so, Comrade Political Officers, a conclusive victory. Put it down in your war diaries. Now we're no more than a stone's throw away from Berlin, unless they give that job to someone else.

During the five days of our advance through a Prussia of burning houses there had been no shortage of celebrations. In the eleven days after we broke out of our expanded bridgehead on Narew and the five days when we moved through Poland there had been some stubborn resistance, but once we crossed the Prussian border it was as if some miraculous curtain had been drawn aside: the German units fell back on both our flanks, revealing an undamaged land of abundance that simply fell into our hands. Clusters of stone houses with tall, steep roofs; soft beds to sleep in, sometimes even under eiderdown; stocks of food in the cellars with sweet stuff and other goodies we'd never laid eyes on before. There was even free drink to be had for those who could find it.

And so we advanced through Prussia in a kind of half-drunken, joyous haze, as if we had lost the precision of our movements and our thoughts. Naturally, after so many years of war casualties and deprivations, we sometimes slackened off a little.

This feeling of enjoying some well-deserved rewards took hold of everyone, right up to the higher commanders. The troops felt it even more. And they found some rewards. And they drank.

After we had cut off Prussia this feeling grew even stronger.

On the morning of January 26, seven of the brigade's tractor and truck drivers died in convulsions after drinking methyl alcohol. There were also some victims from the gun crews, and others who went blind.

So began this day in the brigade. Those who had gone blind were taken to the hospital. Captain Toplev, with a plump, boyish face and only recently promoted from senior lieutenant, knocked at the door of the room where the CO of Second Battalion, Major Boyev, was sleeping, to report on the incident.

Boyev was a sound sleeper, but it was always easy to wake him. With such a marvelous bed to sleep in and with a plump eiderdown as well, he had allowed himself to take off his tunic for the night. He now pulled it on and was standing on the carpet in his woolen socks. His tunic was covered with an amazing array of orders and medals: two Orders of the

Red Banner, an Alexander Nevsky, an Order of the Fatherland War, and two Orders of the Red Star (one came from as far back as the battle with the Japanese at Lake Khasan, the other from the Finnish War; and there was a third Red Star, the most recent, but it had been lost or stolen after he'd been wounded). And so his whole chest was covered in metal, since he wore the orders themselves, not just the ribbons, and it was a soldier's pleasure to feel the weight of them.

Toplev, who just a month ago had moved from head of battalion reconnaissance to Boyev's adjutant, gave a dignified, regulation salute and made his report. His baby face was worried, but his voice still had the warmth of a child's. Two men from Second Battalion, Podkliuchnikov and Lepetushin, had died from alcohol poisoning.

The major was of average height, but his long head with closely trimmed hair stood out like a rectangle whose corners were formed by his temples and jaw. His eyebrows were not quite level and his nose twisted just slightly toward a deep crease in his cheek, as if he were in a constant state of tension.

He listened to Toplev's report with the same tension. He made no reply for a time and then said, bitterly: "Ahh, the slack-brained fools . . ."

After surviving so many shells and bombs in so many river crossings and bridgeheads, only to cop it from some bottle in Germany . . .

They'd have to be buried, but where? Well, they'd chosen their own gravesite.

After passing through Allenstein the brigade had taken up firing positions here, just in case, though it seemed unlikely they would do any firing. It was just for the sake of order.

"We won't use the German cemetery. We'll bury them around our firing position."

Lepetushin. Well, he was that kind of fellow. Talkative, always ready to help, never complained. But Podkliuchnikov? That tall, serious peasant with a bit of a stoop. He just couldn't resist.

2

THE GROUND WAS frozen and stony, impossible to dig very deeply.

Sortov, their carpenter from Mari, built the coffins quickly from some nicely planed planks he'd found nearby.

Should they put up a flag? No one ever saw flags except when the brigade formed up for a medals parade. Their colors were always kept in the stores, somewhere in the third echelon where they wouldn't be captured.

Podkliuchnikov had been in Five Battery, Lepetushin in Six. The party organizer, Gubaydulin—the laughingstock of the whole battalion—showed up to give a speech. He'd been drunk since morning and he strung together the usual glowing phrases about the sacred Motherland, the beast's den into which we had now entered, and the revenge we would take for our fallen comrades.

The commander of one of Six Battery's gun platoons, the very young but solidly built Lieutenant Gusev, listened to this, ashamed and irritated. Did this fellow become a party organizer because of the quick promotion for political officers? Or was it because the brigade commissar had some special liking for him? But over the course of a year and a half, before everyone's eyes, he went from junior sergeant to senior lieutenant, and now he thought he had lessons to give to everyone.

Gusev was only eighteen, but he had already spent a year at the front as a lieutenant, the youngest officer in the brigade. He was so eager to go into battle that his father, a general, had put him into an accelerated course for junior lieutenants while he was still underage.

It's different for everyone. Next to him stood Vanya Ostanin, from the battalion fire control platoon. He was a clever fellow, and he could direct fire as well as any officer. But during the days of Stalingrad in '42 every third person on their course had been yanked out of their academy and sent to the front before his training had been completed. The personnel department selected people for promotion, and there was a note in

Ostanin's file that his family had stubbornly resisted joining the collective farm. Now this twenty-two-year-old, essentially an officer, was wearing the shoulder straps of a senior sergeant.

The party organizer finished his speech. Gusev was driven by emotion to step toward the graves two paces in front of him. This wasn't at all what was needed. The party organizer's speech hadn't struck any sparks. Gusev could only ask in a choked voice: "Why, boys? Why'd you have to end that way?"

The lids of the coffins were closed.

The nails were hammered in.

The coffins were lowered on ropes.

They were covered with foreign earth.

Gusev recalled how a Junkers had bombed them along a road near Rechitsa. No one was wounded and little damage was done, but a three-liter bottle of vodka in the supply truck was shattered by a bit of shrapnel. Lord, how sorry the fellows were about that! Taking some casualties wouldn't have been much worse. Soviet soldiers aren't pampered by too much booze.

Grave markers, still unpainted, were driven into the little mounds.

And who would tend these graves? Gravestones of German soldiers had been standing in Poland since 1915. When they were on the Narew, the signals officer Ishchukov had dug up the German graves and scattered the bones—he was "taking revenge." No one said anything to him: Larin, the SMERSH officer, had been standing right beside him.

Gusev passed by some soldiers standing quietly in a group and heard one of the men of his own platoon, the lively little Yursh from the same number three gun crew in which Lepetushin had served, say plaintively: "So how are we going to get by now, boys?"

How were they going to get by? But that's a soldier's lot: you have to think you'll make it.

But it showed on people's faces, as if a dark cloud had passed over them.

Nikolaev, another man from Mari and the captain of a gun crew, looked on disapprovingly through narrowed eyes. He never touched vodka.

But life goes on, and there's still a job to be done. Captain Toplev went to brigade headquarters to find out how the deaths should be designated.

The chief of staff, the thin and lanky Lieutenant Colonel Veresovoy, had a ready answer: "The commissar has already given instructions: 'They fell while bravely defending their Motherland.'"

He was busy racking his brains: Who was he going to put in the drivers' seats when the brigade moved on?

3

THE STUNNING SPEED with which our tanks broke through to the Baltic Sea altered the whole picture of the Prussian operation, and the heavy artillery brigade could not move quickly and had no assignment for the next day or two.

The brigade commander had been limping about for some time now because of an abscess on his knee. The medical officer convinced him not to put it off and to go to the hospital today for an operation. The brigade commander left, handing the unit over to Veresovoy.

There was no sound of gunfire in the distance and no aircraft—our own or German—to be seen. It was as if the war had ended.

It was not cold that day, but it was very cloudy. Visibility was poor. For the time being, all the troops were pulled back from their pre-arranged fire positions, and the three battalions closed up around brigade headquarters.

The day moved on quietly toward twilight. Even though we had now penetrated Europe, we still kept to Moscow time, and so it didn't get light until almost nine o'clock and it wasn't dark until six.

Then suddenly an encoded message arrived from the headquarters of army artillery: All three battalions were to move north immediately, to the town of Liebstadt, and upon arrival were to take up fire positions seven or eight kilometers to the east, with a general grid bearing angle 90.00.

So they're pulling us out anyway! And just when we're supposed to be getting to sleep. It never fails: just when you're looking forward to a quiet night in your new position and don't want to move. But the 90.00 bearing was a surprise. That hadn't happened since the war began: it was due east! No one ever thought we'd see that. We'd gotten used to angles of 250.00 to 270.00, more or less due west.

Even before this new order the chief of staff had been worrying about replacing the drivers who had died. There were scarcely any replacements. Which ones should he take, and which units should he leave immobile? First Battalion had suffered the most losses, and Lieutenant Colonel Veresovoy requested artillery headquarters to let it stay where it was in order to make up the complements of the Second and Third Battalions.

There was no choice, and he was granted permission.

It's only the first minutes that are difficult in a nighttime move. Already the twenty-four heavy-caliber gun-howitzers had been connected to their tractors, the whole operation done in the open, under the glow of headlights. The auxiliary transport fell in line behind them. All that could be heard was the growling of motors.

The two commanders of the gun battalions in their white fur jackets and the commander of the instrument reconnaissance battalion in his long overcoat arrived to get their exact deployment locations and their objectives from the chief of staff.

As for the objectives, the chief of staff could only guess. Army headquarters had provided absolutely no intelligence data, and they had no way of knowing the situation after such a rapid breakthrough and the cloudy weather of the past day. "Seven or eight kilometers to the east"— that leaves a lot of room for guesswork. A topographical map of 1:50,000 gave some sense of the ground in the area, but couldn't show everything. It did show the main and secondary roads, which places had defenses and which were without; it showed the bends in the Passarge River, which flowed from south to north, and the individual farms scattered across the area. But were they all just farms? And how many small, unmarked roads were there? Were there still people on the farms or had they fled?

The lieutenant colonel assigned the areas at random: Second Battalion would go here, to the south; Third here, farther north.

They marked out approximate ovals for the positions.

Major Boyev stood with his map case opened, looking gloomily at the map. How many hundreds of times over his military career had he had to come like this to be given his objective? And often enough the disposition of the enemy could not be indicated and remained unknown: once the unit begins doing its job, it'll locate the enemy easily enough. But here, twenty-five kilometers away from that town of Liebstadt, how could you tell which ground was unoccupied and where there might be a gap in the German flank? Above all, where was our infantry? And would they be from the division assigned to this sector? Most likely they're lagging. They can't keep up with the tanks and are well spread out. But how far back? And how do we locate them?

Veresovoy's usual firm voice betrayed no doubts, however. There was a rifle division, and yes, it was probably the same one as before. Of course it's spread out. But the Germans are still in a state of shock and will probably be pulling back toward Königsberg. Brigade headquarters will be in Liebstadt or the near vicinity. The battalions' headquarters will be somewhere near there as well.

What would be the sense of taking up fire positions before midnight? You can't fix your exact position in the darkness by survey, and if you just approximate it by local landmarks, your fire is going to be approximate as well.

And all the gun crews are short of men.

Our logistics support is lagging well behind. Well, there's nothing we can do about it. We'll get resupplied sooner or later.

Boyev looked at Veresovoy out of the corner of his eye. There was no negotiating with your commanders, even those closest to you. Just the way your commanders listen to their commander. The commander is always right.

They had to make it safe and sound to that Liebstadt, about three hours away, using a winter road that still had a bit of ice on it. The moon must already be up behind those clouds. Let's hope it won't be all in pitch darkness.

The tractors roared in unison. The whole column, dozens of headlights blazing, moved out of the village toward the highway.

It was nearly half an hour before they all reached it. Then the noise receded into the distance.

4

WHAT A LIFT a victory gives you!

And this silence all around is also a sign of victory, just as are the riches, still warm to the touch, abandoned everywhere by the Germans. Pick up what you can, make a parcel to send home—five kilos for a soldier, ten for an officer, fifteen for a general. But how do you choose the very best and not make a mistake? There's more here than anyone could want.

Every house used for billets was a wonder. Every night you spent in one was like a holiday.

Lieutenant Colonel Vyzhlevsky, the brigade commissar—now he was called the deputy political officer—had taken the most prominent house in the village. The lower level was not just a room, it was a large hall lit up by a dozen electric lights on the ceiling and the walls. The electricity was still coming from somewhere, and the fact that it hadn't been cut off was also a wonder. The radio–record player there (that's going home with us!) was softly playing some dance music.

When Veresovoy came in to report, Vyzhlevsky—broad-shouldered, with a large head and prominent ears—was sunk in a soft sofa by an oval table, an expression of bliss on his rosy face. (A military forage cap didn't suit a head like his; he should have a broad-brimmed hat.)

Sitting on the same sofa beside him was the brigade SMERSH officer, Major Tarasov, always quick-witted, watchful, and active. His face wore a permanent decisive expression.

Both the double doors to the dining room to one side were opened wide, and supper would soon be served there. Two or three women passed back and forth, one wearing a bright blue dress, evidently a German. There was also a woman from the political section who had changed out of her uniform—those Prussian wardrobes were stuffed with clothes. The air was filled with the aroma of hot food.

Why had Veresovoy come here? In the absence of the brigade commander he was formally the senior officer and could make decisions on his own. But after fifteen years of army service he had learned very well that nothing should be decided without the political officer. He always had to know what they thought and not get on their wrong side. And so, what about moving the headquarters? Should he leave immediately?

It was clear, though, that this was absolutely impossible. Supper and other delights were on their way. Sacrifices such as this should not be expected from human beings.

The commissar listened to the music, his eyes half closed. He replied benevolently: "Well, Kostya, where can we go right now? It's the middle of the night—what are we going to do there? Where will we stay? We'll get up early tomorrow and then be off."

And the SMERSH officer, always confident in his every gesture, gave a clear nod of agreement.

Veresovoy neither objected nor agreed. He continued to stand stiffly.

Then Vyzhlevsky, to make his idea more attractive, said: "Why don't you come and eat with us. Another twenty minutes and we'll be ready."

Veresovoy stood and thought. He wasn't eager to go, himself; these Prussian nights soon made you soft. And there was another factor: First Battalion was here, and it was very short-handed; he shouldn't abandon it.

Still, we could catch a lot of flak over this.

Tarasov was the one who found a solution: "Just break off communications with the army and the battalions. Then, as far as everyone else is concerned, we're on the move."

Well, if an officer from SMERSH is suggesting this, he'll hardly be the one to turn me in.

And truly, a trip like that at night was more than he could handle.

5

FINE SNOW FELL through the evening, covering the icy road. They moved slowly, not only because of the ice but to make sure the horses didn't get overtired.

They said their goodbyes in Liebstadt, and Boyev embraced the commander of Third Battalion, who had taken the northern area.

Along the way he used his flashlight to check his map. Boyev had to cross to the east bank of the Passarge River and then follow a dirt track for another kilometer and a half. He would probably position his guns beyond the village of Adlig Schwenkitten to leave at least 600 meters clear between them and the forest. That would make it safe to fire at low trajectories.

The bridge across the Passarge was reinforced concrete and in good shape; there was no need to check that it was passable. The left bank was steep, and there was a ramp down to the bridge.

They left a beacon to mark the spot for the horse-drawn sleds. Motorized units were not authorized to have horses or sleds, and the higher command assumed that such units had none. But ever since the Oryol offensive, all the batteries would collect any stray, German, owner-less and sometimes owned horses as they advanced and use them to haul their supplies in carts. You just had to put a competent sergeant in charge of such a supply train and he would always catch up with his battery. The Allis-Chalmers tractors were wonderful, of course, but if they were all you had you'd never make it. Later, and particularly as we drew closer to Germany, we got hold of the powerful German draft horses to replace our own medium-sized ones. Those German horses were gigantic. Sleds replaced the carts in winter. Today, for instance, without the sleds, every-one from the gunners to the observers would have had to sweat their guts out along these snowy roads.

The snow began to ease, but enough had fallen to reach halfway to your knees. Caps of snow had built up on the covers of the guns.

There wasn't a soul to be seen anywhere. Dead silence. And no tracks.

Using the headlights sparingly, they came to a tree-lined road. There was no one here either. At last, there was Adlig. Again, those foreign build-ings. All the houses were dark, with not a light showing anywhere.

He gave orders for the houses to be checked. The houses in the village were abandoned, but all of them were heated. The inhabitants must have left only a few hours ago. They couldn't be far away, then. You could expect the young women to run off to the forest, but here everyone had gone.

Boyev positioned eight guns along the eastern edge of Adlig, but not all twelve—that would have made no sense. He ordered battery commander Kasyanov to position his Six Battery about 800 meters to the south, falling back at an oblique angle, near the little village of Klein Schwenkitten.

Still, there wasn't a soul to be seen. They hadn't searched Liebstadt, but they hadn't spotted anyone moving in the village. Now where was our infantry? Not a single one of our brothers-in-arms had showed up.

It was a real puzzle: If we positioned our guns here, would we be too far away from the Germans? Or, to the contrary, would we be too close? They might be waiting for us right here, in this patch of forest. For the time being, we'll put in a screening force toward that forest.

What else could be done? The tractors were roaring. Six Battery was extended along the side road to Klein Schwenkitten. Four and Five Batteries were deploying side by side to form a single front. Each of the crews was busy with their own gun, changing over from column to combat formation and setting out their shells. (And, of course, they'd already scouted out the houses on the edge of the village for a bit of shelter and a nice kip.)

This little house was like a toy. Could it really be a farmer's house in a village? It looked like a house in town, everything set out neatly, curtains, pictures on the walls. The electricity had been cut off, but they found two kerosene lamps and set them on the table. Boyev sat down with his map. A map can always tell you a lot. If you look at it long enough, you can always find some way out, even from the most hopeless situation.

Boyev didn't hurry anyone on. They'd have to wait for the sleds in any case. He'd had to work without reconnaissance before. He'd done it, but it had been in his own country.

The radio operator had already made contact with brigade headquarters. They replied that they'd be leaving soon. (They hadn't left yet!) Any news or orders? Nothing for the moment.

Suddenly he heard footsteps in the entry. A man in a neat officer's overcoat, the commander of the sound-ranging battery that was under Boyev's operational command, came in. He was an old friend from the days they had served together near Oryol, a mathematician. Immediately he unfolded his map case by the lamp. Here, he explained, was a direct road leading northeast toward Dietrichsdorf, just over two kilometers away. That's where we'll set up our central station and string out our lines from there.

Boyev looked at the map. He could read a topographical map faster than he could read a book.

"Right, we'll be somewhere nearby. I'll be on the right. I'll run a line out to you. What about the surveyors?"

"I've got a section with me. But we can't do much fixing at night. They'll do a rough fix and then come back here."

So that was how they would be firing—approximately.

There was no time for chatting, he had to rush off. They shook hands warmly, like old friends.

"Later?"

Something remained unsaid. His battery commanders were already busy at their jobs and didn't need him telling them what to do. Now it was a matter of waiting for the horses.

Boyev lay down on the little sofa: It wasn't proper to lie in a bed with your boots on, and with your boots off, what kind of soldier are you?

6

FOR SOME THE war began in '41, but for Boyev it began with Lake Khasan, in '38. Then the Finnish War. And so the past seven years of his life had been nothing but war. He'd been off twice recovering from wounds, but with the war on there was no leave to go back home. It had been eleven years now since he'd been able to get back to his native Ishim steppe, with its hundreds of mirror-like lakes and huge flocks of game birds, or gone to Petropavlovsk to see his sister.

Only when he'd gone into the army had Pavel Boyev seen some real life. What was there for him outside the army? Southern Siberia was a long time in getting back on its feet after the Civil War and the crushing of the Ishim rebellion. In a good many places in Petropavlovsk the fences along the streets and around the gardens still hadn't been rebuilt; many had been burned, and those that had been repaired were leaning. Broken window-panes were stuffed with rags or pasted over with paper. The felt strips of insulation around the doors hung in shreds or had been replaced with straw or bark. Housing was really scarce, and he lived with his married sister, Praskovya. The problem of footwear was no better, and you went on and on mending the soles of your boots but your toes would still stick out. The food supply was worse yet: the bread you got on your ration card did nothing to fill a hungry working man . . . And you had to stand in line for everything, from five in the morning in some places. A mob would rush up to a store, not even asking what they'd be selling. Once a line formed they'd find out. The streets were filled with beggars.

In the army, though, they'd stuff you full of meat borshch and you had all the bread you could eat. The uniforms weren't always new, but at least they weren't full of holes. And the men in the army were the beloved sons of the people. Collar tabs were crimson for the infantry, black for the artillery, and light blue for the cavalry; and there were other colors too (red for the GPU). Life was organized on a precise schedule of drills, forming up, saluting, and marching, and your whole life had a purpose: life meant serving, and everyone had his job. He couldn't wait to get into the army and joined even before he was called up.

And so he never had to adapt himself to anything other than army life, and he never married. Then the trumpet sounded to call him to this war as well.

In the army, Pavel Boyev realized that he was a born soldier, that he'd been meant for the army and it was his home. He knew that army routine—firing exercises, packing up the equipment, moving out, changing your maps, and adapting to new routine—was what life was all about. In '41 they lost some guns and tractors, but that didn't happen again unless a gun had a direct hit or a tractor was blown up on a mine. War was a job, but one with no days off and no holidays, with his eyes peering through a binocular telescope. The battalion was his family, the officers his brothers, the soldiers his sons, and each one of them was a treasure. He had learned to live with the idea that life was a movement from one dodgy situation to another, that happy moments were short-lived, and that now there wasn't a turn of events that could surprise or frighten him. He had completely *forgotten how to be afraid*. And if some extra duty or risky mission came up, he would always volunteer. Under the fiercest bombing and the heaviest bombardment, Boyev never prepared himself for death but tried only to comprehend what he had to do and how best to do it.

He opened his eyes (he hadn't been sleeping). Toplev came in. The horses had arrived.

Boyev dropped his legs to the floor.

Toplev was still a boy, a bit delicate for an adjutant. But Boyev didn't want to pull out any of his battery commanders for his staff and so he took Toplev off his post as head of reconnaissance.

"I want to see Boronets."

The battalion sergeant major, Boronets, was a solid, clever fellow whose eyes never missed a thing. He had already anticipated his orders and had set aside all the unnecessary things—the booty they had picked up and other odds and ends—from the sleds. Three sleds were loaded with gear for the observation points—spools of wire, radios, binocular telescopes, grenades, the weapons and packs of the men in the headquarters platoons, and some rations.

"Did you see anyone on the road after Liebstadt? Any sign of the infantry?"

Boronets only smacked his lips and shook his large round head.

"Not a soul."

So where was the infantry? Had they disappeared altogether?

Boyev went outside. The sky was covered in thick cloud, the ground white with snow. The silence all around was complete and unbroken. No more snow was falling.

All three battery commanders where just were they should be, waiting for orders. One was always with the battalion commander. That would be Myagkov, as usual. Proshchenkov and Kasyanov were each a kilometer away, one to his left, one to his right, at their preliminary observation posts, and they communicated with the battalion commander only through their batteries.

Well, they had all seen a thing or two and they knew their own troops. Now the most important thing was to pick places for the OPs. But first he had to decide how far forward he could and should site them. And how could he decide that in such darkness, silence, and without any screen of infantry? If they were too shallow they'd be useless; if they were too deep they might well stumble on the Germans.

"Just keep in mind, boys, that when it's this quiet and this deserted, things could get very, very serious."

To Toplev he said: "Zhenya, you have to find the infantry. Send out all the runners you've got to look for them. When you find them, have the CO of the regiment come and see me. Something's not right . . . They're taking too long . . . Find out the situation from brigade. I'm going to pick out some OPs and then I'll contact you."

He jumped into the first sled.

7

IN THE ABSENCE of the battery commander, the senior officer of Six Battery was the commander of First Platoon, Lieutenant Pavel Kandalintsev. Nearly forty, he was also senior in age to all the brigade's platoon commanders. He was fairly tall, though without much of a military bearing. His shoulders were somewhat hunched, his hair prematurely gray, but he ran his platoon well. The other platoon commanders called him "Dad."

Oleg Gusev, who had grown up among a group of street urchins in the city, had learned a good many things from Kandalintsev, things that could not be learned elsewhere.

Even before siting all four guns in their fire positions, Kandalintsev had set a screen of outposts in a semicircle fifty meters to their front. The tractors that had towed the guns had moved back and fallen silent, and Kandalintsev allowed the crews to man their guns in shifts. He pointed out to Gusev a small stone barn not far to their rear.

"Let's go there for a bit and rest our weary bones."

By shifting the location of the battery slightly he was able to give easier access to the nearby houses, and it would be easier to fire from here as well.

The gun crews off shift came here to sleep as well. Gusev had gone into two houses and twisted the dials on the radios there, hoping to find one that had its own power supply. But none of them was working. Private houses with radio receivers were something new that they found only in Europe. They took some getting used to: in the Soviet Union all radios had been confiscated for the duration of the war, and if you didn't turn yours in, it was off to prison. But here . . .

Oleg really wanted to find out something about our breakthrough and pick up at least a few more details. But the battery's radios could pick up only one of our stations, on the long wave, and there was no news at all about the breakthrough.

Kandalintsev had been called up from the reserves in 1941. He'd had two hard years at war on the Leningrad front, and after being wounded he'd been sent here, to the brigade, where he'd spent nearly two years.

Kandalintsev would never pass up the opportunity for even a few moments of rest.

They went into the barn and lay down side by side on the hay.

How quiet it was.

"Maybe the Germans have just fainted away, do you think, Pavel Petrovich? They've been cut off and pushed back, so now they're crowding into Königsberg. Is this the end of the war, d'you think?"

Kandalintsev, though, was by no means exhausted by the war, and unlike the others he was ready to keep at it for a long time yet. "A-hh," he sighed deeply.

He was lying there not saying a word. But it seemed he hadn't fallen asleep.

Young officers would dream of what might happen: "People are saying that after the war everything at home is going to change for the better. We'll have a free life! We'll really start living! And they say that they'll do away with the collective farms, what d'you think?"

He didn't care if there were collective farms or not, but the whole fighting army was filled with such hopes. And, in fact, why shouldn't they start living better and with more freedom?

Kandalintsev had heard all this many times before; he had gone through all the party purges hearing about it. In a tired though not contradictory voice, he said: "No, Oleg, nothing's going to change at home. We'll be lucky if it doesn't get worse. The collective farms? No, they'll never do away with them. The state can't do without them. We shouldn't be wasting our time. Let's get some sleep."

8

YES, WAR WAS a heavy burden you bore every day, with times of sudden, violent eruptions when a careless man might easily fall on the battlefield or shed some blood. But even in war his heart was never as heavy as it had been when he was a quiet, well-educated man working in the ravaged countryside in 1930 and 1931. While some maliciously calculated plague raged around him, he could only look at the eyes of the dying and listen to the wailing of women and the weeping of children. It was as if he himself had been vaccinated against this plague but also dared not help any of its victims.

That was what faced Pavel Kandalintsev immediately after his graduation, when he was a young agronomist at a plant breeding station in Voronezh Oblast. He tended the sprouts of the seedlings in the greenhouse, while around him human seedlings of two years or three months were being sent away on sleds in the bitter cold—on a long journey to their deaths. In his own eyes he was also one of the oppressors. And secretly he knew—and could not share his knowledge with anyone—that the peasants who opposed the collective farms were destroying their own stock or grinding up their best seed grain to make flour for their bread. They didn't hide the fact that they were slaughtering their livestock, and they couldn't be stopped. Then the grain collectors would come and scoop up every kernel that remained in their granaries, assemble a train of "Red carts," and drive them into the city: "The peasants bring you their surplus." There in the city a brass band would march at the head of the procession of carts.

The impressions of those months and years had caused Pavel Kandalintsev to become desensitized to the life around him, which now seemed somehow inauthentic. It was as if his nerve endings had grown numb, as if his vision, his sense of smell, and his sense of touch had become less acute and would never be fully restored. He felt he might never laugh again. That was how he lived—and with the constant apprehension that the regional committee would grow angry with him for something and fire this unreliable non-party man from his job. He'd be lucky if they didn't arrest him. More than once they were dissatisfied with him, so with his same benumbed fingers he submitted his application for party membership, and with his same benumbed ears he sat through party meetings. And what a ridiculous chaos of ideas they shoved into people's heads and people's souls, beginning with the abolition of *the week*. The old Monday-Wednesday-Friday-Sunday was done away with, so that no one could count weeks any longer. Now there was the "uninterrupted" five-day week with no common days off. Everyone worked or studied on different days, and there was never a single day when he could get together with his wife and children. Life rumbled over everyone like the continuously moving track of a caterpillar tractor, its oblique treads cutting deep into the earth.

It was with these same forever deadened feelings and sense of detachment that Pavel went off to war in August '41 as a junior lieutenant from the reserves. He had been at war for more than three years now, still unable to feel anything with his whole being, as if alien even to himself and his own body. He had lain this way in a field near Leningrad, seriously wounded, until the medics came to look after him and send him to the hospital. And just as in the pre-war days, when any boorish fool from the regional committee could give Kandalintsev instructions about plant breeding, so in the army he was never astonished when given idiotic tasks to perform.

So now the war was drawing to a close. Had he actually survived it all? But even now Pavel was unable to feel anything fully: they might kill him yet; there was still time enough for that. Someone had to die in the final months of the war, after all.

Only one feeling survived that was still keen: for his young wife, Alina. He missed her terribly.

Well, it will be as God decides.

9

THE SLED MOVED noiselessly over the soft snow, with only the horses snorting from time to time.

The night was becoming brighter: the moon could be seen behind the clouds, and the layer of clouds was growing thinner. You could identify the patches of trees and tell where the land was open.

Boyev kept checking his map, using his sleeve to cover the beam of his flashlight. By the bends in this road across the fields he could tell where he should drop off his battery commanders, each at his own OP in this field covered with fresh snow.

This seemed to be a good spot, right here.

Kasyanov and Proshchenkov jumped from their sleds and came up.

"Just don't get too far away from me, no more than a kilometer. It's not likely we'll have any work to do, and I expect we'll be moved out in the morning. Still, you'd better dig in, just in case."

The three of them went their separate ways. The horses moved off confidently. There weren't many hills in this area, and it took some time to make out where the high ground was. If they don't pull us out by morning, we'll have to look for something better.

And still there wasn't a sound to be heard. There were no black shapes moving across the field.

When there's a tricky job to be done, you get your best man to do it. He called up the clever Ostanin: "Vanya, take one of your gunners and go up about a kilometer, find out what the ground's like. See if there's anyone up there. And take some grenades with you."

Ostanin replied in his broad Vyatka accent: "You see someone moving around out there, best not ask, 'Who goes there?' You'll get an answer from his machine gun. Or you try to fake it and say, 'Wer ist da?' and our own guys will let you have it."

They went off.

Now they brought up some picks and spades and began hacking at the earth. The top layer of soil was as iron hard as it had been on the graves this morning. They led the horses behind some bushes. The radio operator, using his radio on the sled, was calling out: "Balkhash, Balkhash, this is Omsk. Give me Twelve. Request from Ten."

"Twelve"—who is Toplev—replies.

"Have you located any of our 'sticks'?"

"No sticks, no one," comes his very concerned voice.

If there still are no infantry around Adlig, then they haven't caught up with us. Where can they be?

"What about Ural?"

"Ural says you're not looking in the right place. Keep searching."

"Just who were you talking to?"

"Zero Five."

That's the head of brigade reconnaissance. He should be searching for them himself, up here, and not sitting in brigade headquarters thirty kilometers back. And why haven't they moved out yet? When are they going to get here?

The digging was going slowly. Three small trenches should be enough, not even full depth. There's no cover here anyway.

The agile Ostanin returned even earlier than expected.

"Comrade Major. About half a kilometer ahead the ground drops into a hollow, and it looks as if it reaches around to our right. I went off to our left, slantwise, and saw some people crawling around. Couldn't tell who they were till one of them let out a full burst of good Russian curses when his spool of cable got snarled, so they're our guys."

"Who are they?"

"It's the right-hand listening post. One spool of cable will be enough to link up with them, and we'll have a direct line to their central station. So that's fine."

"Right, then let's string out some cable. Your partner can do it."

Still, how are we going to sight in our guns? Nothing's been surveyed in, we'll have to do it all by eye.

"Nobody else out there? No infantry?"

"Not even any tracks in the snow."

"Right. Twelve, twelve, search for the sticks. Send out your people in every direction!"

10

THE VISIBILITY WAS now a little better: you could make out the patch of forest that lay beyond Adlig on the left. The dark, spreading trees on the right could also be seen, but they were probably on the other side of the large hollow there.

Brigade headquarters had stopped responding to calls on the radio. That's fine, they've probably moved out. Didn't let us know, though.

Toplev was very nervous. He was often nervous. He was always concerned for everything to be correct so that no one would criticize him. He wanted to avoid the smallest error, the tiniest flaw in his work, before his superiors spotted it and blasted him for it. But how can you always know the right thing to do?

And now he didn't know where he should be. He had to check the screen of outposts; he had to go to the guns of Four and Five Batteries.

There were just two men from each crew on duty. The others had gone off to houses in the village. Were they getting something to eat? There was food in the houses. Or were they loading up with booty? There was enough of that as well, and it could be packed away in the battery trailer. (There were still a few old men and women in the village, but they didn't dare make a fuss.)

It was a bad move, this letting them send parcels back from Germany. Now every soldier's pack was bulging. And they never knew just what to take: they'd pick up one thing, then toss it aside when they found something better to make up their five kilos. Toplev could understand it all, but he didn't like it because it got in the way of the job.

Then he set off back to the battalion headquarters truck on the edge of Klein Schwenkitten. Next to it was a little house that had a nice eiderdown. Time to stretch out and get some sleep, it was already past midnight. Not likely to get much sleep here, though.

THE SKY GREW lighter behind the clouds. It was peaceful and quiet, as if there were no war going on.

Yet what would happen if some of them crept up from the east? Our shells weigh forty kilos apiece, and what with carrying them and reloading, it was never less than a minute between shots. And we'd never manage to pull out of here with these eight-ton gun-howitzers. It would be great if some other guns showed up, some antitank weapons from division. But there's nobody.

Back at the truck he went to the radio again. He reported to the major: No contact with Ural. And no "sticks" either, though we've sent people out to look for them.

One of the sergeants sent here sprang into action. The hum of a motor could be heard from the road they'd taken to get here. It was a jeep. He couldn't tell who was in it until the last minute.

A man jumped easily out of the jeep. Major Baluev.

Toplev reported: these were the firing positions of a heavy artillery battalion.

The major had a youthful voice, though it was very firm. This news cheered him up: "Do you mean it? Heavy artillery! That's something I never expected!"

They went into the house, to the light. The major was lean, clean-shaven. And he looked quite worn-out.

"That's quite amazing! It makes our job a lot easier."

It turned out that he was the commander of an infantry regiment, the very one they'd been looking for. Now it was Toplev who was cheered: "That's great! Now we'll get everything back in shape."

Not quite, though. It would be half the night before the first battalion of infantry could march here.

They brought a map to examine under the kerosene lamp.

Toplev pointed out the locations of our observation posts. And then there's the sound-ranging battery, over here in Dietrichsdorf. But we still haven't come across a single enemy unit.

The major, his cap tilted over his flaxen hair, focused his keen eyes on the map. He wasn't a bit happy.

He examined the map for a long time. Using a finger, not a pencil, he traced out his proposed lines. Somewhere there, past the artillery OPs, he would position his infantry. He opened his own map case and wrote out his instructions. These he gave to the senior sergeant who had come with him.

"Pass this on to the adjutant. Take the jeep. If you see anything with wheels along the way, do your best to grab it. We have to try to get at least one company up here by transport."

He kept two scouts with him.

"I'm going to see your battalion commander."

Toplev obligingly took the major into Adlig. When they came to the end of the road he said, "It's straight this way, just follow the sled tracks."

They showed clearly on the ground.

It grew lighter. The moon was making its way through the clouds.

11

AFTER BEING WOUNDED in the lung on the Sozh River, Major Baluev was sent on a year-long course at the Frunze Academy. He was afraid he might miss the war, but he came back to the headquarters of the Second Belorussian Army Group just in time for the January offensive. From there he was sent to an army headquarters, then to a corps headquarters, and then a divisional headquarters.

It was only today—no, by now it was yesterday—that he had found this latest post. As it happened, the day before he arrived, a regimental commander had been killed—the third one since the autumn. Now he had taken his place; his orders would be signed later.

He managed to speak to the divisional commander for five minutes. But even that was enough for an experienced officer: he scarcely needed to read the map and could grasp the situation as soon as the artillery officer had moved his fingers over it and voiced a few of his concerns. Do the higher-ups have any idea of what's going on here? They seem to be in a total fog and can't make a decision. And look who gets promoted to general these days! What's more, they have to keep to the nationality quota to make sure each minority is represented.

After working as part of a cohesive academic team fighting a theoretical war, you can't help but be bowled over when you're suddenly dropped into all this. You may have forgotten some of your old habits, but you've got to keep your spirits up.

Baluev, in fact, had managed to grasp something of the situation here while he was on the operations staff at the army headquarters. After 1942, our troops just kept rolling on; they seemed unstoppable! So why shouldn't they seem a bit cocky? It was a wonderful, beautiful cockiness of a triumphant army. They took it with them when they cut Prussia in two. Now their support echelons were lagging behind, the infantry was lagging, but the Fifth Tank Army went rolling on, right to the Baltic. It was something to admire; it was thrilling, in fact!

Just the same, with a forward rush of such scale a single division no longer had the usual three to five kilometers of front. Suddenly a division had a forty-kilometer front! So, you'd better make sure your regiment was well extended. And ask for a couple of seventy-sixes.

That's how it is: An army on the move is an ever-changing structure. Sometimes it can form a wall as hard as marble in twenty-four hours; sometimes it can dissolve like an apparition in two hours. But that's why you're an officer in the regular army, and that's why you've had this academic training.

And in this tempestuous whirl of unexpectedness, bitterness, and harshness, you find the very delight of being at war.

12

IT CONTINUED TO grow brighter, and by one o'clock the clouds had broken up. The moon wasn't yet full, and it wouldn't be out for the whole night. Lacking its left edge and tilted slightly westward, it began floating picturesquely behind the clouds, sometimes shining brightly, sometimes obscured.

It may have been getting brighter, but through the binoculars there was little that could be made out on the snowy field to their front; it did, though, seem completely empty beyond the depression. Yet there were those groves of trees here and there where the enemy could mass his troops.

The moon had had some special power over Pavel Boyev since he had been a child. In his youth, it would make him stop or sit or lie down simply to gaze at it. He would think about the kind of life that lay ahead of him and about the kind of girl he would meet.

But though he was strong, solid, and an excellent gymnast, for some reason girls were rarely if ever attracted to him. He racked his brain to try to find out what was wrong. True, he wasn't very good-looking; his nose and lips were not quite straight. But does a man have to be handsome? Beauty is an entirely feminine quality, even in the least attractive women. Pavel would be simply paralyzed before a woman; he was in awe of her tenderness, her fragility, and he not only feared he might break her but even that he might scorch her with his very breath. Whether or not this was the cause, he didn't marry before the war. (And it was only Tanya, the nurse at the hospital, who had later explained it to him: That's just what we love, the strong hand of a man next to us, don't you see that, silly?)

The moon was shining over his shoulder. He turned to look at it. Then a cloud obscured it again.

It was still the same: not a sound from anywhere. We must have hit the Germans right where they hurt.

Meanwhile, they had strung telephone lines from the guns to all three OPs. Via the listening post they had a connection with the sound-ranging battery in Dietrichsdorf and its posts to the left and farther north. Their battery commander was complaining that there wasn't a soul to be seen anywhere; they had moved their advance post across the lake to their front.

The lake formed a complete gap, and in the moonlight they could spot any Germans who might be there. So, the whole area two kilometers eastward was empty.

He also reported that the surveyors were using the moonlight to fix the locations of the listening posts and some had gone back to Adlig to survey in the guns.

So, an hour from now we'll be ready to fire! But it's not likely we'll be staying here. We'll be moving out.

It didn't look as if there would be a thaw. He was going to spend the night here, so he picked up a pair of felt boots from the sled and changed.

Then Toplev reported: still no contact at all with brigade headquarters. That was odd. How long does it take them to get here? Could the Germans have intercepted them along the road? Then he remembered: the brigade commander had gone off to the hospital yesterday. Vyzhlevsky must be in charge.

Boyev tried to keep his distance from all the political officers; he had little use for such idle people. But he found Vyzhlevsky particularly obnoxious. There was something not right about him; perhaps that was why he was so particularly keen on all his commissar's claptrap. People in the brigade said, on the quiet, that something in his service record from '41 didn't quite add up. He had been in Odessa when the Germans had it surrounded; then there was a mysterious gap in his record for two or three months; and then, as if nothing had happened, he was serving on the western front again with a higher rank. And how was Gubaydulin linked with all this? Why did Vyzhlevsky immediately pluck him out of the group of reinforcements, put him into the political section, and promote him so quickly? (And he saddled Boyev with the job of party organizer.)

Again from Toplev: still no contact with brigade headquarters. But the commander of the rifle regiment had turned up and was following Boyev's tracks to the OP.

Well, about time. Now at least that's been cleared up.

13

"Comrade Senior Lieutenant! Comrade Senior . . ."

"What is it?" Kandalintsev responded immediately, in an alert voice.

"There's a German here, a deserter!"

It was Corporal Neskin who had come into the barn to tell him this. The sentries were holding the German. He had walked straight across the field.

Gusev also heard. Great news! Both platoon commanders jumped down from the stack of hay.

They went outside to take a look. The moon was bright and they could easily make out his German uniform and see that he was unarmed. He wore a warm cap.

The German saw the officers and smartly raised his hand to his temple: "*Herr Oberleutnant! Diese Nacht, in zwei Stunden wird man einen Angriff hier unternehmen!*"

Neither one of them had much German. They could make out a few individual words but couldn't understand them when they were put together.

The fellow was very excited.

Still, he's got to go to battalion headquarters. They gestured for him to go. Neskin led the way, and behind the prisoner marched little Yursh with a carbine (that fellow was always there when you needed him). Yursh passed on more information to the officers as they walked. "We've already tried talking a bit of '*vas-ist-das*' to get through to him. He knows some language that's closer to ours, but we still couldn't make out anything."

The prisoner had something urgent to pass on, by the look of it.

It wasn't far to the headquarters truck here in Klein. While they were walking they tried questioning him again. And the German did his best. He began speaking some language that was not German and sounded somehow familiar. It might sound familiar, but they couldn't understand a damned thing.

There was one separate word that he kept repeating: "*Angriff! Angriff!*"

Wasn't that a word we knew? "Assault"? "Attack"?

Well, that we could certainly expect.

The radio operator in the headquarters truck wasn't asleep, and he woke the plotter, who knew a bit of German, though not much more than the officers. He quickly rolled out of bed and began speaking with the deserter. He translated, but slowly and awkwardly, not word for word.

"So, this fellow here is a Sudeten German. He knows a bit of Czech as well. He came to warn us that in another hour or two, here in our sector, the Germans are launching a big general offensive."

Maybe he's just trying to fool us.

But why should he? That would make it even worse for him.

The German's voice was pleading, plaintive, even imploring.

And he was certainly getting on in years, even older than Kandalintsev. Kandalintsev felt sorry for him. He'd had enough war, the poor fellow. Who wouldn't have enough after so many years?

You poor devil. And now that we've got our hands on you, how many more years before you see your family?

He sent the runner Yursh to Adlig to find Captain Toplev and pass on the information.

14

AFTER QUESTIONING THE deserter, using the plotter as an interpreter, listening to his voice and seeing how friendly and willing he was, Toplev decided that the man was telling the truth. How did he get away? That was easy enough, across an empty field without a single line of troops on it—why not just walk over?

Fine. We'll hold the deserter at the headquarters truck.

But if he's telling the truth and hasn't made a mistake, our guns are completely defenseless. The infantry still haven't arrived!

Toplev was an efficient and thorough officer: Stand at attention! Toe the line! And he always tried to understand the situation, get a full grasp of it, and succeed in what he did.

But now, what should he do? What could he do now?

He had to locate brigade headquarters, and locate it at once!

He told the radio operator to call headquarters at once.

But still no contact.

What's going on with them? This doesn't make sense!

He grabbed the telephone to call the battalion commander—but what was this? There was no contact here either. There hadn't been any shelling, so how could the line be broken? He sent out a lineman, cursing, though not using the foulest words. That he never did. That telephone operator was a scatterbrain. You had to watch him every moment!

And if he used the radio, how could he explain it? He couldn't send a message in clear, but they didn't have the code words to use in a case like this. "Fetch Ten," he ordered the radio operator.

He heard Boyev's voice, deep, always assured and reliable, and he calmed down a bit. Boyev would make the decision now. His eyes fixed on the red eye of the radio, Toplev began a roundabout explanation.

Some old guy has just come to us . . . He's not one of ours . . . From the other direction, you know . . . Doesn't seem like a liar, and I've checked his story from beginning to end. He says that in an hour or two . . . and now it's even less . . . He says *they're coming*! A whole lot of them! That's right, lots of them . . . And there's still no contact with Ural . . . What are your orders?

Boyev took some time to reply. He wasn't very talkative in any case. He was thinking. He asked once more: "Still no contact with Ural, you said?"

Toplev, almost crying, replied: "Not a peep!"

Boyev thought a bit more.

"Here's what we'll do. Move all of Kasyanov's people back across the river. Right away. Have them take up firing positions there."

"And the other two?"

He could even hear Boyev's sigh through the phone.

"The other two? They'll stay where they are for the moment. But make sure, absolutely sure, they're on full alert. Now, what's happened to the telephone line?"

"I don't know. I've sent someone out."

"Everyone is to be ready for action, watching and listening. The minute anything happens, give me a report."

A few minutes later the lineman came running in, swearing it was God's truth: "In the woods over there somebody's cut off a piece of wire this long. Looks like it was done with a knife. And there's tracks off to the side."

The Germans?

Here already?

15

AND SO BALUEV and his two scouts walked along the sled tracks to a group of dark figures on an open, snow-covered spot.

He introduced himself and explained who he was.

Major Boyev, slightly shorter than Baluev, was wearing a white fur jacket.

They shook hands. Baluev thought that he had a firm handshake, but Boyev had a grip of iron.

They immediately established the easy relationship that was normal on the front line.

"So where's your regiment?"

His regiment! He himself had scarcely had a look at it yet. He replied: "Who positioned your guns in this direction?"

Boyev's face broke into a sardonic smile: "Couldn't do it any other way. That was the order."

He explained the situation, as far as he knew it.

Though the moon was out, they needed the flashlight to check the map.

"Petersdorf? Yes, that's where they've stuck me, or my headquarters at least. It's close enough to run a line to you here. And I'd come here to use your OP."

Still, this wasn't much of an OP, on flat ground with no cover.

"Right now I've got about two hours to spare. I'd best get on with my own reconnaissance. Where are the Germans? Where's the best place to put my forward troops?"

Wouldn't it be wonderful to know that!

Boyev was called to the radio. He squatted beside it.

Baluev ran the bright spot of light across the map. If this whole lake is ours, there's no point putting anything here. We have to be farther forward.

Boyev returned and in a deep, quiet voice, away from the soldiers, he passed the news on to Baluev.

"That's quite possible," said Baluev without hesitation, immediately accepting such a situation. "He'll want to come at us on the first day, before we've set up any defenses. He's pushing forward just because he's desperate."

And then we'd have our front line right here.

How soon could he manage to bring up at least a company?

Boyev, with his heavy guns, has a much bigger problem.

But he's not panicking.

Baluev admitted sincerely: "I haven't been at the front for a year. I'm just amazed to see how we're doing in the fourth year of the war. Just as before, they won't make us lose our nerve."

This was only the fourth day Baluev had been in Prussia, but already he had the full sense of being on the front line.

"Still, I'll take a walk up forward, to the right of the lake. I'll let you know what I find. And when I've picked a spot for my headquarters, I'll have a line laid back to you."

They had been together in this bare field for no more than a quarter hour. Now they were parting until a telephone line could be laid and they renewed contact. It might well be that they would never see one another again. It was always like that.

"What's your first name?"

"Pavel, Pavel Afanasych."

"I'm Vladimir Kondratych."

They shook hands warmly.

Baluev went off with his scouts.

Clouds covered the moon.

16

BALUEV HAD SURVIVED even his service in the Second Shock Army in the spring of '42, and he had escaped from German encirclement. But then he'd rotted on the Sozh River bridgehead for the whole of November '43 and was wounded just two hours before the German withdrawal, when they were already pulling back their troops. His wound was such that he could return to duty after two months in the hospital in Samara. And then, off to the Academy for a year.

Now there were few people in the Academy who hadn't been under fire or been battered by the war. Everyone there knew the price to be paid to keep up the fight. Still, that year of study had been a different world: War had now been elevated to something clear, beautiful, and rational. And it was difficult to keep from thinking that in a year or so, the war might be over. Maybe they'll get by without me.

It hadn't ended. But how close the end was now! He had tried to catch up with the troops all through northern Poland and Prussia. He hitched rides with anyone going his way and in regimental command vehicles crammed with troops of every sort. When he did catch up to them, he was happy to enter once again the familiar world of the front line. And at such a sublime moment—the capture of East Prussia! (And on a front that was so broadly extended . . .)

They walked across the broad expanse, breaking through the crust of the snow. The two scouts followed in silence.

He used his compass to find his way.

If something was about to start, then Petersdorf wouldn't do; it was in too much of a salient. And how could he manage to get, if not a company, then at least a platoon to string out for protection of the guns near Adlig?

Could even a single company make it here in time? And if they did, they'd be worn out. Could we even get them back on their feet again?

We just have to hold out through this one night; then things will be better tomorrow.

Now look at that: Over on the left, about four or five kilometers to the northeast, a small red glow had silently come up and he hadn't even noticed when it began. It was a fire, and it was still burning. He couldn't hear any firing.

He stopped and looked through his binoculars. Yes, it was a fire. Burning evenly. Was it a house?

A fire doesn't break out in a war without a reason. It breaks out because there's some action there.

Can the Germans be there already? Or did some of ours make it that far and just were careless?

They walked on, eastward.

Then he remembered the dream of his mother. Baluev's mother died young, so young! And Baluev, now twenty-eight, had been dreaming of his beloved mother for many years now. She had been unhappy, but in his dreams she was always smiling. She never came near to him, though. She would appear briefly, then go away and reappear a moment later; she would be sleeping in the room next door and walk past, nod and smile at him. But she never came close.

Whether it was from the dreams themselves, from something he'd read, or from the stories of others, Baluev had formed the idea that when his time came to die, Mama would draw near and embrace him.

That was what he dreamed last night: he felt Mama's breath on his face and her very firm embrace—where did she get such strength?

Everything in the dream was so warm and so joyous. But when he woke up he recalled the omen . . .

17

THE SNARLING OF tractors violated the dead silence that had continued to reign all around as the four gun-howitzers of Six Battery withdrew from Klein Schwenkitten. Using no headlights, they moved back along the same tree-lined road by which they had come a few hours earlier. Behind the shell trailers came the battalion kitchen and the three-ton supply truck; they had been sent back as well (along with the German deserter).

Lieutenant Gusev, as usual, was sitting in the cabin of Second Platoon's lead tractor. This withdrawal displeased him: whatever the tactical considerations that led to it, it looked like a retreat. And now he would have no part in any sudden rush into battle.

Oleg Gusev lived with the constant awareness that he was not merely a junior lieutenant but the son of a famous general. And he wanted to justify being his father's son with every day of his life in the army and with every one of his actions in the army. He would have been devastated had he in any way shamed his father. So far his only decoration was the Order of the Fatherland War, Second Class, a nice shiny medal. (His father made sure that his son was not being given any preferential treatment.)

The move was easy enough, just a kilometer and a half, and here was that same reinforced concrete bridge across the Passarge that they had crossed yesterday. One after another, the tractors pulled the massive guns up the steep incline beyond the bridge. There was some problem over there, something in the way up ahead. Then the tractors again began to snarl at full volume and moved on.

Oleg jumped down and went ahead to see what was happening.

Kandalintsev was talking to some tall colonel in an astrakhan hat. The colonel was very excited and, apparently, wasn't even aware that he was holding a pistol in his hand. He had drawn it, obviously, to make sure that his orders would be followed. He demanded that the guns be deployed here immediately, facing east and ready to fire—over open sights. Farther back, behind the colonel, the muzzle of an SU-76 self-propelled gun jutted into the air like a crane. A few soldiers sat on the vehicle or stood nearby.

Kandalintsev calmly explained that 152-millimeter guns were not intended for firing over open sights: they took more than a minute to reload and they were not anti-tank weapons.

"We haven't got anything else," the colonel shouted, "so shut your mouth and get moving!"

The issue wasn't the pistol he was holding. When you're in action and your own commander isn't there, you have to obey the senior ranker at your location. And after crossing the river they had lost contact with their own commander.

In fact, it made little difference, since they had intended to take up a position about two hundred meters beyond the river. The only thing is, Kandalintsev coolly and sensibly explained to the colonel, there's not much room here by the bridge and not enough frontage to position four guns. The colonel, despite his excitement, gave some heed to the senior lieutenant and ordered him to position only two guns by the bridge, one on either side of the road.

There was nothing else to be done. Shouting orders in a commanding voice didn't come easily to Kandalintsev, and he simply said: "Oleg, put one of your guns on the left, and I'll put one of mine on the right."

They began turning the guns around and unpacking the assemblies. Gusev put his third crew, under Sergeant Petya Nikolaev, at his position. Kandalintsev assigned his first crew, with Senior Sergeant Koltsov, a man also nearly forty and a Don Cossack. The remaining guns and trucks moved back another two hundred meters, where the dark shapes of the farmstead of Pittenen and its outbuildings could be seen.

It was time to check on the deserter again.

Kandalintsev felt strange when he placed his hand on the man's shoulder and said: "*Gut, gut*, everything will be *gut*. You're coming with us. Now get some sleep."

18

IF TWO METERS of the telephone line were missing, it could not have been cut by accident. Obviously, this is the Germans' home ground; they know every pathway in the area; they've got their own guides and their own reconnaissance and they can hide in all those patches of forest. We'll never spot them, but they're watching us.

Boyev had never been in a situation quite like this. He had made river crossings while being bombed, had sat in an OP on some deathly bridgehead while German artillery and mortars dropped shells around him, and he had lain in a shallow, hastily dug slit trench while the bullets of a raiding party hummed over his head. But he had always known that he was a part of his own brigade of guns and a trusty neighbor of the infantry, and that sooner or later a friendly hand, a telephone wire, or an order from a commander would reach him, and that he'd also have a chance to contribute his own ideas.

But here—what was going on? Not a sound, not a shell; instant death wasn't flying over his head; nothing was clear. There were no infantry and wouldn't be any before morning; in fact he'd be lucky if they arrived by morning. And his own headquarters seemed to have died some time around midnight. What had happened? Had their radio broken down? But they had spare radios.

Once again clouds had obscured the moon; and the moon, in any case, would soon be setting. There was no sign of life in the snow-covered field; visibility was very poor. He had one of his battery commanders right at hand, and two others on his flanks, sitting mutely in the shallow pits they had dug and waiting—for what? The Germans might begin their attack at any moment, yet he had heard no tractor or truck motors, which meant that they were not bringing up their artillery. But what if they move around our flank on foot and go straight for our guns? They're defenseless.

What's the point of staying here? There's nothing to shoot at. Why are we still here?

Boyev had already withdrawn one battery without authorization. Still, he could justify that. (Yes, that's an idea: Kasyanov no longer has a line to his battery, so he might as well make tracks back to his guns across the river. He gave the command.) But should he pull the other two batteries back across the river as well? Now that would be a completely unauthorized change of position, a *retreat*. And there's a sacred principle in the Red Army: Not one step backward! An unauthorized retreat—in our army? Not only did he have no appetite for that, it was simply not possible. That would mean betraying his country. He could be tried for it and even face a death sentence or at least a punishment battalion.

So there was nothing he could do.

Common sense clearly told him to retreat, of course, to pull back his battalion.

What was even more clear was that this was totally forbidden.

You might be killed, but at least it won't be by your own people.

He'd had no word from Baluev since he left. But bits of news were coming in. From his battery commander on the left: a single horseman was spotted about three hundred meters down the small road to our front, going east. Nothing more could be made out. And they didn't have a chance to fire at him.

So, are the Germans using some local people as messengers or for reconnaissance?

Boyev called the commander of the sound-ranging battery via this same OP on his left and the battery's listening post. With two or three connections between them the audibility was only so-so. The battery commander reported that there were Germans right across the lake and they had fired on his advance listening post and killed one soldier.

"Sasha, can you see or hear anything else?"

"Now I can see the glow of two fires over to my left."

"Are any of our troops in your area?"

"Nobody. We've set up in a regular palace here."

"I've got some news for you: they might come at us at any time. You've deployed your 'boxes.' You'd best bring them in before the shooting starts."

"Should I really do that?"

"What do you think you'll pick up on them?"

Toplev reported that now he could see the glow in the sky to his left. Ural still wasn't responding. Were they sleeping, or what? But surely not all of them could have fallen asleep? Toplev was young and on the puny side. If the Germans went round our flank they could bypass the guns. He told Toplev to rouse all the gun crews and not let anyone sleep; distribute the carbines and the grenades. Be prepared to defend the guns from a frontal attack. Maintain contact and keep reporting.

Ostanin arrived: "Comrade Major. I've found a good farm about five hundred meters from here. It's deserted. Should we move?"

Was it wise to move now? By the time we've laid down the lines something more might be happening.

19

ANOTHER HALF-HOUR PASSED.

The glow in the sky on the left and to the north had grown larger. Now there were three fires nearby and something larger a good distance away. But no shelling—no artillery, no mortars. Rifle fire probably wouldn't be heard.

Nothing was happening on the right, where he had removed Kasyanov's OP, but that low ground curving around gave a lot of cause for concern. Then Ostanin returned from the hollow just forward and said that there was no way he could stay there any longer. There were two or three shapes moving around on the slope opposite. He could almost certainly have picked them off but he held back.

HE WAS RIGHT, most likely. With local guides, the Germans here can find every path and byway. And using the low spots in front, they could bring up a whole battalion and their sleds as well.

The visibility was getting poorer all the time. When you sent someone off on an errand, you could make him out—more by guesswork than anything else—for about a hundred meters; then he vanished.

Was that a mass of infantry out there in the darkness, not making a sound? That's not how an attack is made on today's battlefield; it's impossible. Organizing such a silent attack is even more difficult than organizing a noisy one.

Still, in war anything is possible.

If the Germans have been cut off for a whole day, why wouldn't they want to launch an attack?

His thoughts were whirling. Where was brigade headquarters? How could they abandon him this way?

He could not retreat. But he might not be able to hold out until morning either. Staying here was pointless, though. He had to save his guns.

Should he risk pulling back another battery? This would not be seen as just a maneuver: it was an unauthorized retreat. But for the moment, at least, he could do something: Load the binocular telescope, the radio, and any spare spools of cable on the sled. And turn the sled to face the battery. He told Myagkov: "Take the extra drums for the sub-machine guns. Issue all the grenades we've got."

And keep your voices down: noise carries across that open field.

The Germans could move a tank up quickly, of course. And we don't have anything to use against a tank. Our slit trenches are tiny.

The signalman summoned Boyev to the phone. He was only a couple of paces farther down their trench. It was the commander of the sound-ranging battery again. He was very anxious: the Germans had captured his left listening post! All they had been able to report was "They're trying to surround us. They're in white camouflage." And that was all.

He asked Boyev: "What's happening over there, Pavel Afanasych?"

"I can't see anything so far."

"No one's attacking my central station yet. But I'm bringing in my boxes—I don't want to lose them. So you'd best keep your eyes peeled. And you can pull in your line."

Boyev held on to the receiver for a time, as if he was waiting to hear something more.

But there was only silence.

The battle had already begun.

To Myagkov he said: "Take everyone we've got and position them in a semicircle about two hundred meters to our front. Leave one man on the telephone and another with the sled."

Myagkov went off quietly to pass on the orders.

Setting up a protective screen was a risky move: you could find out more quickly when the Germans were advancing, but you couldn't fire from here without hitting your own men. But if everyone stayed in one bunch they'd be caught like a flock of sheep.

He wasn't agitated; his mind was working calmly and clearly. Various scenes passed through his mind: the battles near Oryol, the Desna River, Starodub, the battle near Rechitsa. Each battle was different, and each death was different. One thing he never did was to waste his shells in pointless firing.

There was the triumph of the Bobruisk pocket, the pursuit across Poland, the vicious bridgehead near Pultusk. And still, he'd come through them all.

. . . Just hold on until morning . . .

A few bursts of machine gun fire came from the northeast, about two kilometers away. Then there was silence.

That was roughly where Baluev had gone.

20

THE SHELLS HAD been stacked near the guns at Toplev's position. But it didn't look as if they would have to do any firing before first light. Yet the battalion commander had ordered all the gun crews to get their carbines ready. The carbines were scarcely ever needed, and the men never carried them; they were stacked in ammunition boxes. Gunners in heavy artillery weren't expected to fight with rifles. The reconnaissance men and the headquarters platoons carried submachine guns, and they were all at the OPs.

There was nothing to be seen toward his front or his flanks; everything was lost in this semi-darkness.

Even before this, Toplev had been pacing about, alarmed and uncertain; but now, after the battalion commander's order to distribute the carbines . . .

All eight guns stood in a row, as they were rarely positioned; batteries were always located separately. Toplev paced about nervously, looking very small beside this row of massive guns.

Not every gun had even half its crew; the others had gone to the nearby houses and were sleeping where it was warm and dry. A few of them had even managed to find some German alcohol. The drivers were all asleep somewhere.

He roused all four platoon commanders: Distribute the carbines and get ready to defend our position. Some jumped to follow his orders, others moved reluctantly. If only the deputy political officer, who was usually hanging around, were here: they were afraid of him, at least. But the brigade commissar had kept him with him, on duty until morning.

The Germans wouldn't attack without some preliminary bombardment, though; they'd drop a few shells or mortar rounds on them and give them some warning.

But it was quiet. There was no sound of tanks moving about, either.

He kept listening, but there was nothing to be heard.

He should take another look around the position.

He went to the headquarters truck in Klein. That's where they kept all the files. So if anything did happen . . . then what? He ordered the driver to stay with the truck and the radio operator to keep trying to contact Ural. Then he went back to Adlig, to the guns.

"Comrade Captain!" It was the telephone operator calling him in a muffled voice from the entryway to a house where he had made a place for himself. "It's the battalion commander for you."

He took the receiver.

Boyev said in a steely voice: "Toplev! We're being surrounded here! Get ready to defend yourselves!" He hadn't put the cover back over the telephone receiver, and Toplev could hear shot after shot being fired! Then everything went silent. The connection had been lost.

Then Toplev felt something strange happening to him: His kneecaps began to tremble, entirely on their own and separately from his knees. They were jumping up and down.

Now he had no need to call out all the gun crews. The platoon commanders were rushing along the row of guns: Prepare for action! They've already attacked the battalion commander!

Now the whole place was jumping.

What about the headquarters truck? If anything should happen? He sent a soldier with a jerry can to pour gasoline over it.

If we don't pull out, we'll burn the truck.

21

LOYALTY TO HIS father was the key to Oleg Gusev's character. Who can be more sacred and exalted for a young boy than his father? And how badly his father had been wronged in the 1930s (Oleg understood, though he was just ten) when, for no good reason, he was pushed out of his post as a brigade commander and demoted to colonel. They were living in a two-room communal apartment, and an informer was living in the third room. (In fact there was a reason for what had happened: someone his father had served with had been arrested, though the boy only learned about that later.) And in his teens all he wanted was to follow in his father's footsteps. At age sixteen (these were the months of the Stalingrad battle) he got his wish: after finally getting his father's permission, he donned a private soldier's overcoat.

Loyalty to his father meant not disgracing himself here, beside his two guns, and having his father blamed for his son's actions. It would be better to be killed. Oleg was even happy that everything had turned out this way, that they had been positioned to guard the bridge by firing over open sights, something unheard of for a 152-millimeter gun. So—let those German tanks come rumbling out of the darkness, and the sooner the better!

This had been an unforgettable night for him, and he was anticipating even greater things.

Although each gun was supposed to be allotted sixty shells, there was only half that number, even after collecting shells from the other guns in the platoon. And the gun crews had only seven men, not eight. (Yes, Lepetushin, the missing man . . .) The lieutenant didn't take a soldier from some other crew; that would not have been right. He'd make do with what he had. Better to help them himself, with his own hands.

The self-propelled gun and the fierce colonel had left the area, and the guns from Six Battery stood by the bridge, protecting it. Before them was only an empty, dark expanse; none of our people seemed to be there—and then suddenly people began running toward them.

There were a few surveyors from the reconnaissance battalion, one limping, another with a bandaged shoulder. They had been sent to survey in the guns while the moon was bright, but then they were caught in the darkness. They had been waiting for the clouds to pass. Interrupting one another, the surveyors told their story: It was a strange sort of attack, the Germans simply creeping up silently; some of them carrying shovels, some even knives; they fired only a few shots. There were still a few surveyors left back there.

The sleds from the sound-ranging battery with their reconnaissance equipment came through; they had managed to pull back in time. They had set free the draft horses captured from the Germans; their truck had gotten stuck there and some of them were trying to pull it out.

So how many more people from the sound-ranging battery were still back there?

He asked Kandalintsev: "Pavel Petrovich, how can we fire when our own guys are still pouring in?"

"We'll have to hold off for a bit."

A burst of shooting would come from across the river, but well back; and then things would grow quiet again. Kandalintsev ordered his two free gun crews to prepare to engage the enemy with their rifles. Then he sent them to provide a defensive screen to the left and right of the bridge.

A few more of our troops were climbing up the road from the bridge. Then came a group carrying a wounded man on a groundsheet. They were infantry reconnaissance troops. They were exhausted and could barely carry him. Who was he?

Let's make a place for him over here.

Oleg bent over the wounded man. A major. Hair the color of flax. He wasn't moving.

"One of your people?"

"The CO of our regiment. He's new. They only sent him in yesterday."

"Badly hurt?"

"In the head and stomach."

"Where's your regiment, then?"

"Who the hell knows?"

Some of our gun crews took over from the stretcher bearers and carried the wounded man to the landowner's house. "Have him taken to Liebstadt on our sled, then come right back," Kandalintsev told them.

The town of Liebstadt stood at the intersection of six roads, and the artillery battalion had passed through it yesterday evening with no problems. But if we let the Germans get to it, they'll have control over all the roads.

"So it seems our deserter wasn't lying, Pavel Petrovich."

"I've told the kitchen to feed him," Kandalintsev muttered.

"What's happened to our battery commander? He's not answering our radio calls."

And what about the rest of the battery?

The distant glow in the sky provided a bit of light. They stared into the darkness. Over there, another bunch of our guys. This way!

Then more over there. And over there.

Yes, there's no way we could fire here.

Then, suddenly, to the right and to the left—and what were Four and Five Batteries doing!—some loud machine gun fire, and a lot of it.

Then, a huge shell burst! Another! An explosion behind us! And another!

22

THE UTTER SILENCE of the murky pre-dawn gloom erupted with bursts of machine gun fire raining down on Five Battery. The fire was coming from the forest on the right. There were no mortars, just three or four heavy machine guns that for some reason fired only tracer bullets. Long red streams gave notice of the death they dealt out—a rare occasion when one could see death coming an instant before it struck. A moment later, shouts of "Hurrah! Hurrah!" resounded from the forest—two hundred voices, perhaps. A wave of men, scarcely visible among the flickering streams of red, rushed toward the guns.

Only a few rifle shots replied from the area around the guns; they had no chance for more. The streams of red shifted leftward, to Four Battery, while Five Battery was showered with grenades. Fires flared up here and there.

The attack caught Toplev at the far side of Four Battery. Now it was happening! They were prepared—he had prepared them himself—yet they could scarcely believe it was happening. The tension that had gripped them through the night had just begun to ease; a few had even begun to doze.

Look at them! Three times as many as us! Should he shout? Give some commands? But they'd never hear him, and there was nothing more he could do to rally them.

It all happened in a flash, like the thrust of a dagger in the darkness.

Now Toplev could do absolutely nothing! Should he run? Run to Klein and set fire to the headquarters truck?

Off he ran. He could hear the explosions behind him, close now, and between explosions there were shouts and cries. Ours? Theirs? He could still distinguish a few rifle shots—those were ours.

The plotter and the radio operator were ready for this moment. They splashed the cab of the truck with gasoline and then lit some tinder and tossed it in. The fire caught on all sides. Now go, go! Run!

That's the last we'll see of our firing chart! And they won't get their hands on our files.

They had stopped throwing grenades at the battery. A few isolated shots could be heard here and there.

The Germans were still running toward the fire, bullets whistling around them. It was clear what they intended to do.

Toplev ran on with the two men from his headquarters. He ran, knowing only that he was going in the right direction, but had lost any idea of what to do other than flee. Someone was still running beside him, from the battery probably, he couldn't tell.

Scenes from his childhood and his school flashed through his mind, one after the other, then all of them at once.

A soldier ahead paused for a moment to let the captain catch up. Breathless, he could say nothing, but words weren't needed to understand.

They had saved Six Battery when they'd withdrawn a kilometer down the road and across the bridge. Red flames from their burning truck glowed high above the trees. The battalion commander used to say that we'd get to Germany with this truck.

From the place where the other guns remained came only a few bursts of machine gun fire.

23

LATER, KANDALINTSEV AND Gusev had to help each other piece together as best they could just what had taken place. And then what happened? Whose gun had hit the first tank? What about that third tank? And what set that armored personnel carrier on fire?

They hadn't been able to open fire until six o'clock: there was machine gun fire coming from the opposite bank to their front, but our own boys were still coming in from the German encirclement. None of our units were supposed to be there, yet a good many men had gathered in that snowy darkness.

Then, on the road from Dietrichsdorf on the left, they spotted the sidelights of tanks and APCs. The Germans are on the way! Sometimes the full headlights would flash, the drivers unable to resist turning them on. It was a whole mechanized column on the move. And the rumble of its engines grew louder and louder through the last bursts of machine gun fire.

There it was—the ugly snout of the first tank! Time to fire.

"Gun to the ready!" Kandalintsev's voice barely carried across the road.

"Open sights!" Oleg roared at his crew. "Fire!"

Petya Nikolaev was aiming. Our gun belched. Koltsov's gun belched.

Oleg rushed to help his crew with their next shell. Now we had to move fast!

The Germans weren't expecting any fire from this spot. They began moving to the roadsides.

We weren't going to let them pass. Fountains of sparks showered from the tank's armor! The HE-fragmentation shell had done its job!

The tank stopped. Something behind it caught fire—probably the personnel carrier.

The column was still moving along the road. But we kept up our fire, almost two rounds a minute! We put a shell right into the ugly mug of a King Tiger tank. And what a stroke of luck! We knocked out one tank on the approach to the bridge, another right on it, and they blocked the whole bridge. It was amazing that the bridge itself survived.

The German tanks fired at us, but because our side of the river was so much higher than theirs, their shells ricocheted and passed over us. Our crews would dive down into the ditches along the road and then jump back to reload. Nikolaev and Koltsov never left their guns, and they came through it all unharmed.

At a time like that you don't think of yourself or anyone or anything else, only how to keep pouring fire at them.

The Germans were mixing solid and regular shot, as they'd been doing since autumn. They must be very short of ammunition. Their solid shot didn't cause any wounds from shrapnel, though a direct hit was fatal, of course. Still, young Yursh was wounded, along with two of Koltsov's crew. A shot from one of the tanks cut the equalizing column on Nikolaev's gun.

So that was how they all reconstructed it later; but just who had done what and to whom, that no one could determine.

A NUMBER OF things happened later. Our infantry platoon finally showed up from out of nowhere and took up positions along the river. The bridge was under fire. The Germans tried to squeeze past the knocked-out tanks one by one, but they were mowed down as they came. They tried crossing the ice and clambering up the steep slope while wallowing in the snow, but they couldn't manage it. Then we ran out of shells and had nothing more to fire at the column across the river.

Then, along the road behind us that was still open, one of our own tanks rolled up, a new IS-3 with an angular prow and very heavy armor, sent here from our division. Enemy shells would bounce off it like sunflower seeds. It took up a position between our guns and banged off a few shots at the armored column and two more along the road to Adlig. No more Germans tried to poke their noses out of that place. They pulled their armor back into the forest. Two more IS-3s arrived. That was when things eased up for us.

Still later, more of our boys made their way out of the German encirclement and came back, crossing on the ice and clambering up the snowy bank both upstream and down. Among them was our battery commander, Kasyanov, with a wounded arm. Four and Five Batteries had been captured by the Germans, but some of the crews, those who could still walk, made it back. There weren't many of them.

Captain Toplev had come back, not wounded. All he knew about our battalion commander was that he had been surrounded. We could only hope he hadn't been killed.

When Oleg looked at his watch, he couldn't believe it: How could three hours have passed? How many things had been packed into them; how they had flashed by! They seemed to have disappeared into the battle.

It was already beginning to grow light.

24

THE FIELD KITCHEN fed those who were left.

Captain Toplev was embarrassed and ashamed when he met the platoon commanders. But how could he have done anything better? He concealed nothing and explained to Kasyanov how it had all happened, how unexpectedly the Germans had crept up to them, and how it had been impossible to save the guns. And Captain Kasyanov, who could not be blamed for anything, still felt somehow guilty.

About an hour later two light trucks drove up from Liebstadt in their rear. The first one, an Opel Blitz captured from the Germans, held the deputy chief of staff of the brigade, a major; the head of brigade reconnaissance, another major; and a few lower ranks from headquarters. They could not believe what they saw: This, after only a few hours? After that utterly quiet evening yesterday? And something like this happened? They hurried off to radio brigade headquarters.

The second truck held the deputy political officer of Second Battalion, Konopchuk, and the party organizer, Gubaydulin, who had obviously slept well and was quite sober.

There was also the head of the brigade's SMERSH, Major Tarasov.

They huddled together with the officers: What happened and how? They were furious with Toplev and Kasyanov and heaped abuse on them: How could they allow a shambles like this?

Tarasov gave them a severe dressing down: "I don't want to hear about 'surprise.' We always have to be ready for anything . . ."

But Toplev, utterly worn out, completely forgot himself: "But we did know. We were warned."

"What? How?"

Toplev told them about the deserter.

The full significance of what Toplev said struck Tarasov like a bolt of lightning:

"Where is he now?"

He'd been taken to the landowner's house, over there.

The others who had come with him looked at each other and realized: "Uh-oh, someone's about to get burned. Time to get out of here."

And brigade headquarters had already been informed, *from above*, about a major German offensive in the north during the night, on a broader front than this one. Third Battalion was completely surrounded. They were ordered to pull their survivors out immediately, through Liebstadt to Herzogenwald.

They brought the deserter to Tarasov.

Despite the battle during the night, it seemed that he had been able to get some sleep. He tried to smile. Inoffensively. Anxiously. Expectantly.

"*Kom!*" said Tarasov, pointing ahead with an abrupt wave of his hand.

He took him behind the barn.

He walked behind him, and on the way pulled his TT pistol from its holster.

From behind the barn came two quick shots.

After all the din of the past night they sounded rather quiet.

EPILOG

AFTER THE EVENING of January 25, when the first Soviet tanks broke through to the gulf of Frisches Haff and cut East Prussia off from Germany, the Germans prepared their counterattack in a single day and set it for the following evening. Their tank division, two infantry divisions, and a brigade of Jaeger troops began a westward offensive toward Elbing. During the night of January 26–27, three infantry divisions and the tanks of the Großdeutschland Division were added to this force, whose left flank had now seized Wormditt and Liebstadt.

Given that the wedge our tanks had driven into East Prussia stretched for some hundred kilometers, our infantry divisions had not yet managed to establish even a basis for a front line, and one of their three divisions had been surrounded and cut off. But Elbing, through which our Fifth Guards Tank Army had passed, remained beyond the Germans' grasp.

They succeeded only in holding the territory from Mülhausen to Liebstadt for four days. Their advance was checked in the south by our tank brigade and a corps of cavalry that was brought up from Allenstein—even the horsemen were, at last, of use in moving across the snowy ground.

On February 2 we again captured Liebstadt and the area to the west of it, and reconnaissance troops from our artillery brigade entered Adlig Schwenkitten. The guns of our two captured batteries stood in their former positions at the edge of the village, but all the breeches of all the guns and, in some cases, the barrels as well, had been damaged by TNT charges. They could not be repaired. The bodies of the gun crews, a few dozen of them, still lay unburied among the guns and back toward Adlig. A few had been stabbed to death: the Germans were saving their bullets.

We searched for the bodies of Major Boyev and his battery commanders. A few soldiers and battery commander Myagkov lay dead near Boyev. He had been shot through the head and through the jaw; he lay on his back. His fur jacket had been taken from him, along with his felt boots, and his cap was missing. As well, one of the Germans had taken a liking to his medals and wanted them to prove the success of their attack. He had used his knife to cut out the large piece of the tunic on which Boyev wore all his medals, and the congealed blood of the knife wounds could still be seen on his chest.

He was buried in the central square in Liebstadt, where a monument to Hindenburg stood.

A day earlier the command of the artillery brigade had submitted to the army artillery headquarters a list of those recommended for the Order of the Red Banner for the operation of January 27. At the top of the list were the names of political officer Vyzhlevsky, chief of staff Veresovoy, and the head of brigade reconnaissance; at the end of the list were the names of Toplev, Kandalintsev, Gusev, and the commander of the sound-ranging battery.

The commander of the army artillery, a tall, thin, and tough lieutenant general, realized full well the rashness of his decision to allow a completely undefended brigade of heavy artillery to deploy so early in a place that was an operational void. But when he saw the list his blood boiled. With a thick slash of his pen he struck out all the names of the senior officers of the brigade that stood at the top of the list. And then he added his own instructions in language not normally found in official documents.

Many days later, in March, an official citation was issued for Major Boyev as well: he was awarded the Order of the Patriotic War, First Class. Everyone was satisfied. But no one ever saw this golden medal, and his sister Praskovya never received it.

And, to be sure, did it add much to what some German soldier had cut away with his knife?

IN HIS POSTWAR memoirs, the commander of the infantry division made no mention of his one-day regimental commander, Major Baluev.

He simply disappeared, as if he had never existed.

1998

ZHELYABUGA VILLAGE

1

T HREE DAYS AGO our troops moved through the breach on the River Neruch. For these past days, my central station had been located inside a smokestack by the railway embankment. The brickwork was solid and gave good protection from enemy shelling. Some peasant women with their little ones had crowded in with us, and a couple of dozen gypsies who had popped up from somewhere had also settled in. After two months in areas occupied only by troops, it was odd now to see civilians about. At three that morning my battery got the signal to stand down: we were to pack up and move. By the time we had pulled in all the listening posts, it was already getting light. We rolled in to Zhelyabuga Village before there was enough light for aircraft.

Rolled in isn't quite the right expression. A sound-ranging battery is supposed to have as many as six specially equipped buses; what we had was a battered three-ton truck and a one-and-a-halfer. They could haul only our equipment and supplies along with a small crew, so the rest of the battery had to chase after them on foot. Lieutenant Ovsyannikov, the commander of the line-laying platoon, normally took charge of the battery, while Botnev, who ran the instrumentation and plotting platoon, and I rode in the trucks, hurrying ahead to find a site for our central station.

This was a critical job: the whole setup of the battery depends on the location of the central station. The more quickly it can be sited, the more quickly and safely the battery can be deployed. But it has to be sited absolutely correctly: a shell fragment in this heart of the battery means the whole battery is knocked out. There were times when we had to dig in our station in the middle of a rye field and cover it with a tarp, but this was asking for trouble.

I was nearly burned out after the pressure of the last four days and the lack of sleep. Yet it was a joyous exhaustion. We were making our general offensive, approaching the Kursk salient and taking some giant steps forward.

What a keen feeling we had for the places in this area and for the names of the towns and villages! Though we had never spent much time here, we had been here many times, registering targets from behind the Neruch as we devoured the maps with our eyes and imprinted them on our retinas—every patch of woods, every little ravine and ridge, the stream called Beryozovets, the village of Setukha (we had stayed in it the day before yesterday), the village of Blagodatnoe (we were now passing it on our left but couldn't see it); then Zhelyabuga, and then here was Zhelyabuga Village. We already knew where the houses were situated in every little village.

It's just as the maps show: Zhelyabuga Village is on a gentle slope down toward Panikovets Creek. And here we are, after rocking and jarring along the rutted track from the main road. So long as there are no aircraft we can move about openly. I yell to the boys in the back of the truck: "Dugin! Petyrkin! Kropachov! Scout around and see if you can find a cellar somewhere."

They tumble out of the truck and run off to search. There are already a few troops in the village—trucks here and there, sitting tilted downward with their noses dug in. The mortars have moved on ahead. The divisional artillery is on our right, across the hollow. I'm still searching the map to find sites for the listening posts. In front of us to the west is Mokhovoe, a sizeable place. Just last week the trains were still coming here, offloading supplies for the Germans. They'll try to hang on to Mokhovoe, so we'll probably be here for a while.

I pick out some approximate sites for the listening posts. (Ovsyannikov is the one who'll site them precisely.) They should cover about five kilometers of frontage (the book says as much as seven kilometers, but we've long modified what the book says: we never deploy six posts, and if we're really pushed we'll put out just four; now we'll use five). Ahead of our posts we have to find a place for our forward observer and the warning post. It has to be in a place (and often it's in the infantry trenches) where the observer can hear each sound from the enemy before any of our posts on the flanks can. Then—and this was where the whole art of the thing was—he has to decide for which sounds he has to press the button to turn on a station and which sounds to ignore.

"Found one!" someone is shouting as he comes running. Who is it? Our "regimental mascot," the fourteen-year-old Mitka Petrykin, a lad we picked up from Novosil, a town completely flattened by the war. Once it was a district town, but now it is a pile of white stone that stands as a silent sentry over the spot where the Neruch and the Zusha join. "Comrade Senior Lieutenant! Over he-e-ere! A cellar! A good one!"

Botnev and I walk quickly over to it. Here the cellars aren't under the houses; they are built separately, with bricked roofs and a dozen steps leading down. This cellar isn't cool and stuffy: people have been living in it for the past few days—the owners, perhaps, or some neighbors. They're hiding out here and have brought in their belongings. The brick roof is vaulted, though, and you couldn't ask for anything better.

It's very odd and very cheering for us to see living Russian peasants, to see gardens planted near the houses and grain growing in the fields. On the Soviet side of the front line, all the peasants have been sent some twenty kilometers farther back out of fear of treachery. This is now the third year that area has been without a living soul, no crops planted, and the fields overgrown with weeds as in the time of the Polovtsians.

(And yet your heart still contracts with love for this unworked and unpeopled land. It is clear: You could die without regrets for this Russian heartland. Especially after the swamps of the Northwest.)

But as soon as we crossed to the German side, we saw that people were still living there!

The people in the cellar look at us fearfully. No, we're not going to drive them out, they're our own folk: "Listen, friends, you're going to have to crowd in toward the back. We need to use the front of the cellar."

The women—there are no young men, just one very old fellow and some kids—heave a quiet sigh: How can they squeeze back any farther? But all their faces seem so familiar—our own folk. And they're happy we aren't chasing them out altogether.

"Now my lads are going to stack your baskets and sacks up a bit higher. Let's go, boys!"

We can squeeze in ourselves, but we still need a good bit of space for our equipment and our four small folding tables. But it looks as if we have enough room.

Choosing a place for the central station was the first urgent thing that had to be done. Now there is the second: we have to set up the station in the cellar as quickly as possible. But we have the men here to do it: Dugin and Blokhin, the two who work in shifts at the central instruments, along with some people from the plotting platoon.

I go up the stairs. An ominous rosy glow has covered half the sky in the east, revealing a few small cirrus clouds that weren't visible before.

But then there is also the ominous throbbing of airplane engines. We were absolutely fed up with those damned things. Why can't they leave us alone?

Wait, now. It's all right. They're *our* planes!

Since the spring we've seen many more of our own planes in the sky. We can stop crouching now. When we were in our defensive positions we'd seen more and more large groups of our long-range bombers, engines roaring under their heavy loads, flying off on some bombing mission far away. (And what were we so glad about? Their loads were being dumped on our own Russian cities, after all.) As we neared Oryol we could see it happening sixty kilometers beyond: the intersecting searchlight beams, the silver bursts of the antiaircraft guns, the red trails of the rockets, and the lightning flashes of the bursting bombs. And just in these last days we could recognize the triumphant waves of Ilyushins and their fighter escorts, flying low as they came back from some mission quite near to us. We'd give a cheer as their wings passed over: this was direct help to us, right nearby.

Those planes of ours are flying high. They've chosen their time well: the sun is just coming over the horizon, and the Germans will be blinded.

The plotting platoon is working well; they've done all this more than a few times. They carefully remove the central apparatus from its case and carry it down the stairs. The tables come behind them, along with all the measuring and plotting equipment. The linesmen are stacking up reels of cable outside, each one labeled with the number of a listening post. Once they've hooked them up, they'll run all the lines from here. Sergeant Major Kornev, a capable manager, has found a spot for the kitchen, lower down among the bushes; it doesn't have much cover, but it's well away from the houses in the village. Machine gun fire along the line of houses would pass well overhead. He has the drivers dig ramps for the trucks not far from the bushes; he's a sturdy fellow and lends a hand. The main thing is to get the truck engines down below ground level. All this we can manage to do quickly.

I walk around, smoking and feeling anxious. I keep senselessly opening my map case and checking the map again and again, though I have it almost memorized.

The sun is now fully up. The clouds are melting away.

One of the streets of the village rises up the slope from our position; there are already some fresh, deep black shell holes in it. Beyond the small ravine to our right is a second street, a level one. A battery of seventy-sixes has deployed there. The houses seem to be empty; some of the villagers are in the cellars, some have gone off to the forest. None of the chimneys are smoking.

Come on, Ovsyannikov, you don't have that far to go.

Here they come! An extended line of men is coming up from the little hollow. Even without my binoculars I can sense that they are our boys. They are marching cheerfully along, with Ovsyannikov setting the pace. And once they get here, the third rush job will begin: each listening post will collect its equipment, reels of cable, packs, and dry rations; and while these minutes tick away, Ovsyannikov will be establishing the exact location of each listening post, based on the estimations he made on his map. On the basis of the strengths of each crew, he has to determine which one will man the first post, the second post, and so on. Each crew chief has to hustle away to his post along an exact compass bearing, so as not to go astray. The forward observer has his own job to do. These ten or fifteen minutes when the whole battery is bunched up here are the most dangerous. It will be easier once all sixty of us aren't crowded in the same spot.

Our boys keep coming in, and they go on working just as they have been trained, by the book. The listening posts smartly make all their preparations for deployment. Ovsyannikov and I sit down on a fallen tree trunk to fix the location of the posts more precisely. There's an argument over a reel of cable: someone has walked off with a good reel and left one with a lot of spliced wire.

Everyone looks exhausted, and no one has had enough sleep. They wear their field caps every which way. Yet they move quickly, each of them well aware that we are not in some nameless little local operation, we are part of the Great Offensive! That itself gives them much more energy.

The linesmen are connecting their cables and beginning to lay out double lines. The Germans are already sending over a shot: a heavy shell passes over us and goes on to burst with a spectacular crash. It was probably in Setukha, near the main road. Then comes the first "picture frame," the twin-fuselage Focke-Wulf reconnaissance plane, buzzing about high overhead, looking for a target. Our antiaircraft don't respond: it's basically a waste of time firing at "picture frames," they always manage to dodge the shrapnel. Then a few heavy bombers fly over as well, toward Setukha.

We should be pinpointing our position while the morning is still cool. They hadn't moved us out at the best time.

Each listening post has four or five men, and they have a lot of heavy equipment to carry. A single storage battery is enough to throw out your shoulder; they usually need eight reels of cable, and sometimes more than ten; the sensor isn't heavy, but it's a cube, awkward to carry, and you have to guard it like your life so as not to tear the large diaphragm, and it would be useless if a shell fragment hit it. There's also the transformer, the telephone, and some other small equipment. Submachine guns, carbines, sappers' spades—all that has to be hauled out as well. (We've long since stopped wearing gas masks and just toss them all in the back of the truck.)

Stocky little Burlov takes his crew to post number one, on the left. He holds his compass in his hand like a watch, always checking the bearing to make sure he's on track. The lanky, imperturbable Siberian, Yermolaev, a man who can put up with anything, is in his crew; Ovsyannikov always picks the most reliable people for the distant posts. Then there's Shmakov, who probably has some charges hanging over his head: he'd been in an anti-tank unit and couldn't take the close combat, so he turned and ran and happened on our unit. We've had more than a few deserters of our own, so the commissar just said to hell with it, we'll take him on. And he's been a good soldier.

Shukhov, a quick and capable fellow (we promoted him to corporal to replace a wounded sergeant) leads his crew to post number two. The dark, sullen Volkov is on post five, the other far one, on the right. The central listening posts are closer, with shorter cables and just four men in each.

I go over the map with the gloomy, freckle-faced Yemelyanov (whenever we have an extra map, he's the one who gets it): he's the forward observer and has a delicate job, almost an officer's, but the position means that he wears a senior sergeant's insignia and is always the man at the very front. He has to react to every significant sound of firing and determine by ear the caliber, not wasting a second. (Later, someone closer to the shell burst can still correct him.)

The forward lines are getting livelier, with mortars pounding on both sides. The seventy-sixers from our Zhelyabuga Village are already firing, and we're still not ready. Once they need us, there can't be any delay.

Ovsyannikov is itching to get up to our farthest post: the final selection of a place to dig in the sensor is critical (the soldiers tend to choose the place that's most comfortable, and close to some water as well). He also has to make sure that the location isn't screened by any objects around it. (There was a case when a crew just hauled their equipment into a barn to get out of the rain; meanwhile, we were wondering what the hell was going on and why all the recordings were so blurred.) So Ovsyannikov strides off to catch up with Burlov.

Behind us another little group is walking up to our position. These are the surveyors, carrying their striped poles and tripods. Come on, hustle, we need you right now! The commander of the survey platoon, Lieutenant Kuklin, a sweet-tempered young fellow with the face and the stature of a boy, has brought them up. My Botnev, not much bigger than he, is telling him off: "Where have you been, taking a nap? Without you we have to fix all our coordinates by eye, and what good is that?" And he's right: someone's always on our back, checking such things, and if they miss a target it's always our fault. Would anyone ever walk out and check the surveyor's work? That never happens. If the surveyors make a mistake in one of their fixes, the locations of all the targets will be off.

I sit with Kuklin for a moment to show him where the posts are going, and ask him: "Yurochka, don't be in a rush. But do the three nearest posts first, even if it's just an initial fix. And send us the numbers right away." I explain that I've seen our Third Battalion of guns on the move and they'll be coming in somewhere nearby, but they still haven't arrived.

Kuklin takes his chain to the first clear reference point from which he'll measure the distance to Shukhov's post. (The reference point was taken from the map, and these can also be off. And a trigonometric network in a moving battle is never enough.)

It's hard to say who has the worst job in battle. The surveyors don't really do any fighting, but they walk around with theodolites and levels, dragging their surveyors' chains across the fields straight as the crow flies, and never mind that there might be a minefield there or that you might come under fire at any minute.

And now our signalmen from brigade have found us. They're running a cable to our central station, and the fellows are bringing up the reels of cable from the dammed-up stream below.

Who else has found us? The battalions of guns we'll be working with are still on the move. They're running cables from the brigade headquarters, of course, and it's from there that they'll soon begin asking us for targets.

If only we can get our location fixed in the early morning, before the air heats up. The Germans are already hammering away: there's one gun firing over here, and another ten shells or more coming from over there, and we're still not fully deployed. Our work through the day will be very poor; you can already tell it'll be a scorcher, and that creates a heat inversion: the upper layers of the air thin out as they grow heated, and the sounds won't be reflected downward to earth but will just go higher. The same thing happens with your normal hearing: the shells fall, but the shots themselves are harder to hear. The very best conditions for sound reconnaissance are high humidity, fog, and anytime during the night. That's when the recordings are very precise and the targets—whether they're the sharp blasts of guns or the dull roars of howitzers—can easily be picked up.

The people higher up have never taken this rule into account, though. If they had any sense, they'd have us move by day, not by night.

We, an instrumental reconnaissance battalion, are a separate unit but always operationally subordinate to the heavy artillery; at this moment we're working with a brigade of guns. It'll be hot work for us today: we're serving two of their battalions, the second, on our right, toward Zhelyabuga itself, and the third, on our left, toward Shiskov.

Down in the cellar, people have already crowded around Botnev. They've hooked everything up and run the checks. The needles on the dials of the equipment are already quivering. All six of the tiny glass pens clamped within electromagnetic rings are ready to trace a recording on a strip of paper. The thin, agile Dugin is already at the recorder. (He's good with his hands, and in every spare minute he's busy manufacturing something—a cigarette holder for one person, a cigarette case for another. For me he fashioned some lovely notebooks for my war diaries using strips of sound-ranging records.)

The man on the telephone, the saucy Yenko, has squeezed himself onto the bench beside the recorder. He already has a receiver on each ear, linked by a cord running over his head. One receiver is from the forward observer, the other from all the listening posts; they can hear one another, and if they all start chattering at once, the central operator has to try to keep them in check. But he's greedy for any kind of news: what's going at which post, who's had a bucket knocked over by a shell fragment.

Right behind the recorder is the interpretation table. Beyond that, with scarcely any space to sit, is the table where they determine the time differential. By the other wall are the plotter's table and a map on a slanted frame. The dim cellar is lit up by three twelve-volt bulbs, one hanging over the square-ruled Whatman paper. We're ready.

Fedya Botnev isn't what you would call a bold, intrepid warrior, but in the plotting platoon he doesn't have to be. He's careful, fussy, and very attentive to detail, just what's needed for his job. (He's even very curious about the equipment of the neighboring units and goes to take a look when he has an opportunity. He's been through an industrial-technical school.) He loves to stand at the map board himself and plot the intersecting lines from the sensors.

But the entire progress of any reconnaissance depends on the interpretation. We have Lipsky, a process engineer, and we've promoted him to sergeant. When there's a lull in our work in the battery, he's the only one addressed politely by his name and patronymic. (There's one other man with higher education in my battery, Pugach, a lawyer. He's a good lawyer and can always find some loophole to get him the easier jobs. But you can send him on any detail: "Give the political officer a hand"; "Put together a little news sheet for the boys.")

At the far end of the cellar there's some faint muttering:

"Listen to all that noise! What a commotion . . ."

"You think I might get out and take a look to see they haven't carried everything off? I left a 'nameled basin out there."

"Well, Arfevna, you can't bring it all in here. And if a shell drops down on it, you won't even find your house."

"God spare us that."

It's heating up outside. The light is already the bright yellow of a sunny, hot day. Even those tiny clouds have melted away, and the sky is a pure blue. There'll be a lot going on in the sky overhead today.

Smoke is already coming from Isakov's kitchen in the bushes.

The drivers are sweating to finish digging in their trucks, and a few men who are free are giving them a hand. Lyakhov is a tall, stolid fellow who never gives a sign that he's tired out. Plump little Pashanin, from Nizhegorod, has stripped to the waist, but still his hairy chest and back are covered with sweat and he wipes his brow with his wrist. He was careless enough to tell the battery of his misfortune: the wife he loved so much, a singer in the variety theater, has abandoned him, and Pashanin has become both an object of sympathy and of mockery.

I also have the battery political officer, Kochergarov, usually hanging around; but when things get hot and everyone else is rushing about, there's no way you can make him lend a hand. Before the war he was a driver, though a driver for a party regional committee; and now he doesn't seem to have enough sense to pick up a shovel and help Pashanin.

The first call comes in. It's from post three, the nearest one: they're in position, have hooked up the cable, and are digging in. We test their connection: they give a clap right in front of the diaphragm of the sensor, and our recorder marks it as a shot. Everything's working.

When an aircraft flies over one of our posts, though, its sound spoils the transcription from three other posts.

The cables that now fan out from the cellar are being dug in by the linesmen—each digging the one leading to his post. They bury the first fifty meters so that all the people walking around won't tangle them and also to try to keep them from being hit by shrapnel.

Here come some planes now! Six Henschel bombers. They're flying high at first, then they drop down and turn to our left. We hear the pop of our antiaircraft guns. Missed. Once they've dropped their bombs they withdraw.

Our troops here are crowded into a few square kilometers along the front line. There are light and heavy mortars, forty-five- and seventy-six-millimeter guns, 107-millimeter howitzers, and all kinds of vehicles half dug-in and camouflaged. Drop anything into that area and you'll make a hit.

Meanwhile, we have to find three more seats inside the cellar for the telephone operators from brigade and the two battalions. Our boys saw off three billets from the fallen linden—we're never without our two-man saw—and roll them down the steps. Lyakhov has driven his ZIS truck down the ramp he's dug. Pashanin has also moved his GAZ down. Well, that's a relief.

Shukhov, who has a bit of a lisp, reports that they've arrived at post two. We've tested the system and it's working.

They all take up approximate positions and would like to move to some spot that suits them better, but until Ovsyannikov checks their locations, there's no point in digging themselves in.

A shout comes from the cellar: "Call for you, Comrade Lieutenant!"

I tumble down the brick steps as fast as I can. Yes, it's brigade: we're waiting for targets, Forty-two! "At least let us deploy and get hooked up," I reply. "Give us a break!"

A little nap would be just the thing now. I look at the boys in the cellar. They feel the same way.

"Right, until we've got work to do you can put your heads down on the tables."

They don't need any more invitation, and their heads go down immediately. This will be the last chance for half an hour's rest.

The sun rises higher and the heat grows more intense.

Post four has now hooked up, along with the advance post. A rough estimate, at least, can be made using three posts—depending on the grid square they're firing from.

Two linesmen have been on duty since the central station has been operating. They run out along a line that's been broken and splice the cable. Someone from the listening post runs out to meet them so that there are two people searching for the break (you never can tell which end is closest to it). Repairing a line is one of the most dangerous jobs of all: you're fully exposed and standing, no matter how much you try to bend down; and if there's shelling, all you can do is flop down on the ground. If there's no sign of an artillery barrage, the duty linesman goes out himself; he knows his job. But when there's an urgent need, someone has to decide whom to send out. If Ovsyannikov is here, then it's him; if not, it's me. Depending on the job, it can be done without an officer; the sergeant manning the central equipment can go out himself. He's responsible: without a listening post, we can't locate the target, and that could cause an even bigger loss. Every trip along the line could cost a linesman's life. We've already lost Klimansky that way. And it's precisely when there's firing, when the shells are flying, that we need to pinpoint our target.

Right now it's Andreyashin on duty. He's sat down on the earth floor, his back against the arched brick wall. He's a nimble fellow, short and swarthy, with small ears. Born in 1925, he's only just been called up. He jumps to his feet when I come in.

"Stay where you are, no need to keep getting up!"

But he's already on his feet, and his dark, glittering eyes look imploringly at me: "Comrade Senior Lieutenant, can you let me off to go to Oryol for a few hours?"

He's from Oryol. He grew up on the streets, as a homeless orphan, but he puts everything he has into his job. Though he has no family, he has people he wants to see or look up in Oryol.

"We'll make it to Oryol ourselves before long, Vanya. Just be patient."

"But how long will that be? I can catch up with you, that's for certain."

"I'll let you go, and maybe for more than just a few hours. We'll be in Oryol for a good while."

"Burlovsky's connected!" someone shouts to me from the cellar.

The extreme left! Now we have them all.

Dugin is rubbing his hands. "This is gonna be something. Now we'll have some fun, boys!"

"A queer idea of fun you've got," someone from the depths of the cellar says.

Now we're all right, we can pinpoint a target. But we need to get them surveyed in. (Until that happens the locations of the posts are just rough, as we've marked them on the map.)

Up ahead there's the hammering of a firefight in progress. It comes in waves, though. And if an artillery piece fires in one of the lulls, we can pick it up.

Isakov has porridge ready. The men from our central station go out in turn with their mess tins.

There are more planes flying in the sky overhead, both our own and German, but there are more of ours! We don't see any dogfights; both sides are diving in at the front lines. There's quite a skirmish going on there now, and we can feel the explosions through the ground; that means we can pinpoint them.

Yemelyanov calls from the advance post: "I'm sitting with the infantry for the moment. I haven't dug my own foxhole, they won't let me. And there's no cover. You'll never believe how Ptashinsky just missed catching one—the bullet tore off his shoulder strap."

Ptashinsky is his relief man on the advance post. He's a fine-looking lad, bright-eyed and very steady in battle.

Despite everything, we've now managed to pick up two targets, 415 and 416, using our five posts. Now we have to work out their coordinates. The caliber of the guns we'll figure out just by a well-trained ear, and we can estimate the range.

The brigade is pestering me again: "They're firing now on Arkhangelskoe." (That was not far from headquarters.) "Which one was firing?"

"It was coming from Zolotaryov-3, target 415."

"Give me the coordinates!"

"They'll still be rough—we haven't finished surveying yet."

A hale of obscenities comes by way of reply.

Ovsyannikov comes back from his tour of the posts; he's covered about ten kilometers. I go with him to grab some hot food. We sit on the fallen linden tree.

I love him like a brother, this open-hearted Ovsyannikov with his Vladimir accent. We went through our artillery courses together, but we didn't become fast friends until we ended in the same battery. On the northwestern front, at the last moment before the ice broke up in the Lovat River, he rescued the whole battery by getting it across without breaking through. Then there was the hamlet of Grimov, where we really became friends. It had all been burnt out, only the chimneys still standing, and the Germans could see every patch of it from their OP in a bell tower. Our central station was in a cellar like this one, and Ovsyannikov and I were sitting on the earth floor, our feet in a slit trench, and eating out of the same mess tin between us. While we were finishing off that soup and tinned meat, we had to jump into the trench three times because of the shelling, but the mess tin up top stayed upright. We crawled out and attacked the food with our spoons once again.

The Germans don't have a direct view of Zhelyabuga Village farther down the slope behind us; they can only see it from the air. I roll myself a cigarette from some homegrown tobacco; Ovsyannikov doesn't smoke. He tells me how he's adjusted the locations of the listening posts. Someone coming along the road can see where the various units are located. There's a big fire in Mokhovoe, where the Germans are. We must have set that off.

"They're getting squeezed. We'll be pushing on. We won't be here long."

Before I've finished my smoke I see some vehicles coming off to the left along the road here from the main road, bumping over the potholes. A lot of them! Katyushas!

Eight trucks, fully loaded—a whole battalion. They always travel like that. Closer and closer. They aren't coming here just by chance. Someone has picked out a spot for them here from the map. They're only twenty meters from us, and we've never seen them firing from this close. We know enough to get away from the backs of the trucks and keep off to one side. They wave our boys away and they all tumble out and get busy.

A volley! It begins from the far side and quickly moves down the row; the first one hasn't finished before number eight is already firing. "Firing" isn't the word, though. It's a constant, deafening hiss, like some huge dragon from fairy tales. Fiery pillars slant down from behind each one, hitting the ground and burning everything that grows, scorching the air and the earth; ahead and above them you can see the rockets flying, dozens of them; then you lose sight of them until a huge fiery fan wells up along the German trenches. The power they have! Amazing! (The women in the cellar were frightened to death of the hissing of the Katyushas.)

The last truck barely finishes firing before it's turning around to leave. The second follows, then the third. All eight of them leave with the same rush with which they came. We watch them bumping over the potholes in the road again, though now the guidance rails hold no rockets.

"Well, now they're going to make it hot for us here," one of our boys says. That's not likely, though. The Germans know very well that the Katyushas vanish as soon as they fire a volley.

Ovsyannikov and I go back to our seats on the tree trunk.

When you've had a moment's rest, your thoughts will quickly range farther.

"Yes," I start speculating, "we'll keep on blasting them, and then— into Europe like a spring uncoiling. After a war like this, there's bound to be a revolution, don't you think? It's straight out of Lenin. And this so-called patriotic war will be turned into a revolutionary war, isn't that so?"

Ovsyannikov goes on sitting peacefully, saying nothing. Ever since he found that the Germans were using synthetic gasoline, he couldn't believe that they would soon run out of fuel, as the newspapers said. What worries him now is the advance post: "Things are so hot there they can't even poke their heads out. It's a bad spot. Here, look at the map. How far to the side can I shift them? Or pull them back? I can move them in a minute, and won't even have to disconnect their line."

We measure off the distance with the dividers. They could come back 300 meters, even 400.

Off goes Ovsyannikov, pacing boldly, tirelessly.

I can see that Mitka Petrykin is getting things ready, working as easily as if he were taking a swim in a pond. He calls in the rest of the boys from the plotting platoon who were digging slit trenches.

They've brought in some more cables to us, from the Second Battalion on the right and the Third on the left. They're digging in the cables themselves. With cables fanning out on all sides, our central station looks like some important headquarters. Now three more people have squeezed into the cellar, sitting on sawed-off logs with the telephones on their knees.

Immediately I'm called to the phone. It's Tolochkov, commander of Eight Battery in the Third. I think a lot of him. He's a short fellow, quite reckless, and gets so involved in his job that he forgets everything else. I'm happy to help him make his shots.

"You've got to get me some targets! I'm getting bored here."

"Hang on, I'll have some in a minute. We're waiting for the survey. We're feeling out target 418 right now."

Without any sound reconnaissance, the artillery can rarely identify a target. They can only do it in darkness by direct observation of a muzzle flash, and only if the enemy gun position is exposed.

Then I have another call from the Second Battalion. From the voice I can tell that it's the battalion commander himself, Major Boyev.

"Sasha, we've got some real work to do today, don't let us down."

"I can send you a few coordinates right away, but we're still waiting on the final survey."

"Never mind, just send them. And something else: come and see me at the 'cottage' this evening."

He means the battalion headquarters.

"What's it about?"

"You'll find out when you come."

I'm about to go outside when Yura Kulin comes almost running down the stairs. He hands me a sheet of paper with all of our coordinates.

"If you can wait a minute, we can make them a bit more precise."

"They're OK, thanks." And I pass them right over to the plotter, Nakapkin.

He picks up his measuring device, a metal goniometric rule marked obliquely and accurate to one meter, and sets down the "x" and "y" coordinates for each listening post on the plotting board marked with large blue grid lines, correcting the former temporary coordinates. And now he links the points of all the listening posts with new straight lines, new perpendiculars to them and new angles to the targets. Beginning with target 415, all the targets are indicated with new offsets.

Each of the sensors at the listening posts sends back information that appears as a line of ink traced along the paper ribbon in the central recorder. The movements of the sensor diaphragm at the listening post appear here as squiggles on the paper. By the difference in corresponding irregularities from neighboring sensors we can calculate the direction of the sound on the plotting board. And in ideal conditions, at night or in cool, damp weather, these three or four projected lines will all come together at one point. That's what we're looking for—the location of the enemy gun, and we pass it on to our own guns over the phone. But when there is a lot of sound interference or, as today, a temperature inversion that causes the sound not to be reflected, the sound vibrations are indistinct, distorted, or only weakly transmitted; the moment of movement is imprecise, and so how can we make our calculations? And if we estimate our readings incorrectly, the beams will be plotted on the board incorrectly. We won't get the single point we're looking for, only a long triangle. You might as well whistle for it.

That seems to be the problem now. Botnev is hanging over Nakapkin's shoulder, frowning.

Botnev and I have also been through a lot together. Once we were on the move, in two trucks as usual. The only way to get to our destination was along the dirt track into Belousovo. Then we saw it: a stake by the roadside with a sign: "Suspected minefield." But it was faded and carelessly written. Switching to any of the side roads meant a long detour, even retracing some of the route. Well, what the hell, we'll do it the Russian way—by guess and by God. Pashanin's one-and-a-half-ton jerked forward. I pressed my feet against the floor as if trying to keep a mine from blowing up beneath us and kept my eyes fixed on the road ahead: Could there be something under that clump of grass? What about that patch of loose earth over there? We went on for about 300 meters and then heard the explosion behind us. We stopped and jumped out, knowing an anti-tank gun was no threat to a man on foot, and looked back: the right front wheel and fender of Lyakhov's truck had been blown away, but everything else was still in one piece, including Lyakhov and the men in the back of the truck. Botnev had also survived, though the explosion had been on his side; but he was tearing off, running up a little hill. He came to his senses, though he was raving a bit and had a mild concussion. (The first truck went on to the destination; the rest of the essential equipment had to be carried in.)

No, we've got a sizeable triangle here. Somewhere out there is target 415, but we still can't pinpoint it. There's clearly a one-fifty, and more than one of them. We have to keep looking, but we can't squeeze much out of these recordings. I focus all my attention on the ribbons from 415.

We can't make any reports from this vague data, so let's look for something else. Do the lines on the ribbons show some little spike or flutter that we can use for our calculations?

We pay no attention to the local people here in the cellar, though we sometimes have to shout at them to stop their chattering. Now there's a little boy about ten years old who's trying to make his way to the stairs again.

"Where do you think you're going?"

"I want to have a look outside." His face shows determination.

"Do you know what an artillery barrage is? Before you even have a chance to look around, a bit of shrapnel can go right through you. What grade are you in?"

"Not in any grade," he says, taking in a breath through his nose.

"Why's that?"

It's a silly question: it's war, and there's nothing more to say. But the boy explains sadly: "When the Germans came, I buried all my schoolbooks." His face now shows desperation. "I didn't want to study when they were here."

It's obvious how much he hates *them*.

"And it's been that way for two years?"

He sniffles: "I'm going to dig them up now."

I turn aside for a moment, and he's down on all fours, crawling under the plotting table; then he runs out to his own village.

They call me to the phone. The brigade's deputy chief of staff is impatient: "Where's the target that's firing from Zolotaryovo? Give me the target!"

Well, I'm doing my best to find it. Just give me a minute to think. It would be easier if I just closed my eyes and stuck a needle in the map. They could fire off a dozen shells and calm down. And if there was still fire coming from over there, I could say that it was a new target. But I won't do that. I don't know how many times I've explained to them the problem of interference, passing aircraft, temperature inversions. Just be patient, we're working on it.

Then I'm called to another telephone. It's the chief of staff of Third Battalion. He's got the same question and is just as impatient. I easily recognize this fellow, Captain Lavrinenko, a sly Ukrainian. Once he called me to help him register a gun. He made the first shot and asked for a correction. I passed on the information from the shell burst: left 200 meters and add 150. He took another shot and asked us to pinpoint it. "There wasn't any burst." "What do you mean, no burst—we just fired." "Ah, that's what it was: we recorded an explosion, but it was half a kilometer to the right. What are you shooting at? Are you all drunk over there?" "Yes, we were a bit off on that one, but keep tracking our shots." He didn't trust me after just one shot. The next time, he spoke to our first sound-ranging battery on the sly and then to my second battery, both separately: "Get a fix on my shot!" And once again, both batteries were in agreement. So now he believes me. And here he is, pestering me again: When are we getting the coordinates?

Yes, it's a heavy gun that's lobbing shells, a one-fifty; the bursts are to our left, between brigade headquarters and Third Battalion headquarters.

It's very likely coming from 415, but there's so much noise from the battle going on and from the artillery on both sides in the forward areas that we can't get a proper fix: each time we plot the target on the plotting table it slips away somewhere; we're left with some new triangle.

The advance post keeps starting the ribbon in the recorder. A heap of useless, discarded paper now reaches up to Dugin's knees. We've already replaced one reel.

Now we have to take turns to get a little sleep: "Fedya, you go into the hut and close your eyes for a bit. I'll stay here and keep plugging away at 415."

Yenko, with a telephone receiver on either ear, is something of a joker. He's taken note of the very pretty girl sitting at the far end of the cellar.

"What's your name, sweetie?"

She has fair curls on one side of her forehead and bright eyes. "Iskiteya," she says.

"Where'd you get a name like that?"

The old woman sitting beside her says, "That's the name the good father gave her. But we call her Iskorka."

"How old are you?"

"Twenty," she replies with spirit.

"Still not married?"

"It's the war, you know," the old woman explains on behalf of the girl. "Who gets married these days?"

Yenko, who's almost missed the call coming in, passes me one of his receivers: "It's Lieutenant Ovsyannikov."

Ovsyannikov is reporting from the advance post. He's had to crawl to get there. He's pulled them back a little, to a place where there are two large rocks, and they're digging a little trench behind them. Still, it's a hot spot to be in.

"How do things look overall?"

"Overall. Well, on the right our tanks have gone into Podmaslovo twice. They've just managed to squeeze in a bit, but for the moment they're holding their ground. They're taking a lot of fire."

"OK, that's all we'll need from you right now. Come on back and get some rest. We're going to have a busy night."

"No, I'll stay on with the lads here for a while."

Despite everything, we are managing bit by bit to collect some other targets. None of them are precisely pinpointed, though. When we can get a smallish triangle, we take its center and phone in the coordinates to both battalions. But we just can't seem to pin down the target in 415.

That girl, Iskorka, also just can't sit still and is making her way to the door. Her dress is tightly belted at the waist but is quite full above and below.

"And where are you off to?"

"I want to have a look at what's left up there. They're going to wreck our whole place."

"Do you mean us?"

"Of course. Your guys are stealing our chickens." Anger flashes in her eyes.

"Where's your house?"

She makes a graceful wave with her hand, as if she were dancing: "It's the last one on that row, near the willows."

"That's a long way," I say, taking her elbow.

"What else can I do?"

"Well, be careful. If anything comes over just drop to the ground. I'll stop by later and check if you're OK."

She trips lightly up the stairs and disappears.

We've used up another roll of paper. The sky is filled with noise, from us and from the Germans. Airplane engines are roaring and whining up above as they wheel and dive. Someone's going to get it. And they're firing machine guns at one another.

I hear a wild shout from the entrance up above: "Where's the battery commander?"

Our duty linesman runs down the steps: "Comrade Senior Lieutenant! Someone wants you outside."

I go up the stairs and see a sergeant, well turned out and looking as if he's from some headquarters. His submachine gun, muzzle down, is slung from his shoulder. He's very brisk and in a great hurry: "Comrade Senior Lieutenant, the brigade commander wants you! Right away!"

"Where do I go?"

"It's urgent! We have to run. I'll take you there."

And so off we run, at full speed. My pistol slaps against my thigh and I have to clap my hand over it. We run past all the potholes on the track leading to Zhelyabuga Village. Now I see a Willys jeep parked on the open road. Couldn't he have driven up to meet me? Or is he trying to teach me a lesson? We keep running.

We come running up to the jeep, and I see the black-haired Colonel Ayrumetov sitting in it. I salute and report. He gives me a scorching glare meant to reduce me to ashes: "Senior Lieutenant! For the job you're doing I'll have you sent to a punishment battalion!"

He gives me a full blast. For what? And he *can* send me to a punishment battalion. Such things happen quickly with us.

I stand at attention, mumbling about the atmospheric inversion. (They'll never accept that as an excuse. Why should they even try to understand?) And it would be idiotic to complain about all the extraneous firing: there's a war going on, and you can never eliminate all those noises. His fury abates, and he grins at me: "You need to shave, Senior Lieutenant, even in battle."

Sure thing. Then, as if from nowhere, two single-engine Junkers appear over the rim of the forest. How can they miss the single Willys jeep on the road, a clear sign that there are senior officers about? They've spotted it! They turn and start their dive.

The sergeant who came for me is already sitting in the jeep behind me. But the sharp-eyed driver, not waiting for the brigade commander's order, shouts, "Turn back! Turn back!" So the colonel never finishes his reprimand.

The first Junkers is already in his dive. As always, you can see his front wheels that seem to be reaching out for you like talons; he lets loose the bomb that falls like a droplet from his beak. (And then he comes out of his dive as if he's bending his back and even giving a little shudder of rapture.)

Am I dismissed now? I run back toward my battery. Then I drop down flat in a little depression. Behind me I hear a massive, deafening explosion.

I raise my head and straighten up: the Willys has turned tail and disappeared in a cloud of dust!

What about the second Junkers? He's going on with the turn he began and—is he heading straight for me? He must have realized that the man standing by the Willys was not just a private. Or is he just doing this for spite or revenge?

There's no time to think, it's too late to run, and I've no strength left to look up at the sky. I flop down in that little depression again, face to the earth. How can I protect my head? Even the palms of my hands might help. Is this really where it will happen, out here? And so stupidly, just by chance?

There's a huge crash and I feel the scorching heat. I'm showered with earth. Am I still in one piece? They do miss quite often. There's a terrible noise in my head, and I feel faint. I've got to run, and I do run, stumbling over those damned ruts and potholes. And it's uphill all the way.

They don't seem to have bombed Zhelyabuga Village, and all our lines are still fanned out around the cellar. But will the cellar itself hold out?

No, the Junkers have broken off their attack: they have their own lives to lead, up there in the sky, one racing after the other, and the sky now is no longer concerned with the earth below it.

With all the noise going on, we can't make any recordings at all. So it's off to a punishment battalion for me.

The battery of seventy-sixes next to us is being pulled out of Zhelyabuga and moved forward where things are hotter.

Lord, my head is still buzzing. It feels as if it's swollen, filled with fluid. Things are bad enough even without that: all the stress of these last days—it seems as if there aren't twenty-four hours in a day but two hundred and forty. Yet despite all these sleepless nights, you have an overwhelming sense of power; you even feel light on your feet, as if they had wings.

"Mikhail Longinych, give me all the ribbons from target 415; I'll search through them myself, and you can look at the rest."

I send him off to get my folding table—we have one extra. I set it up near the cellar, in the shade of a willow tree. "And get me a stool from one of the houses." He brings me one immediately.

I sit there, searching through the strips of paper and thinking.

What the training manual said was to calculate the time differential from the beginning of the first oscillation from each listening post. But when these beginning points were indistinct we were taught to do various other things. The peaks of the oscillations could be compared—the first maximum, the second maximum. Or the reverse: compare the minimums. Or you could look at all five sets of oscillations to try to find places with similar characteristics, small squiggles, and calculate the differentials from them.

I try one method, then another one. Mitya takes the ribbons down to the cellar to work on them there. If they can get a smaller triangle among all the intersections, Nakapkin will call me down to look at the plotting table.

Meanwhile, Second Battalion is asking us to help them make corrections. The guns of Four and Five Batteries close on our right begin banging away. We try as best we can to isolate their bursts from all the other noise and send them the coordinates. They make their adjustments, and we check them once more. Myagkov from Five Battery contrives to make his corrections toward target 421. The advance post calls, quite satisfied: the target over there has gone silent.

I couldn't be more grateful for the good work of the plotting platoon.

Lipsky's soft white hands are on the ribbon of paper spread out across the table. He holds it down with his left, and, with his right, using a very sharp pencil like a needle, he goes on marking the proper places to prick the paper where a tiny, slender vertical line shows the beginning of an oscillation. (There are sometimes false results as well. They happen, and there's no time to think about them in the few seconds available, yet the outcome of the operation—good or bad—depends on your results.)

Ushatov, shoulders slightly hunched, concentrates on running his viewer along his Chudnov slide rule, taking readings down to a thousandth.

Fenyushkin, the calculator, uses the tables to make corrections for wind, temperature, and humidity (we take our own measurements beside our station) and passes the adjusted figures to the plotter.

The plotter (the sharp-eyed Konchits has replaced Nakapkin), scarcely daring to breathe, is using these figures to adjust the goniometric rule along its grooved scale. And he transfers to the plotting board the angle of deviation from the perpendicular ahead of each of our posts. Now he'll plot the straight lines, and we'll see if they come together. The fate of those German guns, and the fate of our boys under fire, depends on the scrupulous work of each one of these men.

(When Nakapkin finishes his shift, he settles himself down to make a drawing, using the ink from the apparatus and one of the self-sealing letter cards that front-line soldiers are given, of some Red Army soldiers striking down the enemy. He'll send this home or to his girlfriend.)

Our listening posts are all still in one piece. There was some bombardment near Volkov's, but they've all survived and are now dug in. Our cables suffered a few hits, but they've been repaired. One good thing about dry weather is that our cables, with their fabric insulation, don't get wet. They've got only a weak rubber coating, and when it's damp they will ground or short out. Making a continuity test on the lines when under fire is a lot more than just a hassle. The Germans don't have this problem: their cables have thick red plastic insulation. A reel of captured German cable is worth its weight in gold.

Meanwhile, Konchits phones me: my 415 has produced quite a good intersection, almost a single point. I make up my mind and phone Tolochkov: "Vasya! Here's the 415. Don't try bracketing it. It's best not to make corrections, just give it a volley and scare the shit out of them!"

That's the Russian way! Tolochkov fires off a volley, twenty shells at once, five from each gun. So now what? We'll keep checking.

Now we're having some heavy fire along our slope. I take a look. Along the little ridge where the houses at the upper end of our street stand and where the spreading group of willows is—and where Iskiteya ran off—I see a row of about two dozen fountains of black earth flying up from the ground. They're putting down some accurate fire! One-fifties, probably. Are any of our boys there? The Germans must have scouted out that area, or maybe it's their aerial reconnaissance. There are more of our planes in the sky, though. That means we can walk around with our backs straight.

Back down in the cellar they tell me they've taken quite a shaking. The women had been talking amongst themselves: What are we doing sitting here? Better go and look after our belongings. But now they're hiding their faces in their hands.

Then there's another deep shudder in the earth. That means it's even closer than the volley on that ridge. Dugin is yelling nervously, desperately up above: "The line to the second's been hit . . . ! And the third! And the fourth!"

If they're hitting the spot where the lines fan out, they're very close. And if all three posts send out linesmen, it'll be for nothing—they don't know where the breaks are.

Someone pulls at me from behind. It's the telephone man from brigade, and he seems almost horrified: "Somebody from *the very top* wants you!"

Oh-ho! That means even higher than brigade. It has to be the army artillery headquarters. I take the receiver: "Forty-second here."

The connection is poor, coming from a long distance away, yet the voice is threatening: "Our tanks have been held up in square 74-41!"

I unfold my map case on my knee with a trembling left hand and look up the location: yes, of course, that's near Podmaslovo.

". . . We're getting high explosive fire from Kozinka, 150-millimeter . . . Why can't you give us the coordinates?"

What can I tell him? A man can only do what he can do. But we'll try. (Should I explain about the inversion again? But these smart people in the staff up there should know that already.)

I tell him that we'll do our best.

Once again, very close to us, an explosion, then another! Someone up above is shouting: "Andrey-a-shin!"

The voice on the telephone (I've got my hand clapped over my left ear so I can hear) says: "Listen, Forty-two. When we advance, we'll send a commission to check the location of those German guns. And if you've got them in the wrong spot, you'll be facing charges. I can do whatever I like with you."

Who is this "I"? He hasn't identified himself. Could it be the chief of artillery himself? My throat's gone dry.

While this is going on, there's a huge bustle around our station, with people shouting and running up and down the stairs.

I pass back the receiver and fix the map case that's hanging open. Now, what's going on out there?

Yenko and Dugin shout in one voice: "Andreyashin's been hit!"

I run up the stairs and see Komyaga and Lundyshev running up the slope, carrying a groundsheet. Behind them, limping a little but following readily, comes the medic Cherneykin carrying his medical bag. Someone's lying on the ground about 150 meters away. Lying there, not moving.

What if the Germans repeat that shot? All three of them will be hit.

"Find Pashanin! Get the truck ready!" I shout.

I count the seconds: Please, don't shoot again! But there's still no second shot.

Dugin, forgetting regulations, has abandoned his recorder. His face distorted, his hands spread, he says: "Com' Lieutenant! We've only got the two outside posts left. We can't do anything!"

The three have now run up to Andreyashin and are bending over him. For God's sake, don't shoot! Not now!

There's something white in Cherneykin's hands. He's bandaging Andreyashin and Lundyshev is helping. Komyaga is spreading out the groundsheet. The seconds tick by so slowly.

Pashanin comes running up, sleepy-eyed, his face covered with black stubble.

"Pull out the truck and get ready to move."

The three men are moving Andreyashin onto the groundsheet. Two of them carry him away. Cherneykin, behind them, is carrying something else. He's holding it well away from himself so as not to soil his clothes.

Is that a leg he's carrying?

It is a leg, from the knee down, still in a boot, with a tattered puttee flapping.

They carry him on, treading heavily. Galkin and Kropachov run to help. Mitya comes after them. The lad wants to get a close look at the blood.

The young local boy follows behind; he just won't settle down.

Someone tells me about Galkin: "He was held up for a minute, otherwise he'd have been there. It was his line as well . . ."

So Andreyashin rushed off on his own. And he'd put in for leave to Oryol. People to visit there . . .

He'll have to get by without his leg. And he's got no mother and father to help him out . . .

As they carry him by, I hear him groan: "Just straighten my right leg for me, boys . . ."

His missing leg . . .

The bandage and cotton wool barely stop the flow of blood. Cherneykin applies another bandage.

Lundyshev says: "He's got another wound. Look there, there's some spots on the side of his chest."

Shrapnel. Well, he's got his leave . . .

His swarthy face is much darker than usual.

"Boys," he pleads, "just straighten my leg . . ."

The one that's been blown off.

The ground is uneven and soft, and it's hard to keep him steady. And it's hard getting him onto the bed of the truck. Blood drips down, on the ground and on the open gate of the truck.

"You'd best take it along," I say, nodding at his leg. "Who knows, the doctors might need it."

They take it with them.

"All right, Pashanin, go fast and go easy!"

Over those same ruts and potholes again. But Pashanin's a skilled driver, and he'll take him as if he himself were the wounded one.

There are two in the back with Andreyashin. They've closed the gate, and the truck drives off. And if he survives? We've still lost him. And we're headed for his Oryol—straight there. Gloomily, we go back to our work.

And I remember: I may be facing charges.

Dugin is worried: "Comrade Senior Lieutenant! Should we get them busy repairing the lines?"

The linesmen are waiting, ready to go. They're all afraid, particularly Galkin, who survived just by chance. And out there, our tanks are being shelled.

Who should be spared—the ones out there, or the ones here?

"Just hang on," I say. "We'll wait a bit longer."

It was as if I'd sensed it! We barely hear the shots, what with all the noise and the heat, but they all come crashing down at once—half a dozen one-oh-fives, right in the same spot again, where Andreyashin was hit and a bit closer—a row of black bursts along the slope!

One of the houses is smoking; the roof has been blown off another.

"Don't say anything to them down in the cellar."

That was how the shells fell when Andreyashin was hit.

Mitya comes up from the cellar with a message from Dugin: "They've hit our advance post!" he shouts, as if pleased about it.

All the more reason to hold off.

As my granddad used to say, "Let them croak, the lot of them!" It's one thing after another.

I'm not responsible for the whole army. Even the commander isn't responsible for it all. What I have to worry about are these sixty men right here. As Ovsyannikov says, "We've gotta take care of our people, and take care of 'em well."

We'll wait a bit longer.

I smoke one cigarette after the other, without thinking, but they only make me feel worse. Some sort of dull stupor has taken complete possession of me; my brain has almost stopped working, and I can't cope with even the simplest things.

Twenty minutes go by and there's no more bombardment, so I send Galkin and Kropachov to repair the lines. If they've all been broken at once, then the breaks must be right here, by our station. The two men have telephones on their belts so they can call in and check the lines.

Then I'm called to the phone in the cellar again.

It's the battery commander on our flank: his posts have been knocked out.

Tolochkov thinks that we've taken out 415; nothing's coming from it. There's still no bombardment. The lines have been repaired, at the spot where Andreyashin's blood still lies.

The linesmen come back. Great job, lads!

The sound of the German guns is still indistinct, though. The sun is fierce and saps all our strength. Some cumulus clouds have appeared, but they don't seem to be gathering.

Botnev has taken over the central station from me.

Ovsyannikov is back. He's covered in sweat and his shirt has dark, wet spots on it. He's heard about Andreyashin over the phone. On his way back, he came under some heavy fire. He was lying out on some level ground without any cover. Our forward observer has now found a spot behind some stones but is still having a heavy time of it and can't even raise his head.

Ovsyannikov has taken off his sweaty field cap, and his hair is sticking out in all directions. Still, he gives a very clear account of all that he's done, speaking in his broad Vladimir accent.

"Go grab a bit of sleep, Vitya," I tell him. And he goes.

The hours flow by, and from all the racket, the confusion, and the trying to do three things at once, the extreme strain under which you've been working begins to sink you into torpor. Your whole being seems to be in fog; your head feels swollen, both from the lack of sleep and the effects of the shell bursts that haven't yet passed; your head droops, your eyes are red. It's as if the various parts of your brain and your soul have been torn to pieces and will simply not move back to their proper places.

When night comes, though, you need a particularly clear head. So now I, too, go off to get some sleep in one of the houses. There's a dirty, ragged blanket on the bed, and the pillow is no better. And there are lots of flies. I put my head down and I'm gone. Sleeping the sleep of the dead.

How long was I asleep? The sun has now moved well across to the other side and is sinking.

I hurry back to the station. There's Pashanin with his mess tin, just had supper. "Are they back yet?"

In a voice filled with compassion and sorrow, as if he himself were to blame, he tells me: "He died as soon as they got him to the aid station. He was just full of holes."

So . . . now we know. That's how it is.

I go down the steps to our instruments to check on the work. All the men look downcast. The new shift is already busy at the tables. The women have stopped their chatter; there's been a death in the house.

"Anything that could be coming from 415?"

"Not a thing," says Konchits from the plotting table.

While I was sleeping, it turns out, our boys have twice given the German forward area a heavy shelling, Mokhovoe in particular. And I never heard a sound.

There had been a few breaks in the lines, but our lads were right there to repair them.

Now where's Ovsyannikov?

He's gone to our right-hand posts. There's no stopping that man.

It seems that they've stopped plaguing us with their shelling. Still, the torpor hasn't left me. If they'd just leave us in peace for a bit, I could get back on my feet again. And before it gets dark.

I've got no appetite and don't bother with supper.

A call comes from Boyev to remind me that he was expecting the Forty-second at 2000 hours.

Yes, better not forget that . . . It's just a bit more than a kilometer, and I can walk it. It'll soon be after six . . .

Now the firing seems to have almost died out. Everyone's exhausted.

We're not making any move forward. And there are no planes in the sky, neither ours nor theirs.

I sit down under a tree. Maybe I should jot down a few things in my diary? I haven't added a line since yesterday, when I mentioned the gypsies who were with us. But no thoughts will come to me. I don't have even the energy to move my pencil.

These past four days? A person isn't equipped to cope with so much. What day was it when that happened? The time frame becomes completely muddled.

Ovsyannikov comes back and sits down on the grass beside me. Neither of us speaks about Andreyashin.

"What day was it when Romaniuk shot the tip off his finger?"

"That idiot thought we'd strike him off strength so easily. Now he's in front of a tribunal."

"Kolesnichenko was smarter. He ran off even before we began the offensive."

"And no one's heard of him since."

We go down to the stream, strip to the waist, and wash.

So, evening is coming on. The sun is dropping behind the higher houses in the village, behind the ridge, and will soon be behind the Germans. All our observers will be blinded in a moment.

Seven thirty. In an hour and a half our real work will begin. Seven thirty. I'm supposed to go somewhere at eight. That's right, Boyev called. Should I go? He's not my commander, but he's a good neighbor.

"OK, Botnev, take over for a while. I'll be back in an hour or so."

My head still isn't working properly.

It's easy to find my way there—just follow the wire. (Don't go astray where the wires cross, though.)

I drop through the hollow and then follow the straight road above it. There are about a dozen houses along it, still standing. None of the shells have hit the road. Now that evening's come on, there is the odd villager here and there, tending to their household chores. A few of them still have some livestock. Farther on, there's a small potato field. Then another slope, and among the bushes sits the battalion staff truck, a ZIS, its bed roofed over by a homemade canvas cover. They've obviously come here straight across the fields, not by road.

Battery commander Myagkov and the battalion commissar are standing by the truck smoking.

"Is the battalion commander here?"

"He is."

"Any idea why he called me?"

"Climb aboard, you'll see."

They're also getting in. We climb up the small ladder attached to the back of the truck and go through a low plywood door.

All the map cases, maps, and papers that were on the table in the middle have been cleared away and placed in the corners. The table, bolted to the floor, has been covered with a pair of towels sewn together to make a tablecloth; on it are a white, unlabeled bottle and some open tins of preserved food—American sausages and our own tinned fish; some sliced bread and cookies lie on a plate. And there are glasses and mugs of various calibers.

On the left side of his chest, Boyev wears two Orders of the Red Banner, something you rarely see; on the right he has one Order of the Fatherland and one Red Star; he's not wearing some of his lesser medals. His head isn't quite round and looks as if a bit has been trimmed off each side, which adds to the solidity of his chin and forehead. He grasps your hand firmly and powerfully; it's always a pleasure to shake hands with him.

"So you made it, Sasha? Wonderful. We've been expecting you."

"What are you celebrating? We still haven't taken Oryol."

"It's my birthday, you see, the last one before I turn thirty. And this next year will go by so fast, I just can't put off celebrating."

Proshchenkov, commander of Four Battery, is shorter than Boyev and is both like and unlike him: he has the same unyielding solidity in his jaw and shoulders, a masculine strength. And there's also something very simple and innocent about him.

Yet who among us isn't simple and innocent at heart? Until the war, I had never rubbed shoulders with people like this. Thanks to the war, I came to know them and to be accepted by them.

Myagkov is something else entirely: He is *myagkii*, a gentle, kind fellow. He's like a son to Boyev. Their last names absolutely suit them— Boyev, the *boyevoi*, the fighting man.

The commander of Six Battery has been left at the observation post.

Here I begin to feel myself grow steady and stable. I'm happy I've come.

There are benches fastened to either side. People can sleep on them, but now they are seating six—the battalion adjutant, a captain, had also come.

We don't take off our hats. We are all covered with dust, and the sweat hasn't dried on a few of us.

Boyev calls me by name, but I address him as "Com' Major," though he's only four years older than I. But I can't transgress these army manners and, in any case, I don't want to.

"Com' Major! If there aren't any toasts already planned, may I make one?"

Now at last I feel some relief from this whole day of madness and stupefaction. It's come not from my peaceful walk getting here; it's from this place itself, from the firm handshakes, from the unexpected little gathering around a folding table and, to be sure, from the fact that no one knows where we'll be a year from now (I remember Andreyashin's plan to visit Oryol). Boyev and I have never been close before, yet here we are, friends—all of us, a group of friends.

"Pavel Afanasyevich! In two years of war, I've been blessed to meet people like you! And people like you, one doesn't meet every day."

I look with admiration at his invariably erect bearing and at his face: How can he have such iron determination and self-forgetfulness when life itself now seems so cheap? Yet he never loses his soldier's mannerisms for a moment.

"And how did you ever get a last name like Boyev? No one could have hit on a better one. You seem to be completely at home in war. It's as if you've discovered the happiness in it. I can see you firing on that bell tower as if it happened today . . ."

I had watched it happen next to that hamlet where Ovsyannikov and I lay, unable to raise our heads because of that bell tower. Some of Boyev's clever fellows could see what was going on and, under the same fire we were facing, they came out and lit a few smoke pots. A solid gray smokescreen wafted across, though it wouldn't last long! Boyev himself came out with one gun, using open sights. It was a tricky and risky operation, and he had to make it work: the gun had to be changed from its traveling to its firing position; they loaded it, managed to make out the top of the bell tower when the smoke began to clear, and bang! They reloaded and—bang!—once more. A hit! Then, quick as can be they brought the gun back to its traveling position, hooked it to the tractor, and off they went. The Germans lay down a barrage on that spot, but they were too late. And that was the last of their OP.

". . . For you, war is existence itself, as if you have no existence outside of war. So, may you live through all this . . ."

Boyev listens, astonished, as if he was quite unaware of all this.

We all rise. Glasses clink against tin mugs. All of us feel the fire course through our insides. Vodka after a day like that—you had to watch yourself!

What glorious, rough days! And where were they taking us?

The grand offensive! Over the whole war you could have counted the number of such days on one hand. Our spirits soared. It seemed that we had been filled to overflowing, yet there was still more to come.

Once again we stand, clink our glasses, and drink—to victory, of course!

Mygkov says: "When the war ends, our hearts will all be smaller somehow, just imagine."

The conversation shifts quickly from one topic to another, everyone putting in his word. Boyev says: "They were the ones to lay hands on us, and they'll regret it. We'll make it hot for them."

The adjutant: "We'll put their feet to the fire."

The commissar: "Ehrenburg writes that the Germans are horrified when they think of what's waiting for them this winter. But they should think of what's waiting for them in August."

Everyone is filled with passion, though not with hatred. That's just for the newspapers.

"You try speaking German to the Germans and they switch to Russian. They've learned a lot over two years."

"What do you think, will anyone understand us when we come back home? Or maybe no one understands us even now?"

"Just think, though, how much of Russia they still hold. It's monstrous."

"Why won't they open the Second Front, the bastards?"

"Because they're saving their own skins at our expense."

"Well, they have started the invasion of Italy."

The commissar says: "Capitalist America doesn't want a quick end to the war; that would end their profits."

I suggest something else to him: "It seems to me that we're going too far off course, moving away from internationalism."

He replies: "Why is that? Disbanding the Third International was quite correct."

"As camouflage, perhaps; as a tactical move." But I change the subject: "Well, I can't stay any longer. This is when I have to get busy."

Proshchenkov tells us about an incident from today's firing. He believes that 423 has been destroyed; there hasn't been another shot from that position.

"Maybe they've just shifted the position."

A few more things are said about shifting positions. We don't know about the Germans, but sometimes even when our people are ordered to shift their guns, the blockheads just go on firing and firing from the same spot, out of laziness, until they get blasted to pieces by the enemy.

That's not the only stupidity. What about those who fire at random just so they can report a number of shells expended?

It happens . . .

Proshchenkov says: "We've got ourselves well dug in now that evening's come on. Let's hope they don't move us tonight, at least."

The light coming through the tiny window in the truck is fading, so the battery-run bulb on the ceiling is turned on.

"Not a bad little shop we have here for our headquarters," says Boyev, looking around. "What do you think, will the old girl take us right to Germany?" We begin listing the people who won't be making it to Germany— one, two, three, a fourth sent to a punishment battalion where he was killed.

I've spent time with people who were more educated, but I've never spent time with people of purer heart. I'm happy to be among them.

"Yes, and later when we remember one another . . ."

We hear the distinctive hoarse and hateful crash of a six-barrel mortar.

The mortar shells howl, and then come six explosions in rapid succession.

"Well, thanks to you, friends, and goodbye. It's time for me to go."

And, indeed, it's already twilight outside. I have to get back before dark or risk getting lost.

ALL OUR LINES are still in operation.

Yemelyanov calls from the advance post: "Now we're digging in right and proper. But the German's sending up a lot of flares."

Even back in the village, we're being lit up by red flares and white-and-gold ones that hang in the air for a long time.

We've recorded the six-barrel mortar, though not very accurately— mortars are always difficult to pick up. Then there's a gun, target 428, probably a seventy-six, that fires a single shot. We pick it up at once and get a precise fix on it.

The equipment is in good order, all gauges showing normal. A new tape has been put on the roller. The ink in the pens has been topped up. Everyone on the new shift is rested and in good spirits. Three low-voltage bulbs light up the front part of the cellar. The white paper gleams and the shiny metal sparkles.

Also here are the two duty linesmen, telephones on their belts, carrying extra spools of cable, flashlights, wire cutters, and insulating tape. These men have it tough at night, following the cable to the break at one end and then trying to find the other end.

The far end of the cellar is dark. The children are asleep, the women have also lain down and their faces can no longer be seen. But I can hear the voice of my battery political officer there. I can't tell where he's found himself a place, but I can distinguish his fruity singsong:

". . . Yes, comrades, now we've even let the church come back. Soviet power has nothing against God. Now we just have to liberate our motherland."

"Do you really think you can smash right through to Berlin?" says a suspicious voice.

"Why not? We'll give it to them over there. And all our things that the Germans destroyed, we'll rebuild. Our land will sparkle even more than before. There'll be a *fine* life for us after the war, comrades, the like of which we've never seen."

The tape moves in the machine. The advance post had picked up something. And now all the posts were recording.

Then we hear it ourselves: a long, rolling volley. Right, let's get to work!

2

AND SO FIFTY-TWO years later, in May 1995, I was invited to Oryol for the commemoration of the fiftieth anniversary of Victory Day. Vitya Ovsyannikov and I (Vitya was now a retired lieutenant colonel) were fortunate enough to drive and walk over the routes of the 1943 offensive, from the Neruch, from Novosil, and from our station at elevation 259.0 to Oryol.

Novosil, which we remembered as a wasteland of rubble on a hill ravaged by artillery fire, was now utterly unrecognizable. We also visited our former "regimental mascot," Dmitry Fyodorovich Petrykin, who came out to greet us wearing a felt hat and had his picture taken with us and his whole family, children and grandchildren.

Our underground headquarters at elevation 259.0 had now been completely plowed over; not a trace of it remained, and we had no access to it. Nearby was the wooded ravine where our kitchen and our service area had been and where the unlucky Dvoretsky was killed (he hadn't even come for his porridge; he wanted to see the medic to have a sore treated). He was hit by a tiny piece of shrapnel, but it struck him straight in the heart. The same small Y-shaped ravine and patch of woods had survived very well, both in its shape and appearance: the yearly plowing had not allowed any new saplings to spread beyond the ravine itself.

But what had happened to Krutoi Verkh ravine? It had been about three kilometers long, some fifty meters wide, and had a few gentle curves, like a calmly flowing river. It extended through our area and provided a spacious approach quite hidden from ground observation right to our front lines. Infantry, cavalry, and transport vehicles passed this way all through the day with no need to conceal themselves, and by night there were trucks with ammunition and food; they would move back to the rear by morning or be dug in, nose first, into the sides of the ravine and covered with fresh branches and camouflage nets. After yet another bend, the hill ended directly on the Neruch, and it was here that our 63rd Army was able to assemble and prepare for its breakthrough on July 12, 1943.

But how Krutoi Verkh had changed over half a century! Where had those steep banks gone? Where was its depth? Where were the firm slopes and bottom covered over with grass? It had become shallower, eroded, and had even grown bald; it had lost its harsh contours and was no longer a formidable gorge. It had been our home and refuge! But now, of course, there wasn't a trace of the old dugouts and ramps where trucks had been hidden.

Beyond the Neruch, on the heights, there had then been a fortified German line, and it was very well fortified! There were impassable pillboxes and rows of separately dug-in armored gun turrets. There was something else that was unforgettable: the troops who made the breakthrough immediately faced a minefield. Dozens and dozens of dead, both ours and theirs, had lain there. Ours lay mostly facedown, as they had fallen or crawled forward; the Germans were more scattered, some lying where they had died defending their positions, others where they had turned to flee. They lay, their faces distorted by horror, bodies disfigured, many with half their heads torn away. We had found a German machine gunner sitting in his trench, still clutching his weapon on the spot where he was killed. Scattered across the area were heaps and heaps of scorched metal: tanks, self-propelled guns, all singed red, like living flesh.

And their dugouts were nothing like ours, d'you remember? So deep! Here and there, under ten layers of logs, there would be a little window with a few planted flowers, and to keep them alive, a small ditch dug to bring water. There was a very unpleasant smell inside the dugouts, a doggy smell that turned out to be coming from insect powder. A few brightly colored glossy magazines had been strewn about here, magazines unlike our Soviet ones. Some of them had stories about valor and honor, others pictures of pretty girls. It was a different world, one we had never seen before.

Remember how they launched two air armies at us, from dawn to dusk, to hold back the advance on Oryol for just a single day? That we can never forget. The sky was never clear of German airplanes for a moment: no sooner would one group withdraw after dropping its bombs than we'd hear the drone of another group, coming in on the same course and making the same bombing run. We could see that the same was happening on

our flanks. It was an uninterrupted thrashing from the air, and it continued all through the day. Where were our planes? That day we didn't see a
single one. Between the waves of bombing you might manage to run ahead
a few meters, but trying to deploy the battery was out of the question. Still,
I managed to hunt through the whole of Safonov for a place to put my
station. I tried a shallow little dugout, where I found three signalmen who
had just opened a tin of American sausage and were arguing about how to
share it. No, that wouldn't do. I ran off a bit farther. When I came back
ten minutes later, the dugout had disappeared: a direct hit.

Those things we saw only later in the war. But now we were traveling around in a jeep, much like the one that the brigade commander had
used when he visited me back then (jeeps hadn't changed much over the
last fifty years), and they were taking us to Zhelyabuga Village. The jeep
was the same, though it had a solid roof. We were being escorted by the
heads of the regional and local administrations, carrying out their duty of
hospitality.

Probably no other vehicle could have made it to Zhelyabuga. The
road was nothing more than ruts, and it was good that there had been no
rain for a long time so that they had become rock hard. It could scarcely
be called driving: the whole vehicle was being tossed from one side to the
other, while we desperately clung to the handrails.

Yes! Here was that slope that was so vivid in my memory; it hadn't
changed. Higher up on the crest, the willows still stood as they had before.
There were the few houses clustered around them. But lower down, where
we were, the look of the street was radically different: some of the houses
had been destroyed by the war, others had simply fallen victim to time and
had not been rebuilt. The street was no longer a street but merely a few
islands of houses; and it was no longer a road, either: its center was grown
over with weeds, and the tracks once made by wheels now stood like two
pathways side by side.

The second street to the right and higher up, beyond the hollow, looked much as it had in the past, yet there seemed to be few signs of life on it.

On an open spot on the slope by the side of the road stood a broken-down wagon that had long since lost its function as a vehicle: it had only three wheels, one of the shafts was twisted to one side, and the box had been smashed. New vegetation was growing over the wheels.

What about our central station? Right here, this is where it must have been. But there was no sign of the brick roof and no trace left of the cellar. Had they hauled away all the bricks and filled in the pit?

We left our jeep while the administrators remained in theirs so as not to intrude upon our memories.

Farther down was the pond, a place we could certainly recognize. We walked down to it. The bank was overgrown with sharp, broad-leaved weeds. An emaciated horse was wandering alone, without a bridle and perhaps even without an owner. It seemed to be lonely.

A latticed skeleton of poles stood off to one side: Was it meant for its shelter? It was leaning awkwardly.

The water seemed stagnant, as if it had not moved in years. The bright May greenery around it made it seem bluer than it was. An evergreen branch floated motionlessly on the water along with some fallen leaves. These must have been from last year, since there were no new ones like them yet. No one ever swims here.

Across the brook was a slab retaining wall. Four or five protruding slabs provided enough to hang on to.

Here was a patch of lily of the valley, unseen by anyone, of no use to anyone.

We each picked a cluster.

Slowly, slowly we climbed back up the slope, then farther and higher, past the ruined wagon.

Past Andreyashin's spot . . .

Three houses, side by side. One had been whitewashed and was neater. The two others were made of the same ancient gray logs. How did they remain standing? The roofs were made of crooked gray planks. One would take the houses for barns or sheds.

Somewhere a puppy was yelping in a weak voice. He wasn't barking at us.

A few hens passed by in a row, looking for something to eat.

There were no people to be seen.

Beyond those houses was another piece of waste ground. On it stood something that could not even be called a barn; it had been thrown together in slapdash fashion, the walls covered with rough pieces of slate, the roof a piece of tin. It was already leaning and had been propped up with two logs. What was it for? Who could have needed it?

The sky was utterly silent. Here, perhaps, no airplane would ever fly again, and even the sound of one had been forgotten. Along with the sound of shells.

In those days, though, they had crashed like thunder . . .

A cow, tied by a long rope to a stake, was grazing. She started when she caught sight of us and darted aside.

We went on to the very highest houses.

Here, between two adjoining birches, a crosspiece had been nailed in to fashion a kind of bench; there was even a small beam to support the center. On that bench two old women were peacefully sitting, each nestled against a birch tree. Each held a crooked walking stick made from a peeled branch. Both wore warm headscarves and were dressed in warm, dark clothes.

Though they were under the trees, the leaves on the birches were still so tiny that the sun made its way through the sparse greenery and both could sit in the light and the warmth.

The one on the left wore a dark gray headscarf and a workman's jacket; she had no shoes but wore some homemade footwear of thick felt or rags. Enough for dry weather, at least. She held the top of her walking stick, polished by much use, against her cheek with all the fingers of both hands.

The faces of both women were deeply furrowed; the skin around their chins was sagging; their sunken eyes made it difficult to tell whether or not they had seen us. Neither of them stirred. The second, in a colored headscarf, also clung to the walking stick she had tucked under her chin.

"Good day to you, grannies," we said cheerfully.

No, they were not blind, they saw us as we approached. Without changing the way they held their hands, they replied, "Good day."

"Have you lived around here for long?"

The one in the dark headscarf replied, "So long as we've lived, we've been here."

"What about the war, when our soldiers came through?"

"Right here."

"And how old are you, granny?"

The old woman thought for a moment: "Eighty-five, it must be."

"What about you, granny?"

The headscarf on the second woman was very badly faded, showing only some faded pink patterns on a pale blue background. She was not wearing a jacket but a garment made of incredibly worn black velour that resembled a short overcoat. Her feet were not wrapped in rags but shod in high boots.

She moved her walking stick away from her chin and said slowly: "I was born in the year '23."

Is that possible?—I almost said it aloud. Here we were, addressing her as "granny" and forgetting to look at ourselves, as if we still had all our youth. I tried to set things right again: "So I'm five years older than you."

The sun was on her face and a bit of color came into her cheeks as they warmed under its rays. She was facing the sun but not squinting because her eyes were now set so deeply and her eyelids were swollen.

"Somehow you don't look it," she murmured. "Our folks don't walk about much after seventy, they have to crawl."

When she opened her mouth to speak, I could see that she had only two yellowed teeth left.

"Well, I've also seen a thing or two in my life," I said. It was as if I was trying to justify myself to her. Her lips, now also with a touch of color, moved into a kindly smile.

"Well, may the Lord grant you more years still."

"What's your name?"

"Iskiteya," she said, almost in a whisper.

I was stunned.

"And your patronymic?"

Though her patronymic was scarcely the point. *That* Iskiteya had been five years younger than I.

"Afanasyevna."

"We were the ones who liberated you," I said, growing excited. "I even remember you. Just down the way, over there, there was a cellar and you were hiding in it."

Her eyes were clouded with the mist of old age: "There were a lot of you passing through then."

I didn't know what to say. I had a strange urge to say something cheerful about that time, though there was little that was cheerful about it. Only that we were young. All I could do was repeat foolishly: "I remember you, Iskiteya Afanasyevna, I remember you."

Her lined face was in the May sun, and her words had the warmth of old age: "Well, I forget what I need to forget." She heaved a deep sigh.

The woman in the dark headscarf was more sorrowful: "Everyone's forgotten us. You might buy us a bit of bread."

There was silence. Birds were chirping in the birches. The sun was mild and gentle.

From under her swollen eyelids, Iskiteya examined me with weak eyes, though I couldn't tell if she saw me distinctly. "What was it that brought you here, then? Is there news of some kind?"

The other woman joined in: "You're going to see what you can do about our living conditions, maybe?"

Vitya and I exchanged glances. What was there that we could do?

"No, we're just passing through. We came to have a look at the old places from the war."

"Some of your bosses are back there. Maybe they can . . ."

The woman in the dark headscarf came to life: "Where?"

"Somewhere back there."

Not far away a rooster crowed. No matter what is happening, a rooster's crow is always such a joyful, rich sound that celebrates life.

As for the two of us, what should we do now? Go on with our journey?

We said our goodbyes and walked on, up to the crest of the hill. Our hearts ached.

"Our countryside is still living in misery," Vitya said. "It's been the same all through our trip."

"Yes, people can't get any more now than they did earlier."

The land was open on all sides. Mokhovoe was not far. It was even closer now that the new buildings had crept this way.

Over to our right, toward the second street, five sheep were grazing. No one was looking after them.

We sat on a little mound, gazing straight ahead.

"Just over there was where our forward observer was. How did he ever survive that day?"

"There was the night as well. They had his position pinpointed, and they dropped a lot of stuff on him."

"In the morning they moved us out again."

"The brass were just fussing about. We could have done a lot more here. Why did they shove us into Podmaslovo?"

"Are we going to Podmaslovo?"

"Not likely. There's not enough time."

We sat there, letting the sun warm our left shoulders.

"We should help them, but fixing up one or two isn't the answer. The whole system in the country needs fixing."

But who will do it? Such people haven't been seen for a long time.

A very long time.

We went on sitting.

"I was such a fool, Vitya. Remember how I used to go on about world revolution . . . ? But you were the one who knew the countryside—from the bottom up."

Vitya's a modest man. No matter how you praise him, he never lets it go to his head. And even though life has dragged him through many rough spots, he's still the same Vitya, with his patient smile.

"Over there, on the right, was where we celebrated Boyev's birthday that day. He said that he didn't know whether he'd live to see his thirtieth. And he never did make it to his thirty-first."

"Yes, that Prussian night, that was something," Ovsyannikov recalled. "Dead silence, not a soul to be seen, so how did they mount an offensive? I went across that whole lake, and there was no one and nothing on it. And then—Shmakov gets killed."

"How did we ever pull ourselves out of that Dietrichsdorf? God must have been helping."

Ovsyannikov, now with an ironical smile, said: "And from Adlig, across that ravine, through the snow, running and tumbling head over heels . . ."

We looked to the left and saw our two jeeps coming toward us, bumping and rocking across the fields around the edge of the village. They must have worried when we disappeared.

Both the administrators were in white shirts and ties. The local one was more plainly dressed, with a rain jacket over his suit. The man from the region wore a blue tie and a good gray pinstripe suit with nothing over it. He had a broad, bony face with a rather sullen expression. His hair was pitch-black and very thick; it gleamed in the sun.

"The people here are being neglected," we told them.

"What more can we do?" said the man from the region. "We pay their pensions. We provide electricity. Some of them have televisions."

The local administrator—from what had formerly been the village soviet—had obviously risen from among the local people. He still had a good deal of the peasant in him. He had a long face, long ears, fair hair, and reddish brows. He added: "Some of them have cows. And chickens. Everyone's got a garden. They do the best they can."

We got into the jeeps and, the administrators leading the way, we drove along the bumpy road through the village itself and down our slope.

But what's this? Four women, side by side, had come out to stand across the road in a tight row. They'd brought an old fellow with them, for support, a frail old man in a peaked cap. Three more women came up from various directions, leaning heavily on their sticks. One had a very bad limp. There was not a single younger person.

So, the word about the administrators must have gone round. And it had drawn in a crowd.

There was no way to drive around them. The jeeps stopped.

The place was only about twenty paces above the spot where Andreyashin was killed.

The local fellow got out: "What's the problem? Has it been that long since you've seen anybody from the administration?"

They had blocked the road so no one could pass. There were now six women standing in a row. They would not let him through.

The regional administrator also got out. Vitya and I followed.

The women were wearing gray or brown kerchiefs, and there was one of bright cabbage green. Some had their kerchiefs wrapped right to their eyes, others had their foreheads uncovered so you could see every movement in their wrinkled skin. Right behind the others was a burly, large woman in a red and brown kerchief, her feet planted solidly and not moving. The old man was behind all the others.

The women all began speaking at once:

"Why don't we have any bread?"

"You've got to bring in bread for us!"

"We're living on just one scrap of bread a day . . ."

"We can't last long on that . . ."

The village soviet man was embarrassed, particularly in the presence of the regional administrator.

"Right. First Andoskin was bringing in bread, right from the shop."

A woman wearing a gray and violet kerchief, in a sleeveless sweater over a bright blue blouse, said: "But you weren't paying him enough. When the price of bread went up he said he wouldn't bring in any more for what you gave him. It takes me a whole day, he says, and I don't want to do it. So he quit."

"That's right," said the village soviet man.

"Not, it's not right," said the woman in the blue blouse.

The young man shook his head: "What I'm saying is that's what happened, it's true. But now, for a time, Nikolai will be bringing in the bread. He has to come here to pick up milk and he'll bring bread as well."

"He's not going to do it for nothing, neither. I'll take your milk first, he says, and next time I'll bring your bread."

The woman in the dark gray kerchief, the one we met earlier, was straining to see and hear what they'd say: Were they going to come to some decision?

The one in the light brown kerchief said: "And if you don't sell milk, then what do you do? You ask Kolya—please, just a loaf. I've only got one salary, he says. I can only give bread to those on the list."

A woman in a gray checked kerchief spoke up, with a lot of emotion: "Us folks in the village have come to the end of our rope. There's no living for us here, there's nothing to eat."

The small woman in the green kerchief said: "There's no proper road here, we know that . . ."

The village soviet fellow had to justify himself before the regional man and quickly said: "I always keep an eye on things, you know. Nikolai, I say, are you bringing in the bread? I am, he says."

The woman in blue spoke up now, sharply: "So you keep an eye on us, do you? When did you ever pay us a visit? You, the chairman of the village soviet, haven't been here even a single time . . . None of you people have been here since Adam was a boy."

Others now added their complaints:

"Things have gone to rack and ruin . . ."

"Everybody's forgotten we're still here . . ."

The clean-shaven old fellow in the second row stood silently, not seeming to understand what was happening. He yawned and then went on standing with his mouth open.

Ovsyannikov had bowed his balding head. His peasant heart ached.

"Wait a minute, now," the village soviet man hastened to say. "Why didn't you tell me before that he hasn't been bringing in the bread?"

"We don't quite know how to go about it," said the woman in green.

"We're afraid," said Iskiteya.

At this point the regional administrator joined in, in a powerful voice: "I'm telling you, you have to speak up. You're afraid to tell Nikolai, you're afraid to tell Mikhail Mikhailovich, you're afraid to tell me. What are you afraid of?"

The woman in blue said: "Well, I'm not afraid, and I'd come in to see you. But I can't get around at all anymore. And my old man's in even worse shape."

The woman in the red and brown kerchief leaned her left elbow on her stick, bent over, pressed her fist to her shoulder, closed her eyes, and said: "I don't want nothing to do with any of you . . ."

"But haven't I come to see you now? I keep asking Mikhail Mikhailovich, are they bringing bread for you? Every day, he says. Why didn't you speak up?"

The woman in the gray check made a chopping motion with her hand: "Well, we're speaking up now!"

"We just don't know how to get back on our feet again."

One of the women we met, the one in the dark gray scarf, had black hands on which the soil had forever left its mark; her fingernails were rimmed with black. She stood there, her hands clasped over the top of her stick. She had dozens and dozens of wrinkles on her face—you'd think there wouldn't be enough room for them all. She'd calmed down now and fixed her eyes on something in the distance and stood there, frozen.

The regional administrator made his decision: "Let's agree as follows. Mikhail Mikhailovich will come to you every day for the next week . . ."

"Every day? What for? Every other day, maybe . . ."

"Even if we got some bread every third day . . ."

"I'm not saying he's to bring you bread each day. But for a week, up to Victory Day, he'll come here every day and check that you have all you need."

(But would he manage to write it all down?)

". . . We chose him here, voted for him in the village administration, so he should carry out his responsibilities as head of the local government. At the very least, he has to see that you've got bread to eat. We're not saying that he should start building houses for you—that's something we can't do, given our present circumstances."

"Houses . . . Just imagine . . ."

"You've got water. And you'll have bread. He'll see that you have the essentials. That's his job."

A soft moan came from the women:

"A bit of bread and we could get by and we wouldn't squawk . . ."

"We'd have some hope left . . ."

"Rye bread, now, that's solid stuff . . ."

The village soviet man recovered as well: "Let's agree as follows. Not only will you have bread, but every week I'll send you a mobile sales van."

The women were amazed: "A sales van each week as well! Now that's something!"

The woman in the gray check didn't miss her opportunity: "There's another thing we've been needing. For a long time. While the front was here, some of us went off to do work there . . ."

"From August '43, when the front moved on . . ." said Iskiteya.

The woman in the gray check was somewhat younger than the others; her eyelids weren't swollen, and her gray eyes were wide open and lively. The words poured out of her readily, though only a single tooth flashed in her lower jaw: "I worked for almost three years in a war plant, for example. It was in the town of Murom, Vladimir Oblast. So you know how we worked and what for. Never a holiday, never a day off, never a bit of leave. And what did they tell us then? Your labor will be our victory; it will help us end the war quickly and bring some peace to the country. So why have you forgotten those who toiled away, tell me that? Now even our pensions are less than what other women get . . ."

The regional administrator brushed back his black forelock: "Yes, this year for the first time we have been remembering those who worked on the home front. Almost every day now I award a jubilee medal to our mothers. They're moved to tears . . . Every day they're getting these jubilee medals and weeping. Finally they've remembered us, they say, because we were carrying the whole front on our shoulders. We pulled the plows ourselves, we sowed the grain, we sent our last socks to the soldiers. So if you really were a war worker, in accordance with the Decree you have to either find the documents to show that you worked or find at least two witnesses . . ."

"There's two of us right here. We'll be witnesses for each other."

"You'll need a third person."

"There's one in Podmaslovo."

"If you worked more than six months on the home front prior to 1945 and can document it or get statements from witnesses, we'll certainly give you a medal. And there are certain stipulated benefits that come with the medal."

The village soviet man, though, seemed to have a better knowledge of the regulations. He turned to caution the regional man.

"Unfortunately, I have to interrupt. That's true only when an error is being rectified. In other cases the Decree does not take witnesses' statements into account. If there's no notation in your employment record book the jubilee medal can't be awarded. We've raised this problem a number of times . . ."

The regional man frowned, slightly embarrassed: "In my opinion, this is a case that calls for rectification."

The gray-scarfed woman pressed him again: "How can that be? The Military Committee mobilized us and treated us like serving women. When a few of our girls left their jobs, they were put on trial by a military tribunal. Don't you realize how they treated us?"

Iskiteya could only nod her agreement: "Yes, that's how it was."

The village soviet man said: "Then we'll have to make a request through the Military Committee."

"That's right," said the regional man. "We'll compile a list and send in an official request. They can find the documents from 1943. A lot of cases like this come up."

I could see Ovsyannikov making a terrible face. His head was sinking lower and lower as he listened to all this, and he was holding it with one hand and looking as if he'd lost hope.

The small woman in green spoke up, as if she would not be interrupted: "I've already got a medal for the war years. Not the actual medal, you know, but I've got all the papers, right and proper. And I do get some benefits—like I only pay half for my electricity. But Lord knows what else I should be getting. I went to the office once but they just told me our collective farm is poor and we've got nothing to give you. I didn't even get my seed grain 'cause the chairman never put in for any for the pensioners."

"As for benefits, they're all built into the regional budget. And through the regional budget we can allocate funds to those who should only pay fifty percent. Of course, I can't be here every day to sort these things out . . ."

"We understand," the women said, all smiles.

Then Iskiteya ventured to say a few words. She spoke in that same soft and undemanding old woman's voice she had used with me under the birch tree: "My husband fought in the war. He was wounded, and he got some benefits. But after he died they were all taken away."

Lieutenant Colonel Ovsyannikov roused himself and spoke out indignantly: "You should be getting all the benefits that were being paid to your husband, and unless you've remarried . . ."

Iskiteya looked astonished, and her lips formed a weak smile: "Remarried? How could that be?"

". . . then you should still have all those same benefits! And it doesn't matter when he died."

"It's eight years now he's been gone . . ."

"Well," said the regional man, rousing himself and looking at his watch. "I'll personally look into the questions that concern you, our veterans and mothers. And if I can't do anything, then I'll take it up with the oblast. But we shouldn't bother Moscow with things like this, absolutely not."

1998

TIMES OF CRISIS

1

YORKA ZHUKOV, BORN into a peasant family, could handle a rake at hay cutting when he was seven and helped around the family farm as he got older, though he finished the three-year parish school. Then his father sent him all the way to Moscow as an errand boy and apprentice to a distant, wealthy relative, a furrier. That's where he grew up, starting as a servant, running errands and working bit by bit until he mastered the furrier's trade. (When he finished his training he had his photo taken in a borrowed black suit and silk tie. He sent it back to the village, signed "master furrier.")

But the German war broke out, and in 1915, when Yorka was nineteen, he was called up. Though he wasn't that tall, he was strong and broad-shouldered, and they chose him for the cavalry and sent him to a squadron of dragoons. He learned about horses and he learned to keep his back straight. After six months he was chosen for more training and finished as a junior NCO. In August 1916, his dragoon regiment went to the front. Two months later he was concussed by an Austrian shell, and it was off to the hospital. Then Zhukov became chairman of the squadron committee in a reserve regiment and never went back to the front. At the end of 1917, his squadron simply disbanded itself: each one of them was given a valid pass, all right and proper, told to take their weapons if they wished, and head for home.

He stayed in Moscow for a bit and then went back to his village in Kaluga Province, where he came down with typhus, which was everywhere at the time; the typhus kept recurring. It was now August 1918, and general mobilization for the Red Army began. They took Zhukov into the First Moscow Cavalry Division and sent the division after the Ural Cossacks, who weren't inclined to accept Soviet power. (He saw Frunze himself a few times while serving there.) They crossed sabers with the Cossacks and drove them into the Kirghiz steppe. Then the division was transferred to the lower Volga. They were stationed near Tsaritsyn and then sent to Akhtuba to fight the Kalmyks. Those Kalmyks had gone completely off their heads: not one of them wanted anything to do with the Soviets, and you couldn't hammer any sense into them. Yorka was wounded by a hand grenade there, so it was back to the hospital again. The typhus came back as well—that plague was just jumping from one person to the next. In the spring of that year of 1919, Zhukov, as a conscientious soldier, was accepted into the Russian Communist Party, and at the beginning of 1920, he was promoted as a "Red officer." They sent him to a place near Ryazan on a course for Red commanders. And here, too, he wasn't just an ordinary officer trainee but the leader of his group. Everyone could see he was made to command.

The Civil War was already coming to an end, and Wrangel had been left isolated. The trainees thought they might be left out of the Polish war, but in June 1920, their training was suddenly broken off and they were hastily boarded on trains, some to the Kuban, others to Dagestan (where a good many of them were killed). Zhukov found himself in a composite regiment of trainees in Yekaterinodar. The regiment was sent to counter the landing that the rebel Ulagay had made in the Kuban. Then they fought the Kuban Cossacks, who had scattered into small detachments among the foothills. Those idiots wouldn't surrender even after Denikin had been crushed. Zhukov's unit cut down a lot of them and shot a good many more. With this, his officer training was considered complete, and in Armavir they gave him early promotion as a Red commander. Everyone in his group was issued new riding breeches, for some reason of bright raspberry red. They must have come from the stores of some old Hussar regiment, but they were all that was available. When these new graduates went to their assigned units, they stood out wonderfully, and the Red Army men looked at them like creatures from some other planet.

Zhukov took command of a cavalry troop, but soon he was promoted to squadron commander. They were on the same old operations—"mopping up gangs of bandits," along the coast at first. Then in December, he was transferred to Voronezh Province to wipe out Kolesnikov's band. And they wiped it out. Then to neighboring Tambov Province, where there were more rebel bands than you could count. The Tambov provincial headquarters had to bring in more troops to deal with them: by the end of February, the regimental commissar said, they had 33,000 infantry, 8,000 cavalry, 460 machine guns and 60 pieces of artillery. He was complaining: We don't have any political workers who can explain clearly what's going on right now. This is a war brought on by the Entente, and that's why the link between the city and the villages has been broken. But we'll be steadfast and we'll clear away all this rubbish!

In March, before it thawed, two of their cavalry regiments began an offensive from Zherdyovka Station in the bandit region of Tugolukovo-Kamenka. (The orders from the head of the provincial Cheka, Traskovich, were: Wipe Kamenka and Afanasyevka completely off the face of the earth and be merciless in your executions!) Zhukov's squadron, with four heavy machine guns and one three-inch gun, headed the detachment. Near the village of Vyazovoe, they attacked an Antonov force of about 250 cavalry. Without a single machine gun, the rebels could reply only with rifle fire.

Zhukov was riding his golden-red Zorka (he'd taken her in a scrap in Voronezh Province after killing her rider). Then a strapping Antonov man slashed him across the chest with his saber, knocking him from the saddle. But Zorka fell as well, pinning the squadron commander to the ground. The enormous Antonov man raised his arm to finish off Zhukov on the ground, but the political officer, Nochyovka, rushed up from behind and cut him down. (When they searched the man's body they learned from one of his letters that he had also been an NCO in the dragoons, almost in the same regiment as Zhukov's.) First Squadron on their flank began to fall back, and Zhukov's Second Squadron acted as a rear guard, using their machine guns to hold back the enemy. They barely managed to save their four machine guns, mounted on sleds, and pulled out their artillery piece as well.

Now Zhukov grew truly furious at the bandits. Weren't they peasants just like us? But they were different somehow, not like our Kaluga people. What would make them rise up against Soviet power? His letters from home told of how people there were dying of hunger, while these folk wouldn't give them any bread! The commissar explained that it was true we weren't sending them any goods from the cities, but that was because we had none to send. They can get by on their homemade stuff, in any case; but where can the city get its bread? And the locals in all those backwoods places that our grain collectors haven't reached just go on stuffing themselves.

So we didn't need to waste words when dealing with these people. When we came into a village, we would take their best horses and leave them our worst. When an informer reported that Antonov's men were in such-and-such a village, we would swoop in and round them up, searching the attics, the outbuildings, and the wells (one partisan medical assistant dug himself a hiding place in the side of a well shaft). Or we'd do it another way: We'd line up the whole village, young and old alike, 1500 people in all. We'd take every tenth person hostage and hold them in a barn. The others would have forty minutes to make up a list of all the bandits from that village before we'd shoot the hostages. What choice did they have? They'd bring us a list. It didn't matter much if it was incomplete, the Special Section would find it useful in time to come.

They also had good information. One day we came into a camp that the bandits had abandoned in a hurry, and we found a copy of the same order that had sent us here. Our enemies knew a thing or two as well.

The Red Army's supply system didn't work very smoothly. One day you'd get your ration, the next day—nothing. (The pay rate for a squadron commander was 5000 rubles a month, but what could you buy with that? A pound of butter and two pounds of black bread.) So where could we get food if not in these bandit villages? A cavalry troop would ride into some village that was nothing more than a windmill and a few houses with only the women left in them. The troopers, still mounted, would use their whips to herd all the women into the storehouse at the mill and lock them in. Then they'd go off to rummage through the cellars. They'd drink a pot of milk and then smash the pot, just out of spite.

We'd make some peasant kid drive his cart with the squadron's baggage and an escort of Red Army men, and he'd complain in all seriousness: "I hope you catch those guys soon and let me go back to my mamma." Another kid, too small to understand, asked quite innocently and not angrily, "Uncle, why'd you shoot my dad?"

We captured about two dozen rebels, questioned them all separately, and each one fingered another: "He was the one on the machine gun."

You'd come into a village with mounted patrol and find it all shut tight, as if everyone had died. You'd knock on a door and hear a woman's voice: "Don't be angry, but we've got nothing left. We're starving." You'd knock again: "We can't trust anybody these days. Every bigwig who comes through here just wants to take our grain."

They'd been so terrified by the Soviets and by the partisans that all they wanted was to be left alone.

At our political meetings, they warned us not to antagonize the local population unnecessarily. But they would also say, "Don't let them pull the wool over your eyes. If you suspect anything, just give them a rifle butt in the face."

But even our own Red Army men worried us when they were reluctant to use their weapons against peasants ("We're peasants, same as them, so how can we shoot at our own folk?") The bandits were also spreading leaflets for our troops: "It's you who are the bandits here. We did not invade your lands. Leave us alone, we can live well enough without you." A rumor came from somewhere that within a few weeks, all the Red Army troops would be demobilized. "Why wait that long? How much longer do we have to keep fighting?" (Some of our men also went over to the bandits or deserted, particularly whenever our troops had to be redeployed.) The political officer Nochyovka would say: "Men like that have to be reeducated. Otherwise, when they've had a few drinks and start singing, it won't be revolutionary songs, it'll be 'Stenka Razin' or some filthy stuff. And if they spend a night in a village where all the men are away in the forest, they exploit the women as a class." And he would give talks on the topic: "Spending your life without labor and without revolutionary struggle is parasitism!" (And someone would remind him of our woman medical assistant who was available for the whole division: "I'm not like a bowl of porridge," she'd say, "there's enough to go around, and plenty for the whole squadron.")

We'd hold our breath at morning muster, waiting to see who'd gone off on French leave. We had to keep our own Red Army men in hobbles. The instructor from the provincial military committee told us that there were 60,000 deserters in Tambov Province, all of them now reinforcements for the bandits.

The orders that came from Tambov headquarters and the regiment were never written in strictly military fashion, setting out our reconnaissance sector or giving operation instructions; it was always just "Attack and destroy!" "Surround and liquidate!" "Whatever the cost!"

And we didn't count the cost. But how were we to smoke out the bandits? How could we tell who they were? There were no Soviet authorities left in the villages; they'd all run off to wait it out in the towns, so who could we ask? An army commander would order all the village people to come to a meeting. He'd line up all the men in one rank: "How many of you are with the bandits?" No one said a word. "Shoot every tenth man!" And they'd be shot on the spot, in front of the whole crowd. The women would scream and howl and moan. "Close up the rank. Now, how many are bandits?" Once again, they'd count off every tenth man to be shot. Then the villagers would give in and point them out. A few of them would scamper away. You couldn't pick them all off.

Sometimes a woman walking alone along the road would be arrested and searched to see if she'd been spying or carrying messages. A lot of horse manure along a road told us that a detachment of bandits had passed by.

Our boys also went hungry many times. Their boots were full of holes, and their uniforms were worn-out and bedraggled. They wore them all day and slept in them at night. (And some of them still had the raspberry pants!) We suffered a lot. If anyone had a leg amputated, it was done without anesthetic, and there were no bandages either.

In the middle of April, we in Zherdyovka heard that Antonov's men had swooped in and taken the large factory town of Rasskazovo, just forty-five *versts* from Tambov. They held it for four hours and slaughtered the communists in their own homes, cutting their heads right off. Half the Soviet battalion there went over to Antonov, the other half was taken prisoner. Then the bandits withdrew under fire from airplanes.

So that was how our war with them went. Then, through the winter and spring, things got even hotter. It had been eight months now, and Antonov still hadn't surrendered—in fact, he was even getting stronger. (Even though they sometimes had no bullets and just used bits of iron.)

An order came from Tambov headquarters: "All operations are to be carried out with sufficient severity to inspire respect for Soviet power." Villages that supported the bandits were burned to the ground. All that was left were the skeletons of Russian stoves and ashes.

The Cheka Special Section in Zherdyovka wasn't sitting still, either. The head of the section, Shurka Shubin, walked around in a red shirt and blue breeches with hand grenades dangling from his chest and a hefty Mauser in a wooden holster. He'd come into a cavalry camp (the formation commander was subordinate to the head of the Special Section): "All right, boys, whoever wants to execute some bandits, two paces forward!" No one stepped forward. "Some fine training you've had here." All the people to be executed had been herded into the Special Section compound. They dug a huge pit, made the prisoners sit down on the edge, facing it and with their hands tied. Shubin and his men would walk along shooting them in the back of the neck.

But how else could they deal with them? Yorka had a good friend, also named Zhukov, though his first name was Pavel, and he would cut the bandits into pieces.

It was a full-scale war, and you had to give it all you had, and more. It wasn't like that German War. It was here in Tambov that Yorka turned savage; it was here that he became a hardened, cruel warrior.

In May, a Plenipotentiary Commission from the All-Russian Central Executive Committee headed by another Antonov (though he was Antonov-Ovseenko) arrived from Moscow to stamp out the bandits. And to command the Special Tambov Army, they sent the commander of the western front, army commander Tukhachevsky, who had just settled scores with Poland. His deputy was Uborevich, who had a good deal of experience fighting bandits in Belorussia. Tukhachevsky brought his own staff with him, along with a detachment of armored cars.

Not long after this, Zhukov was lucky enough to see the famous Tukhachevsky in person when he came to the headquarters of the 14th Independent Cavalry Brigade in Zherdyovka along the railway in an armored trolley. The brigade commander, Milonov, ordered all the political officers and commanders down to squadron level to hear Tukhachevsky speak.

Tukhachevsky was rather short, but he carried himself proudly, as stately as a peacock. He knew his own worth.

He began by praising everyone for their bravery and dedication to their duty. (Everyone glowed, chests swelling.) Then he explained the mission that lay ahead of them all.

The Council of People's Commissars had ordered that in the six weeks following May 10, the Tambov rebellion was to be put down. No matter what the cost! We all have heavy work ahead, he told us. The experience of suppressing such popular rebellions shows that we have to flood the whole area of the revolt with troops until it is completely occupied and then station armed units at critical points all across it. Kotovsky's renowned cavalry division has just arrived from Kiev, detrained in Morshansk, and is already advancing on the rebel area of Pakhotny Ugol. When it's done its job, it will come here, to the center of the rebellion. We have a huge material advantage over the enemy, with our air and armored car detachments. One of our first demands to the local population will be to rebuild all the bridges on the roads through the villages so that our motorized units can pass through. (But we must never use local people as guides!) We also have a supply of chemical gasses that we will use if necessary; the Council has given permission for this. In the course of this vigorous suppression of the revolt, all of you commanders will get some wonderful military experience.

Zhukov could not take his eyes off the army commander. This was probably the first time in his life he was seeing a genuine military leader, someone completely different from us simple cut-and-thrust commanders or even our brigade commander. How self-confident he was! And he was able to instill that same confidence in everyone else: it would all unfold just as he had said! There was nothing of the peasant in his face; it was aristocratic and well groomed. He had a long, slender white neck and large, velvet eyes. He'd kept his side whiskers long, but they were carefully trimmed. And he didn't speak at all the way we did. His Budyonny helmet—the same helmet we all wore—truly suited him and made Tukhachevsky look even more like a leader.

Of course, he added, we'll also send more of our agents to scout out the bandits, though the Chekists have, unfortunately, suffered some heavy losses. But we still have our biggest weapon: putting pressure on the bandits through their families.

Then he read aloud Order No. 130, which he had already signed and just now issued across the province so that the whole population would know. The language of the order was as absolutely confident as the young commander himself: "All peasants who have joined the rebel bands must immediately place themselves at the disposal of Soviet authorities, surrender their weapons, and name their ringleaders . . . Those who surrender voluntarily will not face the death penalty. The families of bandits who do not turn themselves in will be arrested immediately, their property confiscated and distributed among the peasants who have remained loyal to the Soviet authorities. The families of those bandits who do not report and surrender will be exiled to remote areas of the RFSFR."

No gathering in which there were large numbers of communists, as was the case on this day, could end without everyone singing "The Internationale," but Tukhachevsky took the liberty of not waiting for that.

He extended his white hand only to the brigade commander and, with the same proud bearing, he left and drove off in his armored trolley.

This audacious display of authority also impressed Zhukov.

Then, even before "The Internationale," all the commanders were given a leaflet from the Provincial Executive Committee addressed to the peasants of Tambov Province: The time has come to rid yourselves of this festering abscess of Antonovism! Until now, the bandits' advantage lay in their frequent exchange of exhausted horses for fresh ones. Now, however, with the presence of Antonov's criminal gangs in your area, you must not leave a single horse in your village. Take them away to a place where our forces can protect them.

As the meeting broke up, Zhukov came away with new feelings: he felt inspired with fresh confidence, he had a new example to follow, and he was envious.

Just fighting a war—well, that was something any fool could do. But now—to be a soldier with every bone in your body, with every breath you took, and do it so that everyone around you could sense it! That was something great.

Zhukov loved soldiering more than anything else.

The six-week period for the final suppression of the rebellion began. The armored cars of Uborevich's detachment had their limitations. They couldn't travel everywhere, and they often broke through the bridges, just as the light trucks and even the cars armed with machine guns did. The peasant horses feared the automobiles and wouldn't go into an attack with them, and when our cavalry was pursuing the rebels, they couldn't lose contact with the vehicles.

We did have one other big advantage. Antonov, of course, had no radios, and so our units pursuing him could communicate with each other without encoding anything, and this made for better coordination and easier transfer of information. The Antonov men would gallop along, thinking that no one had spotted them, but meanwhile messages were being transmitted through all three regions, revealing where the bandits were, where they were going, and where to send a pursuit force to cut them off.

So we went off in pursuit, trying to trap Antonov's main body and force him into a major battle, which he was avoiding. Kotovsky's brigade moved on him from the north, Dmitrienko's brigade from the west; another detachment of Kononeko's Cheka forces was added—seven one-and-a-half-ton Fiat armored cars with their own motorized gasoline carriers. Antonov stumbled into the trap laid for him, but he immediately rushed away; changing horses regularly, he traveled 120 or 130 *versts* a day, retreating into Saratov Province toward the Khopyor; and then he returned. The 14th Brigade, like all the Red cavalry, lagged behind him everywhere. Now only the armored cars were pursuing him. (People told of how an armored car detachment once almost caught Antonov by surprise while he was resting in the village of Yelan. The cars rolled through the village, firing at the bandits from their machine guns. But the Antonov men galloped to the forest, regrouped, and held on, while half our machine guns jammed. Once again, our cavalry was late, and once again the Antonov men withdrew or simply vanished—no one knows.)

Three weeks passed, already halfway to the deadline set by the Council of Commissars, yet Antonov had not been beaten. Cavalry brigades had to feel their way, waiting for news from informants. Both mechanized detachments were waiting for parts and gasoline. An armored train and the armored trolley ran back and forth along the nearby railways, also trying to track down the bandits or intercept them. But they found nothing.

Then came Tukhachevsky's Secret Order No. 0050, to be read aloud to cavalry squadrons and infantry companies: "Effective dawn, July 1, we begin a mass removal of the bandit element from the general population." This meant that we were to comb through the villages and pick up any suspicious people. As Zhukov read this to his squadron, he seemed to see Tukhachevsky; he seemed to become him and, perhaps, he even took on his voice and his bearing. He read in his fullest voice: "This removal must not appear to be a chance event; it must show the peasants that the bandit element, along with their families, are being eliminated and that the struggle against Soviet power is hopeless. Carry out the operation with vigor and enthusiasm. Avoid bourgeois sentimentality. Tukhachevsky, Force Commander."

Zhukov was happy—happy to be under such command. This was how it should be. This was soldiering. Before you can command, you have to know how to obey. And learn to follow orders.

They did remove as many as they were able to scrape up. They shipped them off to concentration camps, and their families as well. But separately.

A few days later, the location of the nucleus of Antonov's force was discovered once more. It was some distance away, in the Shiryaevo forest on the upper reaches of the Vorona River. (There were reports that the last time Antonov was attacked by our armored cars, he had been wounded in the head.) Fresh troops arrived: Fedko's cavalry brigade, another Cheka regiment, and one more armored train. All the escape routes from the Shiryaevo forest were completely blocked. But then a powerful thunderstorm blew in, and the commander of the Cheka regiment withdrew his troops from their positions and took them back to the nearest villages for an hour or two. The armored trolley that had been patrolling the seven-*verst* section from Kirsanov to the Vorona River was shunted aside to let Uborevich's personal train pass, and then the two collided in the darkness. It was as if Antonov's men knew precisely where and when there was a gap in the cordon, and they slipped through it while that fierce storm was raging and vanished into the Chutanovo forest.

Antonov's bandits even had a reply to Order No. 130: they ordered the villagers not to give their names. Now the Red Army men didn't know what to do: no matter how they smacked the peasants around, the bastards wouldn't give their names.

Now we were both deaf and blind. Our headquarters found an answer to this as well, though. On July 11, they issued Order No. 171: "Citizens refusing to give their names will be executed on the spot, without trial. Hostages will be executed in villages that do not surrender their weapons. Where caches of weapons are discovered, the oldest working man in the family will be executed without trial." A family found concealing a bandit or even some of his belongings such as clothing or dishes would have its eldest working man executed without trial. If a bandit's family fled, their property would be seized and distributed among peasants loyal to Soviet power; any abandoned homes would be burned. The order was signed by Antonov-Ovseenko.

So they won't give their names? But then the rebels' families began leaving the villages and going into hiding. To finish the job, the Plenipotentiary Commission of the Central Executive Committee issued a new order: "Any house in which a rebel family has been hiding is to be pulled down or burnt. Those hiding a rebel family in their house will be treated as members of rebel families: the eldest worker in such a family will be executed. Signed, Antonov-Ovseenko."

Five days later, he issued another order, No. 178, to be proclaimed publicly: "Failure to show resistance to the bandits and failure to pass on information about their whereabouts to the nearest Revolutionary Committee in a timely fashion will be regarded as complicity with the bandits, with all the ensuing consequences. Plenipotentiary Commission of the All-Russian Central Executive Committee, Antonov-Ovseenko."

They came swarming out as if we'd thrown boiling water on them, as if we were burning out bedbugs!

The precise, cold-blooded army commander issued one more order, a secret one numbered 0116: "The forests in which bandits are hiding are to be cleared with the use of poison gas. Calculations must be precise to ensure that the cloud of asphyxiating gas is thoroughly dispersed through the entire forest so as to destroy everything concealed within it. Tukhachevsky, Force Commander."

Was that too harsh? No great commander can manage without harsh measures.

2

PEOPLE BELIEVE THAT it is entirely appropriate and proper to begin writing your memoirs when you turn seventy. What I did, though, was begin seven years early. It's so quiet here, and I'm of no use to anyone, so what else should I do with myself? One year passes after another, and all I have left is the spare time that has been forced upon me and that drags by so slowly.

No one phones me anymore, and they certainly don't visit. The world around has gone silent and shut me out. And I may not have enough years left to live out these times.

There are some good reasons why I must write. Let it be for the record. Many others have already rushed to write memoirs; some have even been published. They're in a hurry because they want to grab a bit of glory for themselves. And of course they want to dump their mistakes on someone else.

That is dishonorable.

But what a job it is! Just sorting through your memories wears you out. Some of the blunders I made tear at my heart even now. But there is also much to be proud of.

Of course, I also have to weigh my words carefully: there are things that *can't* be brought up at all. The things that can be brought up have to be said with great caution. I might write something that could blow up in my face later and take away what peace I have left, and take away this marvelous dacha on the bank of the Moskva River.

What a view it has! It's on a high bank, right among the pine trees— real beauties, with trunks rising toward the sky, some of them two hundred years old. The land slopes from here, and the little road is sandy and covered in pine needles. The bluish river makes a lazy bend. The water, downstream from the Rublyovo Reservoir, is clean, and it's all within a nature reserve. If you see someone out in a rowboat, you know that it's one of our people or a neighbor. No one's doing any poaching here or causing trouble.

From the back gate there's a path down to the river. But Galya doesn't go there, and she certainly won't let Mashenka, who's only seven, go without her. And for someone pushing seventy, it's more pleasant to sit up here on the veranda. These days I have to use a stick just getting around the yard. My hearing's not what it used to be, either. I don't pick up the sound of each bird and every rustle in the forest.

The dacha itself is wonderful, though it belongs to the state, and every stick of furniture has an inventory number tacked onto it. I have possession *for life*. And so when I die, Galya, who's forty, and our little daughter and my mother-in-law will be moved out immediately. (My first family is gone, and my married daughters have set up on their own.)

I've had two heart attacks already (and let's hope they were only heart attacks). I was laid up for a long time, but then things settled down and now it's over. It was after the second attack that I took up my memoirs.

It's the last freedom left to old age: to spend your time thinking, gazing at the river, and writing a few more lines. Otherwise, my head will ache. (I get headaches at times.)

The most boring part is writing about times long past, about the times I was growing up. About the Imperialist War. And even about my younger days in the squadron. What should I say? How did I distinguish myself?

The real interest begins from the time the Soviet system got well and truly established. My settled soldier's life began only in the 1920s, with training in all the many aspects of the cavalry, tactical drills, and, the best thing of all, maneuvers. You are the complete master of your body, the sweep of your saber on horseback, the horse itself. Then, you get your own squadron, then your own regiment. Your own brigade. At last, your own division. (It was Uborevich who gave it to you—he could see you were a soldier.) And you feel yourself even stronger as part of one single great organism—the iron Party. (You had always dreamt of being like that amazing Bolshevik, Blyukher, a working man from Mytishchi who was given, as a joke at first, the name of the famous German general.)

You get absorbed in the study of tactics and, of course, feel yourself much stronger in the practice than in theoretical matters. Then they send you to cavalry staff college for a year, where they make you write a report on the topic: "Basic Factors Influencing the Theory of Military Science." And here you crumble into little pieces like a dried-out biscuit: "What's all this mean? What factors? What am I supposed to say? Who can I ask?" (His friend on the course, Kostya Rokossovsky, helped him out. As for his other friend, Yeryomenko, well, he was a total blockhead.)

Then you go on serving with real success as a cavalry commander, a horseman who knows his stuff. The one thing you really want is for your division to become the best in all the Workers' and Peasants' Red Army. People often accuse you of being much too demanding, of being a slave driver, but that's a good sign; that's the way military service has to be. Suddenly, you're promoted from your division to be deputy inspector of all the cavalry, working under Semyon Mikhailovich Budyonny. You're given the job of writing the training manual for cavalry, and you do it. This is work that makes sense. And who supervised your work? You can hardly believe it: Tukhachevsky himself! That same handsome and smart soldier you once saw in Tambov Province. Now you worked together for

two months. (And being such a devoted communist, you're chosen as secretary of the party Bureau of Inspection of all branches of the military.)
You're forty years old. In the years ahead, of course, you'll be promoted
again and given even more important posts.

When you look around the country, you see how much we've achieved:
Industry is working at full speed, the collective farms are flourishing; the
country is united. What more could you want?

Then come 1937 and 1938. Military service, once such a direct, plain-
and-simple matter, now is a treacherous road with twists and turns that
take real cunning to navigate. There's a summons from a fellow named
Golikov, the senior political officer of the military district: "Do you have
any relatives among those arrested?" "No," you answer confidently.
(Your mother and sister are in a Kaluga village, and they're all you have.)
"Any friends among them?" Now "friend" can't be as precisely defined as
"relative." Some you know, others you've met—does that mean they are
"friends"? How can you answer that? "When Uborevich visited your division, he had dinner at your house." Well, there's no denying that. (He did
a lot more than have dinner! Uborevich was his mentor and patron.) Then
there was Kovtyukh, "legendary" until a few months ago, then suddenly
"an enemy of the people." Then they locked up Rokossovsky as well . . .
"And did you not change your opinion of him after his arrest?" Well, of
course. You're a communist, so how couldn't you change your opinion?
So, yes, I did change my opinion. "Did you have your daughter baptized
in church?" Here the answer is confident: "That's a piece of slander!"
They've gone too far with their accusations. (No one ever baptized Era.)

Now all sorts of accusations are being hurled at party meetings. Once
again he's accused of being too harsh (as if this is a flaw in a military
commander), of cruelty, of boorish behavior, of failing to show leniency
(but how else can you run a military unit?), even of *a hostile approach
to the training of cadres*: that he had held back valuable personnel by

refusing them promotion. (That from those same slanderers he'd refused to promote. Then there are those who slander not out of malice but to whitewash themselves in advance.) But here, too, he somehow fought off his attackers.

Then more trouble: a promotion to command a corps. But it's the Belorussian Military District, where almost every single corps commander has been arrested. So it's not a step toward advancement, it's a step toward ruination. Is this how I'm going to be finished off—not in some battle, not from the slash of a saber? Yet there's no way of refusing.

The only thing that saved him was that at this very moment, the wave of arrests ended. (Only after the Twentieth Party Congress did he learn that in the Belorussian Military District in 1939, they had opened a file on Zhukov.)

Suddenly, there's an urgent summons to Moscow. Well, this is it, they're going to arrest me. But no! Someone had advised Stalin, and they were sending him to Khalkhin-Gol for his real baptism of fire. Once again he showed his unflinching will in commanding "at any price!" Without waiting for artillery and infantry, he threw a whole tank division directly at them. Two-thirds of them never made it back, but he gave the Japanese a roasting! Comrade Stalin himself took note of what he had done, particularly by comparison with the Finnish War that had been so badly messed up by incompetent commanders that it seemed an entirely different Red Army was fighting there. Stalin took note of him, and kept him in mind for a long time to come. Stalin received him right after the Finnish War, and he was assigned to command the Kiev Military District—a post of huge importance!

Just six months later, however, and a new order came: Turn over the Kiev District to Kirponos and return to Moscow. But Zhukov had nothing to complain about: now he was to be appointed chief of the General Staff! (And all of it because of Khalkhin-Gol.)

He was sincere when he tried to decline the post: "Comrade Stalin! I've never had any staff experience, even in a low-level job." And now, all at once, the General Staff? He'd never had a bit of military-academic or operational and strategic training in all his forty-five years. How could a simple, honest cavalryman manage the General Staff, particularly now, with so many different branches of troops and new technologies?

Something more made the job frightening: chiefs of the General Staff were being changed every six months. After half a year, Shaposhnikov was replaced by Meretskov; now Meretskov had been sacked and, rumor had it, arrested—so now is it your turn? (The same sort of leapfrog was going on in the Directorate of Operations.)

Never mind, just take the post! And you'll also be a candidate member of the Central Committee. What trust Stalin had in him!

That meeting with Stalin left a very warm, tender impression.

It was precisely here that he saw the biggest obstacle to writing his memoirs. (Maybe he should just give up the whole thing . . . ?) *How* was he, a general who had had long and close contact with Stalin during the Great War and who had seen his many moods and who had even become his closest deputy, to write about the man who was the head of government, the general secretary of the party, and soon the Supreme Commander of the armed forces? As a veteran of that war, he could scarcely believe how the Supreme Commander had since been dethroned and how a few dimwits were trying to stain his reputation by telling cock-and-bull stories—how he "commanded the front lines by looking at the globe . . ." (It's true, he did have a large globe in the room next to his office, but there were also maps on the wall, and he would lay out other maps on the desk when he was working. The Supreme Commander would pace from corner to corner, smoking his pipe, and then go to the maps so as to understand clearly the report he was being given or to indicate what he wanted.) Just now they've thrown out the biggest windbag of them all, kit and caboodle.

And maybe, little by little, they'll be able to restore proper respect for the Supreme Commander. Still, some irreparable damage was done.

And so, if you don't count the members of the Politburo, it was you who had closer professional contact with him than anyone. There were some very bitter moments, to be sure. (Stalin never minced words when he was angry and could offend people undeservedly; the target of his wrath had to have a thick skin. A certain sign that he was in one of his cold-blooded, brutal moods was when he carried his unlit pipe in his hand. Then his wrath could pour down on your head at any moment.) But there were also moments when he showed you his amazing, heartfelt trust.

So now the problem was to find a way to write an honest, worthy account of it all.

Something else to think about: the many things that the two of you shared in those very tense—and deceptive!—months before the war also meant that you shared the responsibility for what happened. Was the Supreme Commander wrong? Did he blunder? Did he miscalculate? Then why didn't you set him right? Why didn't you warn him, even if it cost you your own head? Didn't you see that this dogma of "Attack! Attack! Attack!" which was hammered into everyone in the 1930s and practiced in all the maneuvers till 1940 and 1941, left the enemy with a huge advantage? It meant that we rarely practiced the defense, never practiced the withdrawal, and breaking out of an encirclement never entered our heads. Did you support these dogmas as well? You completely ignored that huge concentration of German forces near the border! German aircraft kept flying over Soviet territory, while Stalin accepted Hitler's apologies for his "young and inexperienced" pilots. What about 1941, when the Germans suddenly needed to look up their World War I cemeteries on our side of the border? It's all right, go ahead and look . . . What an intelligence coup they made out of that! But at the time, Zhukov believed that there was no man on earth better informed, more profound, and more shrewd than

Stalin. And if he hoped to the last to be able to delay a war with Hitler, then who were you to cry out, "No!" even though it might be your last word?

Who was not paralyzed, even from a distance, by the fearsome name of Stalin? And going to meet him in person was always like taking the final steps up to the gallows. (Still, he did persuade him to release Rokossovsky from a labor camp.) Zhukov was also paralyzed by his lack of confidence in strategic matters, his sense that he was in over his head as chief of the General Staff. He was paralyzed even more, of course, by never knowing how the Supreme Commander might react. He could never guess why he had been summoned. What was the safest way to answer when he was asked, "So what do you propose? What are you afraid of?" Stalin had little patience for listening to reports and sometimes even seemed disdainful. And there were many things that others reported to Stalin that he did not share with his chief of the General Staff. For him, Zhukov was like Stalin's personal fire department—someone he could suddenly call and send off to deal with some emergency.

During these first hours after war broke out, Stalin was in a state of confusion that no one had seen before and that he could not conceal. Four hours passed before anyone ventured to order the military districts to resist the enemy, and by then it was too late. What he did was send Zhukov, his chief of the General Staff, rushing to Kiev to save the situation there ("We can get by without you here," he told him.) But the whole of the high command was operating simply by hit-and-miss. Three days later, Zhukov had to rush back to Moscow: What needed saving, it seemed, was not the Southwestern but the Western Army Group. Stalin began in a tone of complaint: "In a situation like this, what can be done?" (Zhukov had the foresight to offer a few pieces of advice, one of which was to form unarmed divisions from the people of Moscow. There were more than enough people available, and going through the Military Committees would take too long. Stalin announced on the spot the formation of a Home Guard.)

Given Stalin's obvious unsteadiness, Zhukov ventured to offer more strong advice. At the end of July, he was bold enough to suggest that Kiev should be abandoned and the troops withdrawn beyond the Dnieper: this would keep some major forces intact and ensure they would not be surrounded. Stalin and Mekhlis both bawled him out for his policy of capitulation. It was then that Stalin dismissed Zhukov as chief of the General Staff and sent him to push back the Germans near Yelnya. (It could have been worse: in those same weeks, about a dozen highly placed and excellent generals who had won victories in the war in Spain were executed; on the other hand, Meretskov was suddenly let out of prison.)

The battle near Yelnya was a meat grinder, to be sure, but it was a real operation, not just staff work, and Zhukov won it within a week. (Of course, it would have made more sense just to cut off and surround this Yelnya salient, but in those days we still were lacking confidence.)

As for Kiev, it had to be abandoned in any case, but now with masses of our troops caught in the pocket. (Vlasov did manage to bring a good many of them out and pull back some 500 kilometers, but nowadays his name can't even be mentioned.) And so if Zhukov had remained in command of the Southwestern Army Group, he might well have had to shoot himself like Kirponos.

Something extraordinary happened: when Stalin summoned him at the beginning of September, he admitted that Zhukov had been right about Kiev. And then he went on to dictate an order, top secret, numbered 001919: *Blocking detachments* were to be formed from regiments of NKVD troops; they were to occupy a line in the rear of our forces and fire on anyone who retreated. (How about that! But what else could you do if they would not stand and fight to the death but ran off?) And then he sent Zhukov to save Leningrad, which had been cut off. Zhukov had to hand over to others the central sector of the western front that he had saved. The whole time, though, Zhukov held on to his post in General Headquarters, and this allowed him to learn a great deal from people like Shaposhnikov, Vasilevsky, and Vatutin, all of them with a solid military education. (And he wanted to learn, and had to—it was urgent.) He picked up a lot from them, but still remained their shield or battering ram or blunt instrument: they would send Zhukov charging into the most dangerous sector.

Stalin managed the war in its first weeks by giving orders that were not to be questioned, and his mistakes piled up, one after another. He had no idea of strategy and operations and no sense of how to coordinate the operations of various branches of the army (what he had were a few ideas left over from the Civil War). But then he became more cautious. Boris Mikhailovich Shaposhnikov was again named chief of the General Staff. He was the only one of the military leaders whom Stalin addressed politely by his first name and patronymic and the only one allowed to smoke in Stalin's office. (Stalin rarely greeted the others even with a handshake.)

But Stalin respected the members of the Politburo, particularly his favorite, Mekhlis (until Mekhlis made a complete mess of the bridgehead in the eastern Crimea), far more than any of his military leaders. Often when he and a few other members of the Politburo had heard some general give his report, Stalin would say, "Leave us for a few minutes while we discuss this." The general would leave and meekly await a decision on the fate of his project or even his head but not feel slighted in the least. We were all communists, but the members of the Politburo, and even Shcherbakov, were the highest among us, and it was quite natural that they would make decisions without us. If Stalin was angry at any of them, it was never for long and never final. Voroshilov botched the Finnish War and lost his post for a time, but when Hitler attacked, it was he who was given the whole Northwestern Army Group. He botched that as well, along with the defense of Leningrad, and was dismissed once more. But he came back again as the lucky marshal and most trusted member of Stalin's entourage. It was the same with the two Semyons, Timoshenko and the hopeless Budyonny, who made a mess of both the Southwestern and the Reserve Army Groups; yet they all remained members of the General Headquarters as before. Stalin had still not included Vasilevsky or Vatutin in the GHQ, but all the marshals kept their posts there. Zhukov was not promoted to marshal either for saving Leningrad or for saving Moscow or for the victory at Stalingrad. Still, what did rank matter at a time when Zhukov was running operations far more significant than any the marshals ran? Only after lifting the blockade of Leningrad was Zhukov suddenly promoted. It was not just that he had felt hurt by the delay; he couldn't understand *why* he hadn't been promoted. Was it to make him strive all the harder? Was Stalin afraid to make a mistake, to promote someone prematurely and then not be able to get rid of him? He needn't have worried. The Supreme Commander could not see into the guileless soldier's heart of his Zhukov. In fact, when could he have learned anything about a soldier's heart? He never spent so much as an hour at the front during the war and had never chatted with an ordinary soldier. He would summon Zhukov, who would make a long flight back to Moscow, and after many weeks in the constant roar of the front lines, the silence in Stalin's Kremlin office or at a private supper in Stalin's dacha seemed quite agonizing.

Then there was something he could not help but learn from Stalin: the Supreme Commander was always interested to hear about enemy casualties, but he never asked about our own. He simply shrugged them off with a four-fingered wave: "That's what war means." He certainly didn't want to learn how many had surrendered. He ordered that the surrender of Smolensk not be announced for almost a month, still hoping that it might be won back and frantically sending more and more divisions there to be ground to pieces. Zhukov learned that if you first consider the potential casualties and then the actual losses, you will truly never be a military commander. The commander cannot weaken himself by compassion, and all he needs to know about casualties is the number of replacements to be sent up from the reserve and when to send them. There's no point calculating whether the casualties suffered in winning over some little Yelnya Salient were justified.

He had to learn how to instill in all the generals serving under him the cold-bloodedness he had himself achieved. (More and more stories were repeated about him: How harsh he was! A will of iron! Give him your hand and he'll want your whole arm! A voice that rings like steel! But how else could you manage such a huge military machine?)

And so Zhukov saved Leningrad in September 1941. (The blockade, though, went on for 900 days . . .) Then, the day after Guderian took Oryol, Stalin called him back, now to save Moscow itself.

Before a day had passed, our troops had been caught in the huge encirclement at Vyazma, more than half a million of them . . . a catastrophe. (Stalin had decided to put Konev on trial for the collapse of the western front; Zhukov stood up to him and saved Konev from Stalin's rage.) All the roads to the capital were open to the enemy. Did Zhukov himself believe that Moscow could hold out? He no longer hoped to maintain a defensive line along the Mozhaysk-Maloyaroslavets arc and was preparing a defense from Klin to Istra and Krasnaya Pakhra. But after summoning up his iron will (what about Stalin's will? He had one, though it was shaken more than once. In October, he would bring up some of the benefits of the Brest-Litovsk Treaty and speculate whether it now might be possible to arrange a truce with Hitler . . .), Zhukov rushed here and there (and it must have been the finger of fate that led him past his own Kaluga village, from which he managed to extricate his mother, sister, and nephews). He summoned up strength he never realized he had, and after five days of battles near Yukhnov, Medyn, and Kaluga itself, he had broken the German advance on Moscow.

At the same time, twelve divisions of the Home Guard were marching westward (to be swallowed up, some at Smolensk, others in the encirclement at Vyazma). They were all in addition to the regular mobilization. And now, squelching through the autumn mud, a quarter million women and youths had hauled up three million cubic meters of heavy, wet earth as they dug trenches. A scorching wave of panic from the approaching front blew over them. On October 13, the diplomats and staff of the central administrative bodies began being evacuated from Moscow; at the same time, some of those not being evacuated began running away and, shameful to admit, there were even some communists from the Moscow regional committees among them. Uncontrollable panic broke out in Moscow on October 16, when everyone believed that the city was already lost.

It had always remained a mystery why, precisely during this terrible, decisive week, the Supreme Commander never once gave Zhukov a sign, a word, or even a telephone call. Zhukov never dared approach Stalin himself. And it remained another mystery just where Stalin was in the middle of October. Certainly he did not appear in Moscow until the end of October, when Zhukov and Rokossovsky (and even Vlasov) had stopped the Germans along the arc from Volokolamsk to Naro-Fominsk. At the beginning of November, Stalin was on the phone demanding an immediate counterattack along this whole line so as to have a victory in hand for the November 7 anniversary. He would not listen to Zhukov's objections and hung up the receiver as he had done more than once before, simply crushing your soul.

A counterattack like that now, given our weakness, was utterly senseless. Zhukov decided not to do it. The Germans themselves were exhausted and had temporarily halted their advance. And Stalin, as if nothing had happened, called Zhukov to ask him to release some troops from the front for the parade through Red Square on November 7.

And now here he is, sitting on his veranda with a view over the peaceful Moskva River, looking at the meadows on the opposite bank where the water laps at the city beach in Serebryanny Bor, trying to make sense of it all. So this is the problem: Should he write about *all this*? In fact, *could* he write about it?

It's not easy.

But a communist should be able to do it, because a communist sees by the light of a truth that never fails. And always and in everything you tried to be a worthy communist.

That was so from the beginning. In those days we had a weak grasp of Marxist-Leninist theory. Studying it was a long and hard job. It was only later that I achieved a deeper understanding of the organizing role of our party and realized that the brain of the Red Army, from the very first days of its existence, was the Central Committee of the All-Russian Communist Party (Bolshevik). Young people today, unfortunately, don't have much of a grasp of statistics, but they show that our growth rate before the war gave solid evidence of our progressive system. Industrialization, though, can't take place without some limits to mass consumption. (And long before that, when I was young in the time of the tsar, there was poverty and starvation in the villages, and the kulaks were sucking the blood of the village poor. Isn't that true? It certainly is.)

What about that awful year of 1937? You know it yourself, and you have to remind others, that those groundless violations of legality were not an expression of the essence of our system. The Soviet people trusted the party and followed steadfastly in its footsteps. The damage came from the unprincipled suspicions of some of the leaders. But the superiority of the socialist system and our Leninist principles still emerged victorious. And our people were unequalled in their endurance.

And what happened when war broke out? Sending *political officers*—communists with years of training in propaganda—to the army meant a decisive strengthening of our ranks. Then there was the important directive from the Political Directorate of the Red Army—to strengthen the role of communists in the leadership. Yes, I remember what a huge effect that directive had. It's true, there still were cases when our troops didn't put up as much resistance as they should have. Yet why did our GHQ emerge stronger than Hitler's? Precisely because it was based on Marxism-Leninism. And our troops showed amazing fortitude. They fought to the death, just as the Central Committee and the High Command expected them to do.

The Germans, though, had a first-class army. We never write about that or, if we do, it's done with contempt. Yet an attitude like that only cheapens our victory.

In the middle of October, when the Germans halted their advance because their front lines and their communications had grown too extended, we should have been doing the very same thing in the smaller arc that we were holding: bringing in reinforcements, weapons, and supplies, and strengthening our defense. Then we could have faced the next German offensive in mid-November, perhaps without having to fall back much at all. But the Supreme Commander clung to his unfortunate idea of winning some quick victories by November 7, and he insisted on a counterattack on *every* sector of the front, from Klin to Tula. Who could ever accomplish that? Zhukov now felt bold enough to object and argue, but the Supreme Commander wouldn't listen. And so he had to throw poorly armed and completely untrained divisions into battle. We wasted those precious two weeks on unnecessary counterattacks that achieved nothing; they won us not a single kilometer of ground, but they did sap our last strength. Then, on November 15, the Germans began the second stage of their attack on Moscow, and on the 18th they attacked near Tula. Guderian took Uzlovaya and was advancing on Kashira. He had come as far as Mikhailov, in Ryazan: he was moving eastward to encircle Moscow! That would have ended it all.

On November 20, Stalin phoned Zhukov. He could not hide his alarm. In a tone that Zhukov had never heard before, his voice cracking, he asked: "Are you certain that we can hold Moscow? I ask with pain in my heart. Tell me frankly, like a communist."

Zhukov was shaken that Stalin was unable to conceal his panic and his pain and was not even trying to do so. And he was moved to hear the trust he had in his general. Summoning up every single ounce of his truly iron will, Zhukov, as if swearing an oath before Stalin, the Motherland, and himself, replied: "We will hold it!"

Carefully calculating the days remaining, Zhukov set the possible date of his counteroffensive for December 6. Stalin at once tried to bargain with him: it had to be December 4. (This was not because he had made his own calculations; he wanted it for Constitution Day on the 6th, that was it.)

Meanwhile, every day brought news of more defeats: Klin was lost; Solnechnogorsk was lost; the Germans had crossed the canal near Yakhroma, and now the way to the eastern parts of the Moscow region was open to them. It was one huge mass of confusion and catastrophe; we were no longer fighting in military units but in chance groups of soldiers and tanks. And he had scarcely any will left to believe, to force himself to believe: No, we will not let it collapse! We will hold on. (During these days of the battle for Moscow he slept only two hours a day, no more. When Molotov phoned and threatened to have him shot, he gave him a very insolent reply.)

Stalin's call was a final blow: "Are you aware that Dedovsk has been taken?"

Dedovsk? That's halfway between here and Istra. Absolutely impossible.

"No, Comrade Stalin, I'm not aware of that."

Over the phone came Stalin's malicious jeer: "A commander ought to know what is happening on his front. Go there yourself, immediately, and take back Dedovsk!"

To abandon your command post, your communications with all the units on the march, to leave all your preparations at a time like this? No, the Supreme Commander has learned nothing over these six months of war. (Zhukov himself treated the generals under him no differently, however. That was the only way to win battles.)

"But Comrade Stalin, abandoning the army group headquarters in such a critical situation is not a wise move."

Stalin's reply, now with an angry sneer: "Never mind, we'll get by somehow without you there."

In other words, you count for nothing. That's what he thinks you're worth.

Zhukov rushed to phone Rokossovsky and learned that, of course, Dedovsk had not fallen. As Kostya guessed, they probably meant the village of Dedovo, much farther away and in a different area.

You needed a lot of courage to argue with Stalin. But now Zhukov hoped that he could ease the tension and even offer Stalin a bit of amusement with his phone call. But Stalin immediately flew into a rage: Go at once to Rokossovsky, and the two of you will recapture Dedovo! And take the army commander with you!

It was pointless to make any more objections. He went to Rokossovsky and with the divisional staff they established once more that, indeed, a few houses in the village of Dedovo, on the far side of a ravine, had been taken by the Germans; the rest of the village, on our side, was still ours. A shot across the ravine would be enough to drive the Germans out of the houses they had taken there, but four senior generals had to plan the operation and send a rifle company supported by tanks to carry it out.

All of them had wasted a day.

Still, Zhukov began bringing up all his reserves according to plan, and on December 5 he moved into the major offensive that Stalin wanted so badly. Within a few days he had been able to push the circle of German forces a significant distance away from Moscow. (Vlasov also made some fine moves with his 20th Army, but that mustn't be mentioned.) And the Germans never managed to take Moscow.

A resounding victory! The whole world was amazed, and rejoiced. But the Supreme Commander himself was more amazed than anyone, and it seems that he never believed it would happen. Dizzy from the victory, he didn't want to hear that we had used up our last reserves, that now we were completely exhausted and could barely hang on to what we had taken. No! The triumphant Stalin, in an expansive fit of desperate courage, ordered that we immediately begin a massive *general* offensive with *all* our forces, from Lake Ladoga to the Black Sea. We must liberate Leningrad and Oryol and Kursk, and do it all simultaneously!

The months passed—January, February, March—in a backbreaking and unnecessary effort by all our exhausted troops just to realize Stalin's rosy dream. And so we sent out tens and hundreds of thousands of our men in pointless attacks. (Among them were the men of Vlasov's Second Shock Army, who rotted in the swamps of the northwestern front and were abandoned without any reinforcements—but no one should ever write about *that*, and you'd better just forget about it yourself. Vlasov, in any case, later turned out to be a traitor.) We reached the point that our artillery was allowed only one or two shells per day.

Nothing was achieved anywhere. All we did was to spoil the picture of our Moscow victory. There was a single notable success, however, and it was achieved by the Western Army Group under Zhukov. Then Stalin took away the First Shock Army from him. Zhukov telephoned him, confident that he could convince him that he had prospects of a victory, but Stalin wouldn't discuss it; he only heaped him with abuse and hung up.

He had to master the art of speaking to Stalin, an art no less complex than the art of war. Many times he would hang up on Zhukov or shower him with obscenities. (Yet when Stalin summoned him from some faraway front, more than a day's travel away, and if he was down with a fever or the weather was too poor for flying, he still had to fly to the Supreme Commander, and he'd better not be even ten minutes late. Once, when the plane was descending over Moscow—there was a thick fog, but he couldn't wait for it to clear—the wing barely missed a factory chimney.)

Yet in some incomprehensible manner, Stalin's blunders were always covered up and glossed over by history. Obviously, it was to show the superiority of our system and our ideology. Even our enemies have no business objecting to that. This is a good time to repeat that the Central Committee had insisted that we show the party's political activities on a broader scale. This gave rise to the widespread heroism of communists and Komsomol members, and our entire population rallied even more closely around the Communist Party.

Yet Zhukov did not take Stalin's treatment of him personally. The Supreme Commander not only had to manage the war; he had to look after our industry as well, and he kept both in his iron grip—along with the entire country.

It might have been one of Stalin's flaws—or, perhaps, one of his virtues—but he did not like to change his mind. All our winter counteroffensives failed. Mekhlis's landing near Kerch was a bloodbath (but since it was Stalin's own idea, no one else was harshly punished for it). And yet, ignoring the objections of his generals on the staff, the Supreme Commander undertook a misguided attempt to recapture Kharkov in May. The result was the pointless squandering of our reserves and all our efforts. In the summer, the now reinforced Germans began a major offensive (but not on Moscow, as Stalin was expecting). It was then that Golikov, another of Stalin's favorites (and the same political officer who had questioned Zhukov in 1937 about his contacts with enemies of the people), almost lost Voronezh. The Germans flooded across the Don and the northern

Caucasus, and by September they had already taken the mountain passes. It was only then, it seems, that Stalin realized he was the one to blame for the failures of 1942. And so he did not look for generals to take the blame. At the end of August, he appointed Zhukov (still not a marshal) as Deputy Supreme Commander, and once more he admitted with obvious pain: "We could lose Stalingrad." He sent Zhukov there. (A few days later, when he learned that the next counterattack was set for September 6, not September 4, he again hung up the phone on Zhukov. He also sent him an ominous telegram: "Your delay looks very much like *a crime*.")

It was at Stalingrad, though, that Stalin for the first time kept his impatience in check. Zhukov and the clever Vasilevsky were able to win themselves almost two months for the very detailed planning of an enormous encircling operation (Stalin was also captivated by the beauty of this plan), including the systematic assembling of forces, setting up a command system, and planning joint operations. Stalin had learned from his earlier mistakes; he was patient and did not interrupt. And so they achieved the great victory of Stalingrad.

One other thing was achieved there, something that few expected. Though he'd never had any formal training in strategic planning, something had obviously found its way through his thick skull. It was only here, for the first time, in the pressure of that great struggle, that Zhukov turned into a *strategist*. He became a different Zhukov, someone he had not been aware of before. He acquired a real insight into the mind of the enemy, along with a constant sense, both intellectual and instinctive, of all *our* forces simultaneously—their personnel, their variety, their capabilities, and the qualities of their generals. He acquired the confidence that came from his ability to see farther and more widely than the others, an ability he had never had before.

And so it was all the more deeply insulting to read, some years later, Yeryomenko's lies of how he had planned the whole Stalingrad operation

. . . together with Khrushchev. Zhukov looked him in the eye and asked, "How could you do that?" "Khrushchev asked me to do it," was the reply.

After that it was Chuykov, the commander of only one of the Stalingrad armies, who claimed the glory for all three fronts. He also made a jab at Zhukov, now in disgrace, when he wrote in his memoirs that Zhukov had "only confused things." Zhukov thought his heart would burst—he'd have another attack for certain. He called Khrushchev: How could he allow such lies to be printed? The "Corn King" promised to put in a word for him. (What did Chuykov's memoirs matter, anyway? Did he, Zhukov, have nothing to say for himself? He pulled out some old army newspaper articles in which he was mentioned and used them to defend himself.)

After Stalingrad, still working with Vasilevsky, Zhukov confidently set about planning a new battle at Kursk. He took a very risky decision: He would *not* hurry his offensive. He would not even begin an offensive; he would first give Manstein a week to smash himself against our well-prepared defense in depth (it was almost a reckless decision: What if Manstein should break through?), and only then stun the Germans with our offensive on Oryol.

It turned out to be yet another strategic masterpiece with the beauty, power, and resounding success of Stalingrad. Zhukov's powers as a strategist grew even stronger, and he became confident that he could smash Hitler even without the Allies' Second Front. Now he could actually feel himself guiding this enormous process of retribution and also feel himself a component part of it: the process itself was guiding him. (And he became ever stronger in his arguments with Stalin. He even weaned the Supreme Commander from his habit of post-midnight telephone calls: you can sleep until two in the afternoon, but we have to get to work in the morning.)

Stalin's restraint did not last long, however. The process of destroying the forces of the surrounded Paulus dragged on. Stalin was edgy, pushing him to move faster and showering him with insults. After Kursk he would not allow him time to work out encircling operations. He insisted on frontal attacks, hitting the Germans head-on, achieving nothing and allowing them to maintain their fighting capacity. All Stalin wanted was to clear them off Soviet territory as quickly as possible, even if they left fully intact. (Though when they met now, he would shake Zhukov's hand and even joke with him. After promoting him to marshal, Stalin gave him the Order of Suvorov, First Class, then the gold stars of a Hero of the Soviet Union, three in all. He would transfer Zhukov to every spot where there had been a setback or a delay, and on one occasion, Zhukov, not without a good deal of satisfaction, was able to dismiss that same Golikov, who had once interrogated him, as commander of an army group.)

After that, we made the leap across the Dnieper and held on to the ground we captured. We rolled southward right to Romania, then Bulgaria. There was the Belorussian operation, where we easily took the Bobruisk pocket. And then another torrent of troops rolled into Poland, across the Vistula and to the Oder.

Zhukov grew in stature with each operation, and his confidence increased. His very name would now strike terror into the hearts of the Germans when they heard he was coming to *their* front. Now he could imagine no obstacles he could not overcome. And so on Stalin's orders he was to take the burned-out ruins of Berlin—something Hitler could not do with Moscow—and take it quickly! They were to take it themselves, with no help from the Allies. Zhukov was to crown his war, and his life, with the Berlin operation.

Berlin was about halfway between us and the Allies. But the Germans had concentrated all their forces against us, and there was the risk that they might simply fall back before the Allies and let them through. That must not be allowed! The Motherland has demanded that *we* make the attack, and make it quickly. (Zhukov had absorbed something from Stalin, and now he also wanted to get this done before the May Day holiday. But that didn't quite work out.) Zhukov was left with no choice but to attack head-on once more, never counting the casualties.

People will say that we paid a high price for the Berlin operation, with about 300,000 dead. (Perhaps even half a million.) But what about all those who fell earlier in the war? Was anyone counting casualties then? It's useless to keep on about that now. Of course it was a hard thing to lose fathers, husbands, and sons, yet people staunchly bore these inevitable losses since they all understood that we were writing the most glorious pages in the history of the Soviet people. Those who survive will tell their grandchildren about it, but now we must move forward! (After the war, the Allies, more from envy than anything else, insisted that not only was the Berlin operation unnecessary, so was the whole spring campaign of 1945; Hitler, they claimed, would have surrendered without it and without any more battles. He was already doomed. Yet they were the ones who inflicted an unnecessary bombing on Dresden, an unmilitarized city. They also burned to death about 150,000 people, and they were civilians.)

Zhukov, in fact, was prepared to keep on waging war. His was like a machine: his grasp of strategy and his steely will demanded new obstacles to grind up. But his whole life suddenly changed, as if he had been a ship sailing along at top speed and then had run aground on a soft and comfortable shoal. Now he was appointed commander-in-chief of Soviet occupation forces in Germany. The sleepless nights spent planning operations were exchanged for long, elaborate, and drunken banquets with the Allies (they couldn't get enough of the caviar and vodka). He struck up a kind of friendship with Eisenhower. (At one late-night banquet, he performed a Russian dance to show him how it was done.) A flood of decorations moved between the Allies and the Soviets. (He had to wear those huge medals of theirs on his belly.) Now his tasks were more economic than military—disassembling German factories and shipping them to the USSR. And, of course, he had to try to do something to help the German population. We did a lot for them, and our sense of internationalism did not allow us to take revenge. Ulbricht and Pieck the Younger also helped us understand a great deal. (Eight years later, Zhukov was astounded at the inexplicable uprising of Berlin workers: it was we, after all, who had struck down all their Nazi laws and given complete freedom to the anti-Fascist political parties.)

There was one thing he could take pride in: in June he went back to review the victory parade through Red Square, mounted on a white horse. (Stalin, obviously, wanted to do this himself but was not certain that he could keep his seat on the horse. It was also obvious that he was envious: he seemed to be gritting his teeth. And once, suddenly, he made an exceptional confession to Zhukov: "I am the unhappiest of men. I'm even afraid of my own shadow." Did he fear an attempt on his life? Zhukov could not believe such frankness.)

In the summer the ceremonious Potsdam Conference took place (it was in Potsdam because no place could be found for it in Berlin, utterly ravaged by our artillery and bombing). And then there were the worries about how to make the Allies return to Soviet "organs" our Soviet citizens who, again for inexplicable reasons, did not want to return to the Motherland. (How could that be? Either they have some serious crimes in their pasts or they've been seduced by the soft life in the West.) It meant making a stern demand that the Allies allow our representatives—professional criminal investigators— to meet with these people. (These were very capable and practical people who had always been a part of our army, but Zhukov's high rank meant that he had had little contact with them previously.)

There were many such things to do. Zhukov did them all, but without much energy, almost sleepily. His former inspired ability to discern what the enemy would do and to devise his own plans would never return.

In any case, it was time to give up this honorary and boring post in Berlin and go home to revamp and strengthen the Soviet Army (no longer called the Red Army) to deal with possible future conflicts and to update it with the latest military technology. Now that the war was over, Stalin would scarcely want to keep his post as the People's Commissar (now called the Minister) of Defense, and he would give the job to Zhukov. Staying on as Stalin's first deputy, Zhukov would have control over military affairs in any case.

But when Zhukov returned from Berlin in 1946, he was stunned by the news that the post of deputy minister of defense was given not to him but to Bulganin, a civilian through and through. As Stalin explained, waving his hand with his smoking pipe as if to indicate his powerlessness to interfere, Bulganin had already structured the staff of the Ministry of Defense with no place for a second deputy.

Zhukov felt as if he'd been thrown off the back of a galloping horse. Who cares what Bulganin has done in the ministry? What about me . . . ?

But how could he oppose the Supreme Commander? It couldn't have been Stalin's idea. To do that after all the victories they had won, after all the meetings in his own home, after all the work they had shared, the one-on-one dinners! It was that two-faced Bulganin's doing, of course. (Zhukov had seen similar cunning and dexterity from other members of the Military Council—the ones who managed the political side of the fronts and the armies. They would sit quietly until the main battles were over and only then would they act. Khrushchev was such a person: on the surface he seemed simple and straightforward.)

The chief of the General Staff was now Vasilevsky, and that was only as it should be. Zhukov was offered the post of commander-in-chief of land forces. That meant he would have no control over the air force and navy; he would have no role in strategic planning and, even more, he would be directly subordinate to Bulganin and without the right to appeal to Stalin (so it was stated in the ministry's new table of organization).

Here it was: from a full gallop to flat on the ground. It was painful. Like the time in Tambov Province when he had been knocked from his saddle. And Zhukov was just now turning fifty, at the very peak of his strength and abilities.

His heart ached for his vanished military past . . .

But his current sentence to inactivity turned out to be a good deal more involved than he had expected. He still had not foreseen all the troubles in store for him.

In late 1945, at a Kremlin meeting in which Stalin reproached Zhukov for claiming responsibility for all the victories, Zhukov readily responded that he had never claimed responsibility for *all* of them. And when in April 1946 he had the bitter experience of Bulganin's treachery, he still did not realize the extent of his troubles. He lasted only one month as commander-in-chief of land forces. The Supreme Military Council suddenly began reviewing the testimony of Zhukov's former adjutant (he had now been arrested!) and the chief marshal of the air force, Novikov (also, it emerged, recently arrested!), as well as statements from some other arrested officers. These indicated that Zhukov had supposedly been organizing a military conspiracy. What utter nonsense! Who could ever have invented such a thing? But Rybalko, Rokossovsky, and Vasilevsky stepped forward and spoke up in Zhukov's defense, for which he was grateful. They convinced Stalin, and Stalin saved him from Beria's vengeance. Zhukov was merely sent to head the Odessa Military District.

It was a hard fall, and it was painful; still, it was better than prison.

To describe in his memoirs, in his own hand, how after all his famous victories and his three Heroes of the Soviet Union (the only person in the country who could claim that!) he was cast aside to command a military district—no, that he could not do. He could never put that down on paper; he would be shamed before history. He would have to gloss over it somehow.

But that was still not the limit of his troubles. Before two years had passed, General Telegin was arrested. He had been a member of the Military Council with Zhukov at the end of the war. (And, as it came out later, they had knocked out all his teeth after his arrest, and he lost his mind. Novikov was also tortured—and then released.) It was then Zhukov realized that Beria was after him. And it was then that he had his first heart attack.

Beria and Abakumov suddenly burst into Zhukov's suburban dacha (a gift from Stalin for saving Moscow, the place where he was now writing his memoirs). They came supposedly to check that the documents in his possession were being kept securely. They rummaged through cases of documents and opened his safe; they discovered some old operational maps that had to be turned in—and this from a commander-in-chief! And then they slapped him with a severe reprimand.

No, they still hadn't arrested him: Stalin interceded and saved him! But he was exiled to the Ural Military District, not even on the border and with little strategic importance. This looked very much like Tukhachevsky's exile to the Central Volga Military District in 1937, though he had been immediately arrested on the train. That was what Zhukov was expecting now. He kept a little suitcase ready, with some underwear and a few toiletries.

His fame might never have existed. His power might never have existed. He was cast aside, forced into idleness, an agonizing idleness, when he still preserved all of his powers, his will, his mind, his talent, his experience as a strategist.

There were times when he thought: Might this really be Stalin's own idea? (Has he not forgiven me for that white horse at the Victory Parade?) But no, it has to be Beria who's pulled the wool over Stalin's eyes and slandered me.

On the other hand, there were anti-Soviet forces in the world that found it useful to create a Cold War climate. And Zhukov was quite useless fighting a Cold War, that was true.

In those years, however, it never entered his head to sit down and write his memoirs. That would be as much as admitting that his life was over.

But Stalin never forgot his slandered but faithful commander and hero. In 1952 he admitted him to the party congress and as a candidate member of the Central Committee. He transferred him back to Moscow and was preparing some very important post for him in this new and complex situation that was developing.

But then, suddenly, he passed away . . .

May Eternal Memory be his! And the situation became more and more complex. Beria was one of the ruling circle, but he was not alone. Zhukov once again became commander-in-chief of land forces and the first deputy minister of defense.

Two more months passed, and Zhukov proved to be most useful. He was summoned by Khrushchev and Malenkov: Tomorrow in the Politburo (they had now given it a somewhat softer name, the Presidium), there will be a military issue on the agenda, and you will be called in and will have to arrest Beria immediately! For the moment, only the three of us know about this. Bring two or three trusted generals with you and some adjutants, of course. Make sure you're armed.

At the appointed hour, they were sitting in the reception room awaiting their call. (The generals were speculating on why they had been called in. He explained their task only moments before they were to enter the chamber and assigned people with drawn pistols to guard the doors.) He entered, took a few paces and then rushed at Beria! He took him by the elbows and with the strength of a bear jerked him away from the table— Beria might have a button there to summon his guards. And he barked at him: "You're under arrest!" Got you at last, you bastard. You snake in the grass! (The Politburo just sat there, no one moving a muscle—none of them would have dared interfere.) Then he remembered what they used to do in Tambov when they took a prisoner. He told his adjutant to remove the prisoner's belt and cut off all his trouser buttons: let him use both hands to hold up his pants. And they took him away. They put him on the floor of a large limousine, tightly rolled up in a carpet and with a gag in his mouth; otherwise, the guards might stop them as they drove out of the Kremlin. Four generals got into the same car, and the sentries only saluted them. They took the son of a bitch into a bunker in the inner courtyard of the military district headquarters; they also brought in some tanks with guns trained on the bunker. (Konev was given the job of running the tribunal.)

But still, you can't put this very sweet moment into your memoirs. It's not appropriate. It does nothing to support the work of the Communist Party. And above all, we are communists.

After this operation, the Collective Leadership again summoned Zhukov to do a real job. It was only then that he became minister of defense, with all the powers that went with the post. He was running the army. And at what a crucial moment: the development of atomic weapons! (He and Khrushchev made a friendly flight to the Tots Camps in the Urals where a test was being made on the survival potential of our troops, 40,000 of them in the field immediately after an atomic explosion. They were working out a tactical warning strike against NATO.) He was preparing the army for great tasks, even against America, if need be.

Now he made trips to Geneva for summit meetings with the Allies. (And there he met his old colleague, Eisenhower. Imagine: now he's the president!)

And so it happens in life: one trouble follows another, one happiness follows another. He married a second time, to Galina, thirty-one years younger. And another daughter was born, his third and all the more dear since she was still a child. Like a granddaughter . . .

He had no anger left toward Stalin. All that had happened over these last years he simply erased from his memory. Stalin was a great man. And how well he had worked with him in those final years of the war, how many things they had pondered together, how many decisions they had made.

But the Twentieth Party Congress shook him: The crimes of Stalin they had uncovered! So many! Absolutely unthinkable!

At the Twentieth Congress, he became a candidate member of the Politburo.

And in the wake of the Congress, a number of generals began approaching him, the all-powerful minister of defense. Some came alone, others in pairs: "Georgy Konstantynych, we don't need these political sections and commissars in the army anymore. They only tie our hands. Can't you get rid of them? These days, no one would dare try to stop you." "And let's get rid of these SMERSH people who are always trying to arrest someone, and the Special Sections as well. That would be completely in the spirit of the Congress."

People came to him like this more than once, and also on the sly or at parties (though Zhukov never drank to excess), saying, it was a *Russian* army that finished off Hitler, yet they're treating us like a pack of idiots again. Hasn't the time come, Georgy Konstantynych . . . ? And some even said plainly: Now that you're minister of the armed forces, you've got more power than the whole Politburo taken together. And so . . . ? Perhaps . . . ?

Zhukov even gave it some thought: Perhaps they were right. All the power was in his hands, and he was as sharp as ever as a soldier; toppling all of *them* wouldn't be difficult in the operational sense.

But if you're a real communist? How can you even think about it when we owe our victory to . . . yes, even to the political apparatus and the people from SMERSH? No, gentlemen, that's not for me.

But word still leaked out and spread through Moscow, if not through the army as well. He was asked some anxious questions about it in the Politburo. He assured his comrades: "How can you even think such a thing? I was never against the institution of political sections in the army. We are communists and will always remain so." And with that they survived the ideological crisis of 1956.

Zhukov was now sixty, in the full prime of his life, and once again he was needed when some discord broke out within the Collective Leadership. They rose up against Khrushchev almost to a man, saying that he had become authoritarian, that he was trying to become another Stalin, and that it might even be necessary to depose him. Khrushchev rushed to Zhukov, saying, "Save me!"

Saving him meant collecting votes in the Central Committee, because Khrushchev had only a tiny minority of support in the Politburo and his enemies had refused to convene the Central Committee.

This was a ridiculously simple job. Zhukov sent out about seventy military aircraft and brought all the members of the Central Committee to Moscow in flash. With their support, Khrushchev won out. He declared the Molotov-Malenkov-Kaganovich group and those siding with them an anti-party faction. (Bulganin and Voroshilov had also supported them.)

Saving his homeland from German fascism, saving it from the degenerate Beria, and saving it from the anti-party faction were victories that gave Georgy Zhukov, a worthy, beloved son of his Fatherland, a triple crown.

It would never have occurred to him to indulge in such a frivolous pastime as writing *memoirs*.

It was then that he had to pay an official visit to Yugoslavia and Albania. He went with a flotilla of several warships via the Black Sea, the Mediterranean, and the Adriatic. It was a wonderful voyage, something he'd not experienced before.

While visiting Albania, he found out that he had been *removed* from his post as minister of armed forces! What was going on in Moscow? Was it some misunderstanding? Were they simply changing the name again or making reforms in the ministry? Would there be some new post for him, one just as important or even more so?

He felt his heart contract. His chest felt empty and all the official visits meaningless. He hurried back with the hope of getting an explanation from Khrushchev: Was he incapable of remembering the good that Zhukov had done in *twice* saving him?

Not only was Khrushchev incapable of remembering, it turned out that he had already declared in the Central Committee and in Kremlin circles that Zhukov was "a dangerous person"! A Bonapartiste! Zhukov wants to topple our own Soviet power! Back in Moscow and fresh off the airplane, who should meet him but Konev! He escorted Zhukov to the Kremlin, and there he was removed from the Politburo and from the Central Committee.

There was nothing he could have done from Albania. And when he came back to Moscow, he had been rendered harmless; everything had been altered here, and he had no lines of communication left open.

It was only now, only with hindsight, that Zhukov understood: he was too large a figure for Khrushchev. The man was incapable of keeping such a person near him.

Where could he defend himself? *Pravda*—it was Konev again!—published a vile article against him. Konev! Saved by Zhukov from Stalin's tribunal back in October '41.

Never in his life had he been so insulted, so humiliated, so wronged. (Stalin, now, was a legitimate Boss; he was above all of them, and he had a right to power. But what right did this little speck of cornmeal have?) It was so painful that he tried to deaden his feelings with sleeping pills. A pill at night, then another, and when he awoke in the morning his heart gnawed at him so that he needed another pill. And again at night. And again during the day. And so he deadened himself for more than a week, simply in order to survive.

But this was not the end of it: he was thrown out of the army altogether and sent "into retirement." Even this was not the end of it: Khrushchev made that same Golikov, Zhukov's old enemy, the head of the political administration of the army and navy, and now it was Golikov who ensured that all the movements of the disgraced marshal were blocked, as were the visits of any of his friends—those who had not turned away from him—to his dacha in a suburban forest, this home with the ridiculous colonnade. (He should be thankful that they didn't take away his dacha.)

It was then that Zhukov suffered his second heart attack (if not something even worse).

When he recovered, he was not the same iron man he had been. His entire body seemed to weigh him down, and he had grown weak beyond recovery. The skin on his neck grew loose and flabby. His unyielding chin, familiar to the whole world, now had grown soft. His cheeks had swollen, and his lips seemed to move unevenly and with difficulty. For a time he had nurses at the dacha watching over him twenty-four hours a day.

Now Zhukov only had his wife (a doctor, and most often away at work), his little daughter, his mother-in-law, and his old, faithful driver from the war. He became very involved in following Mashenka's progress when she began studying in her music school. (He himself had always wanted to play the accordion, and after Stalingrad he found the time to work at it a little. And now, with time on his hands, he would play a few tunes. He would happily play "The Peddlers," "Baikal," and the old wartime tune, "Dark Night.") The only long trips he made were to go fishing, which he loved. The rest of his time he spent on his own wooded lot, taking walks, tending the flower gardens, and, when the weather was bad, wandering about the spacious dining hall, from the huge oak buffet to the bust of himself sculpted by Vuchetich and the model of a T-34 tank.

Life outside went on in its own way, as if he'd never been a part of it. A multivolume *History of the Great Patriotic War* appeared, but no one ever came to ask Zhukov for any information . . . They passed over his achievements and did their best to omit his very name. He heard that photographs of him had been removed from the Armed Forces' Museum. (Everyone had turned away from him, apart from Vasilevsky and Bagramyan, who still visited. Rokossovsky would have come, but he'd been sent to take charge of the Polish Army.)

This was the time when so many marshals and generals were rushing to write and publish their memoirs. Zhukov was struck by how jealous they were of each other, how they put themselves in the limelight, tried to take away the glory from their neighbors, and dumped their mistakes and failures on others. Even Konev had now dashed off his memoirs (or did he have someone else write them?). And he emerged as pure as the driven snow, while he shamelessly stole all the glory of the achievements of the modest and talented Vatutin (killed by Bandera's Ukrainian nationalists). Knowing Zhukov was defenseless, the lot of them, almost, would badmouth him. The artillery marshal, Voronov, even went so far as to claim responsibility for planning the operation at Khalkhin-Gol and take credit for its success.

It was at this point that Zhukov sat down to write his own memoirs. (And he did it in his own hand, without any secretaries, working slowly, carefully, and gradually. He was grateful to have some help from his former personal assistant, an officer who could help him check dates and facts in military archives: it was awkward now to go to the ministry's archives himself, and he might well have been refused entry.)

War memoirs are something inevitable and necessary. Just look at how many the Germans have turned out! And then there were the

Americans, though their war over there wasn't much compared with ours. The memoirs of some of our ordinary officers, even junior officers, sergeants, and airmen, were coming out as well—and they all have their use. But when a general or a marshal sits down to write, he has to be aware of his responsibilities.

And so he wrote, not finding the anger or the rashness within him to dispute with all the others. (Vasilevsky had given a rather sharp dressing-down to one or two of them.) You have to be relentless in battle, but not here. He had no rancor either toward Konev or Voronov. As the months and then years of his time of disgrace passed, the anger in his heart also passed, and he became reconciled to his situation. The injustices, however, could not be allowed to remain in the historical record. He had to correct the accounts of his comrades, even if only gently, and set the record straight. Do it gently, so as not to make them go on to reach for an even bigger share of the common fruits of victory. And those things he had not done or had left incomplete must not be left out of his memoirs either, for it is from such mistakes that future generals can learn. What he had to write was the full, unvarnished truth.

The problem was that the truth itself somehow steadily and irreversibly altered with the passage of time: under Stalin, the truth was one thing; under Khrushchev it was another. And there were many things that it was still premature to mention . . . Yes, let it be about the war, and leave it at that. He didn't even want to talk about what happened later, and he couldn't, in any case.

Then, suddenly, they got rid of that gasbag Khrushchev! This time there was no Zhukov to save his skin.

But the situation of the disgraced marshal did not change after a week or after a month: the cloud of disgrace still hung over him. No one confirmed it anew (Golikov had passed on), but no one lifted it either. Who would be the first one brave enough to say the decisive word?

One thing he did allow himself: he made a trip to Kaluga Oblast, back to his native village. He had been longing to go back, and it had been—what?—fifty years since he'd lived there. It upset him deeply: he met women he had danced with in his younger days, and now they all looked so old, like beggars; and the village itself had become so impoverished. "But why are you living so badly?" "They won't let us live any better . . ."

But then came the twentieth anniversary of Victory Day, and the new rulers had no choice but to invite Zhukov to the ceremonies in the Kremlin Palace. It was his first public appearance in seven years. Not long after that, he was unexpectedly invited to a banquet in the Writers' Club. The marshal was both surprised and touched by the warmth of his reception. Once again in that same year he was invited back to the Writers' Club for an anniversary of a well-known writer of war novels. He went in civilian clothes and was seated at the head table. What followed was just a regular celebration at which he was an outsider, but when, among the half-dozen speeches, his name was mentioned in passing, the whole hall full of writers—the Moscow intelligentsia—applauded furiously, and twice they all rose to their feet to honor him.

That was something to remember!

Then Zhukov permitted himself to make a trip to Podolsk to the Central Archive of the Ministry of Defense to go through some documents from the war years, including some directives he himself had issued. And now there were archivists to help him. Then a trickle of correspondents and filmmakers began appearing at the dacha that everyone had forgotten and where he was spending his years of disgrace. A woman from some publishing house of the Novosti Press Agency arrived with a contract for his memoirs. They were to be finished within six months (and he had already written them as far as Berlin). His book could come out for his seventieth birthday. And would he give them the rights for publishing abroad? Well, of course he would.

Not all that long before, no one even asked about these pages of memoirs; scarcely anyone knew about them. Now they wanted them, and quickly, and for the whole world to see!

But could he push himself to meet the deadline? This reflective, meticulous work at his desk was not at all what a professional soldier was cut out for. It seemed an easier task to move a whole division five kilometers forward than to drag his pen through another line of text.

The woman editor became a regular visitor; then a second woman came. They suggested he use a tape recorder; they could supply all the words he needed, even whole sentences, and they sounded fine. For example: "The political work of the party was a most important factor in the development of the battle-readiness of our ranks." At first you wanted to say no to this: you yourself had prepared your troops for battle enough times to know all about the necessary factors. But then you think for a time about the political work. Well, it may not be the most important factor, but of course it's one of the most important. Or: "The party and Komsomol organizations provided an enormous moral force to increase the combat-readiness of our forces." You think about this, and it's also true, and it doesn't diminish the operational work of the commanders. They also brought in materials from the archives for which you never had any responsibility and which you can't verify now. Here, for instance, were some reports from the political sections stating in plain black and white: "In the year 1943, our glorious partisans blew up 11,000 German trains." How could that be possible? But then it can't be completely ruled out: the trains might have been only partially destroyed—a few freight cars here, a wheel or a platform blown up there.

He asked the Press Agency to find out if the KGB would give him access to the reports that Beria and Abakumov had submitted on him. He was informed that all these files had just been destroyed as being without any historical significance.

He did learn something, though: There was an account, printed a fairly long time ago, by a former army translator in Berlin. She wrote that in May 1945, she taken part in the identification from false teeth of the corpse of Hitler, which had been discovered near the Imperial Chancellery. How was that? You mean they found Hitler's body? Zhukov, the commander-in-chief, the victor in the battle of Berlin, neither then nor later knew about it! At the time, he had announced in Berlin that nothing was known of Hitler's whereabouts. What a fool he must appear now! His subordinates had secretly reported the discovery directly to Stalin, behind Zhukov's back. How dared they! And Stalin not only kept it from Zhukov, but in July 1945 had asked him directly whether he knew where Hitler was.

Zhukov could simply not conceive of such treachery. It was incomprehensible. And he had thought that after the years of war he had come to know Stalin through and through . . . And now how could he admit this in his memoirs? It would be politically improper as well. He found this additional deception very painful to endure. (He asked this translator to find him the documents that he himself could not get.)

Zhukov was not readmitted to the Central Committee. (He heard that Suslov opposed him.)

But Konev did come to see him. And he apologized. Zhukov forgave him, though it cost him an effort.

Good or bad, he submitted the manuscript to the publisher by the deadline. But when it came to books, there was always another obstacle. Now the Press Agency created a group of consultants "to check the facts." Month after month they made their "suggestions" and their revisions—fifty typewritten pages in all. ·

Now there was no way he could expect his book to come out for his seventieth birthday. The work dragged on, and time after time he would give his assent . . . Many things had to be deleted or reworked. His descriptions of Tukhachevsky, Uborevich, Yakir, and Blyukher were all deleted.

This was something new: you didn't write what was in your heart, you wrote what would *get through*. Would they let it pass or not? What could now be said, and what could not? (And so you give your assent: Yes, that's right. That's fine.)

Until now he had written simply for himself, quietly and peacefully. But now he had become so eager to see his book in print! He made the concessions and wrote the revisions. He toiled with these editors for two and a half years, but still there was no book. Then he learned that for some reason the newly hatched Marshal Grechko in the Army Political Directorate had spoken out against his memoirs. But Brezhnev stepped in and proposed a solution: "To create a committee of experts to review the contents of the book."

Meanwhile, in his own month of December (the month he was born, the month he had won his victory on the outskirts of Moscow), Zhukov and Galya went to a sanatorium in Arkhangelsk. There he suffered a severe stroke.

The recovery was slow. He would get out of bed, but less often than before. At first he could not walk at all without someone's help. The massages and physiotherapy took up more than half the day. He also had an inflammation of the trifacial nerve. He had dizzy spells.

By now he couldn't rouse much interest in his future book. And yet he wanted to live to see it in print.

That summer our troops invaded Czechoslovakia. That was the right thing to do: we couldn't put up with the shenanigans going on there. Zhukov always took the problems of the Motherland more to heart than he did his own. And in the military sense, it was a first-class operation. It's a fine thing—they haven't forgotten the lessons of our old school.

The third year of editing was coming to an end. He was informed quite plainly that Leonid Ilych wanted to be mentioned in the memoirs. How's that for you . . . ? How was he to remember anything about Political

Officer Brezhnev when he had never met him during the war, not even on that tiny bridgehead near Novorossiysk? But he had to save his book, and so he put in two or three sentences.

After that, Brezhnev himself approved the book.

In December again, though in Zhukov's seventy-second year, the proofs were sent to the publisher.

Should he rejoice or not?

Sunk in his deep armchair, overcome by weakness, he sat. And he remembered—he remembered the furious applause in the Writers' Club (was that three years ago?). He remembered how everyone in the hall had gotten to their feet again and again as if they were using the palms of their hands to make an imprint of his immortal glory.

Their applause was like a stubborn repetition of the disappointments and hopes he had heard from the generals right after the Twentieth Congress.

There was pain in his heart. Perhaps it was *then* that he should have done something. *Then*, perhaps, then was the time he should have acted.

Can it be that I was really such a fool . . . ?

1994–1995

FRACTURE POINTS

1

WHO DIDN'T GO hungry that year? Though his father was a shop foreman, he never "picked up" anything extra and never allowed anyone else to do so. In the family were his mother, grandmother, sister, and Mitya, almost seventeen, and all of them so hungry! He would stand by his lathe all day and then at night it was off in a boat with a friend to catch some fish.

His father's shop produced shell casings for the Katyushas. The people in the Kharkov Hammer and Sickle Factory kept working—they weren't allowed to stop—right until the city itself was in flames. They almost were caught by the Germans and left the city while bombs were dropping around them, going all the way back to the Volga.

The war? Well, by now it seemed to be coming to an end. The front lines had all moved westward, but then what would happen? Mitya was only a whisker away from his call-up. But he already knew what he could achieve, given his character and his brain, and in that spring of 1944 he passed not only his ninth but also his tenth grade as an external student, and passed with honors. In September he could make a run for some college or institute. But which one? He and his friend got their hands on a booklet, *The Colleges and Universities of Moscow*. Wow, what a lot of names, and then there were all the faculties, departments, and specialties. What did they all mean? Who could make sense of it? How to decide? They had almost made up their minds, but then they read that the Energy Institute on Enthusiasts' Highway provided three meals a day! And that outweighed everything else. (Though he kept it to himself, he had been thinking about law or history.) Still, with the breeziness of youth, he applied there.

He was accepted. The student residence was in Lefortovo. The trouble was the way they calculated the three meals. Cabbage soup was one meal, a scoop of rotten mashed potatoes another. Then 550 grams of poor-quality bread. That meant they would spend the day studying and the night unloading trucks. They were paid in cigarettes. Then it was off to the market to trade a pack of "Ducats" for some potatoes. (His father helped him out as well.)

Those born in '26 were now all being grabbed for the army. Those born in '27 were ducking here and there. He managed to keep out of the way. And then the war was over.

The war was over, and yet it wasn't over. Comrade Stalin declared that now we have to *rebuild!* Life went on in the same rigid military fashion as before, though without the military funerals. Rebuild! A year, two years, a third year of rebuilding meant that you had to go on working, living, and feeding yourself as if there were still a war on. He was already in his fourth year and had saved 400 rubles for a new pair of pants, but then the rumor went round of the currency reform. People rushed off to the savings banks, and immediately two lines would form, one to deposit money, another to take it out; but there was no telling which was the best. Mitya Yemtsov guessed wrong, and his pants vanished into thin air. There were some immediate gains: student grants and salaries weren't divided by ten, and there was no more rationing. With his January grant money he bought up enough rye bread to stuff himself, and some tea and sugar as well. The head of their institute was a woman with reputation and influence—Malenkov's wife, in fact—and she was able to get some supplemented grants. Yemtsov's grant increased as well. He was thriving.

He was thriving not only because of the food and not only because he was doing well in his studies. (They were selecting students to specialize in atomic energy and automated aircraft guidance systems. He chose the latter, without giving it a great deal of thought. Had he taken the nuclear option, he would have been locked away in secret laboratories for years on end, as if he'd gone to prison.) He was also thriving in his community service, in the Komsomol.

It happens imperceptibly and not by any intention: we learn our own worth only with the passing of years and by the way that others regard us ("he's exceptional"). Everyone notices that you're energetic by nature, that you're the first to make proposals on how the collective should handle a certain issue, that your opinions prevail over others'. So, why don't you preside over the meeting? Will you make the report? Well, why not? And your words come together easily when you make a speech—these people must be supported, those must be denounced. Everyone applauds. And they vote for you. It all proceeded so smoothly, as if it had happened of its own accord: Komsomol leader, faculty secretary in your third year, deputy secretary of the whole institute in your fifth. (For this post, you had to be a candidate for the party. But an instruction had come from the Central Committee: Party intake is to be suspended effective 1948 [during the war they had taken in too many people]. And so the proposal was "that Comrade Yemtsov be accepted, as an exception." There were now some war veterans at the party meeting, and they began to murmur: Why him? Why the exception, and for a young puppy like that? The meeting was against the proposal. But the head of the institute, this imposing and confident woman, rose to her feet—and remember who her husband was. Was anyone unaware of that? Her words fell weightily on the auditorium: "There are some *special considerations* in this case." And that was enough. Even the veterans voted in favor.)

Very soon—you still hadn't graduated and hadn't yet been given your job assignment—they took you into the Moscow City Committee of the Komsomol as deputy director of student youth. (You still had to travel to the institute, but why take the streetcar? Call the city committee and you can ride in a Pobeda; call again and the Pobeda will bring you back, but not to the student residence: now you have an apartment.)

Yes, you had favorable winds behind you, to be sure. But you weren't the least bit embarrassed in front of your classmates because there was nothing dishonest in any of this: you never pushed for it yourself, you never plotted and schemed, it just happened all by itself. And even more: the work of the Komsomol was honest, true, even sacred! (The first time you came into the Komsomol City Committee's offices, it was like a religious person entering a church—with reverence and awe.) This was the living, throbbing center of a resplendent life for all our people: after the world-renowned victory we had won, the streams of energy directed to reconstruction simply poured through the whole country! And the news of our grandiose construction projects resounded through the land. And you are a part of this, and you are helping guide your generation of students toward those projects and those achievements.

He wrote proudly to his father (who had remained in his factory shop, now on the Volga—they were never sent back to Kharkov). His father could appreciate what it meant to succeed through your own talents. He was the son of a blacksmith who had risen to become an engineer. He had married a girl from a Poltava landowning family who in the early 1920s was looking to shelter herself under someone's wing. (Later, his father would get very angry when his wife spoke to her mother in French.) In

1935 he suffered the misfortune of being arrested when someone spread slander about him. (Their family immediately had to begin living in straitened circumstances, and their Schroeder grand piano was put into a cellar on its side.) Six months later, however, his father was acquitted. Being freed in such a wondrous fashion only strengthened his proletarian faith in the soundness of our system and reinforced his lifelong dedication to the path of Lenin.

But wasn't it true that something had changed in the Komsomol City Committee? Not everyone entered there with reverence. And some were clearly deficient in ideological enthusiasm; their affectation was obvious and could not be hidden. It was true, to be sure, that once a person yields even a little to his personal interests, it's very difficult to put him back on the right path. One person is scheming against another to get a better job. Suddenly, the second secretary of the City Committee gets caught on his office sofa with a secretary. Well, measures were taken . . .

Like it or not, there are also certain *facts* that slip into each of our lives. Here was a fact: Beginning with his promotion to deputy director of the section and continuing with each promotion, a long envelope, always of the same greenish brown color, would slip into his hands each month. It was called a "package." Inside was the equivalent of a month's wages, the full amount, without any deductions, taxes, or payments for state loans. And you'd be lying if you said that you found this awkward, unnecessary, or unacceptable. In fact it was very acceptable: there's always a use for a bit of extra cash.

He married one of his classmates, but they had no honeymoon: like all party and government officials in Moscow, he had to be on duty in the City Committee until two or three in the morning, wide awake because of the will and the habit of Stalin. He would come home in his Pobeda sometime before four a.m., and why should he wake his wife? She had to get up at six to catch the suburban train for work.

His work and his responsibilities expanded in a big way. They set up the International Union of Students (he worked in it with Shelepin himself) and made it a part of the international struggle for peace. Here he also had a support job, writing speeches for the big bosses: "We will not allow the clear sky of our homeland to be darkened once more by the clouds of war!"—that sort of thing. Some tasks were secret, some quite open, but he was in the public eye and he held his head high.

Then his father came to visit him while on holiday. He stayed for a week. He listened to what his son had to say and took a close look at everything. But he expressed none of that fatherly pride that Dmitry had expected. Even worse: he sighed and said, "So, now you're one of the straw bosses. You'd be better off back on the shop floor. *Production*— that's the only real job."

Dmitry was wounded and offended. He felt that he had always been flying high, and if he did touch the earth he walked about it like a bigwig. Then suddenly to hear that he was a straw boss?

His father read only the newspaper *For Industrialization*. And he lived "for the good of the people," as he was fond of saying.

The son rejected what he had heard as merely a father's grouchiness. But as the weeks passed, something began to gnaw at him inside and to weigh heavily on him. His father's censure lay on his heart like a stone. It would have been easy to brush it aside had it come from anyone else. But from his father . . . ?

Perhaps his father was right: What sort of "job" did he have? He could see it himself: talk and more talk, sitting through meetings, plotting and scheming, too much drunkenness. When he looked at his colleagues, he could see they were all blockheads and bureaucrats. And if you yourself had such abilities, why not find a place where they could be better used? (But where should he go? That he didn't yet know.)

Still, parting with his "packages" and his Pobeda wouldn't be easy.

Something kept gnawing away at him. And it wasn't easy to decide what to do about it.

Suddenly, just like that and with no real consideration, he put together a letter of resignation and sent it in.

Then he learned what such a letter meant. How could a member of the party send in his *resignation*? Against the will of the party? He's an unreliable element in our midst! And they made him out to be such a troublemaker, and they gave him such a going over and chewed him out at the party meeting so that he could only sit there like a boiled crayfish and go on apologizing for his error.

Perhaps it was for the best. His career took a positive turn again. (He was given some very odd assignments: the students at one institute had established, supposedly in jest, the Society for the Protection of Bastards and Bootlickers. When you looked into it closely, though, was it not a case of political subversion?)

Then there was a major shake-up in the party in Moscow. At a plenum of the Moscow City and Oblast Committees, the longtime first secretary, Popov, who was so solidly entrenched, so imposing and so unshakeable, was suddenly ousted. (His enemy, Mekhlis, had been plotting against him, and Stalin had decided to purge those who had done well by the war. There was no shortage of accusations against Popov, either: How was it that a paved road outside the city reached just as far as the home of Popov's mistress and no farther?) Khrushchev was designated to take his place.

Then came Komsomol Day. A group of Komsomol activists were invited to a reception and a banquet in the St. George Hall in the Kremlin. The lively and generous Khrushchev, whose round head looked as though it had been shaven, made a promise to them: "Keep working! Keep working, and you all can be secretaries of the Central Committee!"

Suddenly—and what in blazes ever made him do it?—Yemtsov spoke up. Recklessly he jumped to his feet: "Nikita Sergeych! May I ask a question?"

"Of course."

"It's been two years now since I graduated, and my diploma is still lying idle in my desk. Don't we need people to work in manufacturing? I'm prepared to go anywhere the party wants to send me."

(Now how did that sound! Right in the St. George Hall. He had to admire his own courage.)

Khrushchev barely paused before he nodded his bald head: "Comrade Sizov, I believe that you can look into this request?"

"Look into it!" Why that's as good as an order when it comes from the mouth of one of the country's leaders! (Mitya never expected such a sudden and irreversible turn of events. Had he been too hasty in jumping up like that?)

Sizov called him in to discuss the matter. He said expansively: "Why did you take that approach? You should have said something to us earlier. We could even have moved you up to the Central Committee." Well, I've lost that chance. "So where do you want to go?" "Somewhere in the aviation industry." "The Aviation Materials Research Institute? Or the Central Aerodynamics Institute?" "No, I want to go directly to the manufacturing sector."

The request went through the ministry's personnel section, and he was assigned a place in the provinces. True, he was able to choose the city he had come from and where his parents were living. The names of such factories are made deliberately obscure to conceal their purpose. This one was called the "Modular Assembly Plant"—try and figure out what's going on in there. What was going on was the manufacture of aviation electronic equipment, autopilots, and fuel metering devices, but the plant was also supposed to produce consumer goods. They were to get busy producing household refrigerators, for example: We should be ashamed to be lagging so far behind Europe!

People there knew that "Khrushchev himself had sent him," and this helped him become head of a factory department rather quickly. (But now he had only a fifth of the salary and the "package" he had earned in the Moscow City Committee, and that really pinched; he even felt the loss of his thirty-ruble "bread increment.") His department, though, had been assigned the task of producing refrigerators! They had a refrigerator from England right there, and their only job was to make a copy of it. Lord knows, they made an exact replica, but there must have been some secrets that they still hadn't grasped: a tube in the condenser coil would clog, or it would produce so much cold that everything would freeze. Buyers would return the refrigerators with complaints and curses: "The damned thing won't stay cold!" The stores would submit claims for replacement.

What made his job easier, though, was that in those years—the early 1950s—the factory still maintained the unquestioned discipline of wartime—this despite the fact that the townspeople called it the "booze factory" (they were allotted a good deal of alcohol, intended for cleaning their equipment).

Stalin's death was shattering! It wasn't that they considered him immortal, but he had seemed some eternal Phenomenon that could not simply *cease to exist*. People sobbed. His old father wept. (His mother did not.) Dmitry and his wife wept.

Everyone realized that they had lost the Greatest of Men. But at the time, Dmitry still did not fully realize how great he had been. It would take many more years to grasp fully the Impetus that Stalin had given to move the whole country into the future. The sense of a war still being fought would pass, but the Impetus would remain, and only through it would we achieve the impossible.

Yemtsov, of course, was much more than a common man. He had an uncommon mind and uncommon energy. His work at the factory demanded not so much the knowledge he had acquired in his institute as the knack of handling equipment and people skillfully. Once again, he was spending very little time at home. Now, though, he had a new son, and when could he find time to help bring him up? He didn't have a moment to spare. His greatest life lesson, however, he learned from the factory manager, Borunov.

Managers came and went, staying for a year or eighteen months at best. The latest manager, along with the chief engineer, had been replaced "for producing poor-quality goods": review commissions from the merciless Office of State Inspection showed up unexpectedly, as did commissions from the Office of the Prosecutor; the factory's work was halted; one office after another was interrogated; everyone lived in terror. And so Borunov came in as the new manager. He was a strapping, handsome man of about forty, a Russian original. His face seldom wore a smile, but it radiated an assured superiority that said that he could remedy any problem.

And, indeed, it was amazing! Within two or three weeks the whole factory and the refrigerator department were totally changed. It was as if people had entered some powerful electromagnetic field: they all seemed to turn in the same direction and look the same way and understand things the same way. All sorts of fabulous tales were told about the new manager. (Yemtsov was away on a week's holiday at the time, doing some ice fishing, and did not return when called. When he did appear, Borunov's secretary said: "He told me to say that he doesn't need you any longer." Borunov refused to see him for three days.) In January Borunov suddenly declared: "As of February 1, the factory will work by a balance sheet system." Every day each department had either a red column (plan fulfilled) or a blue one (plan not fulfilled) posted on their bulletin boards. When a department had a series of blue columns, its life wasn't worth living. Sweat and slave was what it meant! He seemed to have solved the technical problems with the refrigerators, but then the electroplating shop couldn't supply the wire shelving in time. A small thing, but the refrigerators couldn't be finished without them. The head of the electroplating shop begged him: "Just sign that you received them today and I'll have them for you tomorrow morning." This happened again, and then a third time, and the shortage kept building. Yemtsov refused to sign, and his department was given a blue column. At the next planning meeting Borunov told him: "Yemtsov, get out of here!" Yemtsov even threw up his hands to beg his boss for mercy: he'd done the right thing, after all. But no, he might have been talking to the wall. He gave up.

At the planning meetings he watched how Borunov did it. He never shouted or pounded his fist. But he was confident that he was better than any of his subordinates. He was intellectually better. He had a quicker grasp of detail. He had a keener mind. He had better judgment. (But Yemtsov had all these qualities himself!) It was impossible to argue with Borunov. It was impossible not to produce results.

What was possible for Yemtsov, though, was to get ahead of him and suggest something of his own. The opportunity came when the relays from Kursk began arriving irregularly and disrupting the plan. He came to Borunov with his idea: "Get me an airplane and a bit of money! I'll fly to Kursk with a group of electricians." The manager beamed and immediately gave what was needed. At the Kursk factory, Yemtsov sent in his team to sort out the problems with the relays and met with the local engineers. We need the relays, whatever the cost! Thereafter there were only red columns.

Borunov did not stay long as manager. He wasn't sacked, though; he was promoted to secretary of the Oblast Committee.

Yemtsov matured so much and absorbed so many things through that brief experience. What had happened at the factory was due not so much to Borunov personally but to the fact Borunov (or anyone like him, or you yourself) was riding the crest of that great Impetus that Stalin had begun and that would grip us all for another fifty or a hundred years. This was the only rule: *Never listen to anyone else's excuses* (you'll lose your momentum, begin to slacken, and ruin everything). This is the only thing to think about: *The job either gets done or it doesn't get done*. And if it doesn't get done, look out!

People have no choice! They'll do the job, without fail! The whole system is easily managed as well.

Soon he was the head technologist in the factory, before he had even turned thirty. Barely past thirty, he became the chief engineer.

Now there was a new task assigned by the party: to begin producing magnetrons—powerful generators of ultra-high-frequency waves that were to be used in the radars of antiaircraft defenses. Were there any examples to follow? Of course, here is a German one, here's an American one. Copy them as much as you like, though a magnetron is a lot trickier than a refrigerator: How can we prevent overheating? How can we regulate the power? And simply generating high-frequency waves wasn't enough: it had to be done across a very narrow spectrum, otherwise the target couldn't be recognized. (Several groups of theorists in the design offices were working on all these things.)

A few years passed, and the complex of defense industries, scattered across the country but linked by reliable delivery channels, solved one problem after another, problems that had so recently seemed to be insoluble. The words of Khrushchev (his godfather) were now being repeated: "We're turning out missiles like sausages on a conveyor belt." But to ensure that these missiles could fly on an absolutely accurate course, we needed gyroscopes. The gyroscopes had to run constantly so that the missiles could be quickly launched, and this caused them to wear out. But when laser technology came into being, a way was found to make a laser gyroscope with no moving parts, that could be ready in an instant. Yemtsov, who had become unaccustomed to sitting still, needed no urging to go into action and seek out new possibilities on his own. He suggested that the minister and head of the defense section of the Central Committee, who was visiting his factory, should entrust them with a laser. (It was a desperate act, but he took it on, like a kamikaze.)

The minister agreed. And immediately thereafter, at age thirty-three, he became manager of the factory.

This was in April 1960. On May 1, one of our missiles shot down the aircraft of Francis Gary Powers.

But how did it happen? Several days later Ustinov, then deputy chairman of the Council of Ministers and Khrushchev's deputy for defense, held a top-level meeting. Ustinov still very much had a hand in the business of his former post, the Ministry of Defense Industries. (This was the first time this fresh young factory manager had been among such a high-ranking assembly.) There was also a group from the Ministry of Defense. The head of that group, Baydukov, made serious accusations that the military-industrial complex was making a mess of Soviet defense.

Those damned American U-2s (it was an amusing coincidence that our old low-altitude plywood "crop-dusters" had the same name) could fly at altitudes beyond the reach of our fighters and could jam our radar or confuse it by throwing out metallic chaff. Our system could not reliably distinguish the nature of targets and we could not accurately direct our weapons. Our technology, clearly, wasn't advanced enough to shoot down these aircraft.

And now Powers had passed through our air-defense system with no resistance and had flown directly over our air-defense testing area of Kapustin Yar on the lower Volga. From Iran he had flown halfway across the USSR, and though we'd taken some shots, we hadn't been able to bring him down. (We did manage to shoot down one of our own planes, though.) Only when he was over the Urals did we hit him, and then it was essentially by chance. (Powers, by the way, preferred captivity to killing himself with an injection, as stipulated in his contract. Then he published his memoirs and made a lot of money.) The whole incident was made public, but the story was that Khrushchev, out of compassion, hadn't wanted to shoot him down at first. But we knew very well that our systems were flawed.

It was obvious how difficult and unpleasant this was for Ustinov. Yemtsov was sitting quite close to him, not at the main table but in one of the chairs arranged along the wall. Ustinov, his long face twitching, was clearly trying to find a way to justify himself and to find someone who could speak and come up with some ready answers.

At this point Yemtsov was seized by a sudden burst of inspiration, as he had been with Khrushchev some years earlier or when he undertook the manufacture of laser gyroscopes. He was simultaneously both terrified and fearless, as if he were flying through the air without wings: Would he soar upwards or crash to the ground? With a bow to Ustinov, he raised his hand to speak. (But inwardly he was hoping, please don't give me the floor! Those high-level meetings were more deadly than a battlefield or a minefield: a single careless remark or a tiny break in your voice would be enough to ruin you. His engineers, though, had assured him that a solution was at hand.)

Ustinov saw his raised hand, but he wasn't ready to risk letting this scrawny young upstart speak: He was so young, and who knew what he might blurt out? One general spoke, then another; one factory manager, then another. After each speaker Yemtsov would raise his hand (though he was still trembling inside). Ustinov looked questioningly into his eyes, and then Yemtsov sensed how his eyes had lit up, sending a clear signal to Ustinov. And Ustinov understood and accepted that signal. He gave him the floor.

Yemtsov jumped to his feet and began speaking in a voice filled with energy. He was also relying on his experience with the galvanizing shop: yes, there were times when you had to declare something done that was not yet done. And the business with the Kursk relays as well: we can make up for the failure in time, but we have to have our red column! Though he knew that the system of selection of moving targets had not yet been perfected, it *would* be perfected! It would—by the law of the great Impetus!

He tossed his head haughtily and assured the room full of generals in ringing tones: "We have already solved the problem of high-altitude target selection. In a very short time, we will be making the equipment to do it."

Everyone in the room froze, mouths half agape.

Should he stop at this? No, his victory wasn't yet complete. Now, in a very concerned but also haughty tone, he added: "Actually, we have been working on another problem, one that concerns us all: We want to create a system for identifying low-flying targets. Every now and then the Americans reduce their altitude . . ."

The meeting was stunned. During the break Ustinov grinned approvingly at him: "Well, you didn't disgrace the defense industries." Another prominent general took Yemtsov by the arm (Yemtsov couldn't understand why he had come to him, but later he learned that the general's influence was on the wane and he was trying to strengthen his position) and led him to a group of even higher-ranking officers: "So, the two of us have been talking . . ."

And so it was all very satisfying but also terrifying: *What if we can't pull it off?* Indeed, it was quite possible that we might not be able to pull it off . . . We *might* not be able to, but for the Great Impetus! That summer he had to repeat at another top-level meeting (the heads of the military-industrial complex were burning with impatience) that everything was going according to plan—yet the equipment still had not been developed.

In a case like this you wouldn't just destroy your career, you'd go to prison . . .

But he had Borunov's example to follow: be quicker and sharper than your subordinates; don't allow them to take the initiative (but pick up anything useful from them at once). Use psychology on your subordinates: those blue columns are useful for all sorts of situations! He already felt that he was a ruthless industrialist and an inspired manager. From time to time a car would come during the night to fetch him from home: "The conveyer's broken down!" or something of the sort, and he would rush back to the factory. (Now they were telling fabulous stories about him as well.) He believed that miracles could be worked. It would seem that the normal laws of nature would not allow a process like this simply to be ordered up in advance; the whole project might fall apart. But there was also a psychological law: "Push on regardless!"

So they kept pushing. For the fourth quarter of that year, the factory was awarded the banner of the Central Committee and the Council of Ministers, and the manager was made a Hero of Socialist Labor.

After that he went on soaring higher and higher. (He could see his inexorable triumph reflected in the eyes of any factory girl—and can we advance very far without feeling this sort of pride? He had some aristocratic blood in his veins, after all, and it showed in the way he held his head high.) His factory, now renamed "Tezar" for security reasons, expanded as more and more buildings were added and thousands of new workers hired. It produced UHF generators, radar transmitters, and the complex power supplies for them; other of his divisions were producing wave guides for antennas and calculating systems for radar sets. (The signals sent out by radar had to be of varying frequency so that the enemy could not detect them and take preventive measures.) The first anti-missile defense system was under construction. The "Moscow umbrella" had already been set up: 140 complexes for each of the four corners of the earth (an attack over the North Pole was particularly anticipated) to detect the flight of a missile from a thousand kilometers away. The complexes were arranged in three belts so that the inner ones would pick up anything missed by the outer ones. A thousand targets could be processed simultaneously. And later, computers were used to assign targets for each missile. (With this "umbrella," we had left the Americans behind!)

Still later came multiple warheads, and here we again caught up to the Americans. We learned to use radar signals to distinguish warheads from dummy missiles.

Yemtsov was heaped with rewards. And he lost count of the number of these high-level meetings he attended, the places he had flown, and the high-ceilinged offices he visited where, as they say, all the doors were open to him (not every door, of course). He even served on a commission editing the decrees of the Central Committee. And how many of those grim faces with their flabby cheeks, double chins, expressionless eyes, with lips that barely opened when it was time to utter a few phrases—how many of them reluctantly changed their innately hostile expression when they faced Yemtsov? (They found this defense plant manager alien: he was too young, too slender, and too lively; he had those eyes that glowed with inspiration and an aristocratic forehead.) Dmitry Fyodorovich Ustinov, though, had simply fallen in love with Yemtsov.

(There was a time, however, when Yemtsov's career ran onto the rocks. One of his close friends, a scientist and electronics specialist initiated into many of our secrets, went to Europe for a conference—and never returned! He rebelled against our System! Yemtsov was placed on the list of those not allowed to travel abroad—for twenty years! It could have been much worse, though; he might have lost his job altogether. But how could he comprehend his friend's sudden and completely unanticipated about-face? There was no comprehending it, in fact: he had simply lost his head. Surely it wasn't for the blessings of life in the West—he had more than enough of them right here. Freedom? But what freedom had he lacked? Was it *personal*—an act of treachery? Yes, it must have been "personal." Because of this turncoat, the whole anti-missile defense system had to change all its codes, its names and its numbers . . .)

YET OVER THESE twenty years Tezar continued to expand. The factory headquarters was a marble palace. Even the new workshops were luxurious buildings, a feast for the eyes. There was never any shortage of money for new buildings. Now it was no longer just a factory but five factories combined, all enclosed behind a stone wall, along with three design offices (these had even tighter security than the factories). There were 18,000 workers and office staff. Yemtsov had presided over it all for almost a quarter century now, still sitting in the same old office chair (he had taken it with him into the new building). He maintained his slim figure, his brisk gait, and his rapid, intelligent gaze. He had lost much of his hair, but what remained on his temples had not gone grey. He gave all his orders forcefully, and there was no one who could get the better of him. He was now past fifty.

At such an age a wife is hardly likely to present her husband with a second son. But his new son was the focus of his pride, his love, and his hopes and showed promise of continuing in his father's footsteps in the years to come. It was as if Yemtsov was taking his first steps along with him. His elder son had been on his own for some time and had made many missteps, but this one, who had arrived twenty years after his first son, would go on to astonish them all! And how much meaning he was to give to Yemtsov's life in the years to follow.

Tezar continued to lay its foundations ever deeper in the land along the Volga, swallowing up the acres of nearby houses and farmland. But it was its output, its mission, and its activity that made it more and more of a colossus among the defense industries of our nation. Its manager never missed an opportunity and never tired of staking out new areas of production. (Yet he was still not allowed to travel abroad. The Central Committee trusted him—and how could they not?—yet it seemed the security organs still had reason to be cautious . . .)

Yes, the Soviet defense systems—and its offensive capacity as well—continued as indestructible and effective as before. Still, a sharp mind, one that also was aware of the details contained in secret reports coming from across the ocean, could begin to see in the early 1980s and the Reagan era that we were no longer the same contender in the race that we had once been: we were beginning to fall behind. That could not be tolerated; we must not allow ourselves to pause! But those wrinkled old fellows in their armchairs, with their dead eyes and lowered brows, squinting at you as they listened with only one ear, hostile to anyone subordinate to them—how could they be moved? How could anyone reach their benumbed minds? (Even Ustinov had changed in his old age.)

Then, suddenly, a new figure appeared on the scene and displayed his talents: Gorbachev! From the first plenum of the Central Committee he roused hopes. We will come to life again! With him was Ligachev, and he allowed Yemtsov to speak to the Politburo! And Yemtsov, as far back as the failed reforms of Kosygin in '65, had been aware that the time had come for us to rebuild our economy; but we were timid and halfhearted, and in our indifference we let an opportunity slip through our fingers. In those days the industrial managers felt themselves in fighting trim and believed in the slogans of planning in a totally new way and creating new incentives for labor. And Yemtsov was speaking not only for himself when he eagerly took on the task of speaking to party audiences and even to the Higher Party School on what a new economic system should be and how it would save the country. They listened and were amazed. Then a local university invited him to give a series of lectures on "The Foundations of Socialist Economic Policy." Yemtsov accepted the challenge. At that time, for his own interest, he had become thoroughly fascinated by the then-forbidden science of cybernetics; he had read much of the work of W. Ross Ashby and included in his course those elements of cybernetics that he had managed to master. He himself was amazed that one might approach absolutely everything from the point of view of complex systems! How about that? (The grateful university awarded him a PhD.)

But then the swell of reform simply fizzled out as if someone had pricked it with a pin. And it remained dormant for twenty years. Still, we managed somehow. But were we to live out our age without any reforms?

No, here it was now! Gorbachev! Yemtsov's faith, which had grown cold, began to glow hot once more. He went back to the university to lecture on the contemporary system of industrial management, using his old but now updated basic ideas (though without mixing in his former ideas from cybernetics—he hadn't been able to keep up with developments in that field over the past twenty years).

But Gorbachev the reformer? What are you talking about? What did he do, this nearsighted, clumsy oaf? The orders he gave caused nothing but damage, just one blunder after another. He introduced Councils of Working Collectives! They were to study the plan sent down from the ministry and decide *whether or not to approve it!* I ask you now, is there any cook (never mind the manager of a powerful and renowned factory complex) who would allow something like that to go on in her kitchen? Wait, here's something even better: this so-called working collective from now on will *elect the manager!* Half of what I do goes on outside the factory: all the deliveries, relations with the other enterprises, dealing with government, foreign currency purchasing—and tell me who in this working collective or any other riffraff is capable of deciding all these things? It's raving lunacy! And then some wretched little newspaper—and one that focused on literature, besides—began a series of articles under the title "If

I were the manager . . ." Just tell them what you want to do . . . Have you ever seen anything like it? Maybe your memory is better than mine. But I, at least, know how to draw conclusions from what I've seen. And so, what I think is—*this is the end!*

But whatever the end might be, those alive have to go on living. (And you have a second son who's growing up. Isn't that music for your soul? Now you have to live! And go on living for a long time!)

And so we floundered around through five years of *perestroika*. We tackled our problems through the "trial and error" method, as experimenters call it. And we had to do it ourselves, working far away from those who ruled over us, without making a nod toward Moscow. By the end of the eighties all the lines of communication among the industrial enterprises of the USSR had so deteriorated that you could no longer rely on your suppliers. And the giant Tezar was looking for ways to manufacture as many of its supplies as possible on its own.

But we still hadn't felt the full misery of it all. Then we found out that they had driven out the party. Yes! I can say that I was the first one to dislike these beetle-browed people at the very top, despite all the orders I wear on my chest, despite my gold stars, despite the many times I spoke in the former Central Committee. Just think of me as a humble man, a simple professor of cybernetics. Still, the party was our rudder. It was our pillar of support. And they knocked it out from under us.

And so we rushed into the Great Reform, just as the old fisherman said as he sat by his hole in the ice: we'll drop in a line and see what happens.

This was how it came to Tezar. Exactly three weeks after the brainy fellows began the reform, on an overcast day in late January, Yemtsov was given a telegram from the Ministry of Defense: "Cease dispatch of production number so-and-so and number so-and-so due to lack of funds."

Alone in his large office but seated in his same old chair, Yemtsov looked at the telegram and felt the goosebumps rise on his scalp.

It was as if some evil spirit or demon had flown over, just brushing his head.

Or it was as if some enormous bridge, a marvel of engineering spanning a river broader than the Volga, had collapsed in an instant, leaving only a cloud of concrete dust slowly settling over the ruins.

For forty-one years, from the time in the St. George Hall, Yemtsov had been an industrial manager. For thirty-two years, since Francis Gary Powers, he had been manager of Tezar. And this telegram proclaimed: *it was all over* . . .

If the Ministry of Defense, three weeks after the start of the "reform," had no money left for something like *that*, then they had no future. A wise man has to be able to see through everything, right through to the last wall at the back. This really was the end of it all. And the most unwise thing to do would be to flounder about trying to save yourself, to send off imploring telegrams, to deceive even yourself, to delay the final resolution. The telegram said only to "cease dispatch," not to "cease production," and there was still capacity in the shops and warehouses to go on producing for a time.

But no. Best to cut it off at once. Don't prolong the death throes.

Had he sat there for a whole hour? He hadn't turned on the light, and now his office was almost dark.

He switched on his desk lamp. He called in his three senior managers. In an aloof, emotionless voice, as if speaking of something unrelated to him, he told them that as of such-and-such a date, no further supplies were to be issued to the factory shops.

In other words, the Great Impetus was over.

DURING THOSE WEEKS, ninety-five of every hundred managers of defense plants rushed to Moscow to argue: "We will lose our technological expertise! Give us some government contracts, and in the meantime we will go on producing for the warehouse!" They all feared one thing: that they would be excluded from the system of supplying the military: "Don't cast me aside to be privatized." The word "privatize" was as frightening as a sea monster.

Yemtsov saw it as clearly as if he were at absolute zero, -273 degrees: our electronics industry is finished. Our advanced technologies will die because sectors or factories cannot be maintained independently; there will always be some element missing from the whole complex. The system as a whole will deteriorate. Our advanced military technology will begin to collapse, and when that happens, no one will be able to restore it for decades.

Yet the whole reform led by Gaidar, Yeltsin, and Chubais was correct and brilliant! There were none of Gorbachev's half-measures: the whole thing had to be destroyed, all of it, right to the last bit! And then, sometime in the future, Carthage will be rebuilt, though not by us, and it will certainly not be done in our fashion.

But when Yemtsov announced to an anxious and tight-knit band of managers who were all supplying the state that he was going to privatize his factory, these defense contractors erupted with rage: "Have you lost your mind? How can you even imagine privatizing the things that we do? There'll be no privatization as long as we're alive!"

"Really?" Yemtsov smiled with his usual air of assurance, though his smile was a bitter one. "Fine, let's discuss it so I can crush your arguments. If I've understood you correctly, you think that despite all this, our metallurgical industry, for example, will continue to grow. Do you think we can go on churning out low-grade steel when the market for special steels has disappeared? You're all thinking of the past. But you'd better forget it. There'll no longer be any head office for the defense industries, and there'll no longer be any employees in the defense industries. And before long, we'll be unable to match the level of our current production."

Among all the idiotic buzzwords and phrases of the time—
"*perestroika*," "accelerated development," "a socialist market," and then
"reforms" (but no one knew just what sort of reforms)—there was one
that was remarkably intelligent and perceptive, if one truly grasped its
meaning. It was addressed to factory managers: "Become the masters of
your production!"

Absolutely true! It captured it all! That was the key.

BUT IF YOU are the "master of production," in name at least, then why not
become one in practice?

Becoming a *master*, though—how does that happen?

It's always more difficult for the first one who has to blaze a trail
through unexplored territory. Still, he had won some time for the reconstruction of Tezar.

In fact, there were a few others like him in the "party of economic
freedom." He joined the group, but what he encountered was either a lot
of empty talk or people who wanted political power. No, politics was not
going to solve this problem.

At first, Yemtsov believed that he could get help from Western investors. When a group of Western bankers visited Tezar, he received them
graciously and trustingly and entertained them lavishly, in Russian style.
They smiled and were very polite; they enjoyed the caviar; but they offered
not one penny of help.

Nor could the Russian government provide more than small change.
He had to hurry.

Now that there were no travel restrictions, he decided to go to America
himself. He was received very graciously, as a "progressive entrepreneur."
There were meetings and business breakfasts and lunches; he took advice
from specialists. But there wasn't a penny for investment. What he did
hear, again and again, was the same piece of advice: No one would be

willing to invest in such a giant as your Tezar; that could only be a losing proposition. You have to take it apart and create many separate enterprises; then each one of them will have to sink or swim on its own.

From his childhood in Poltava he recalled what Gogol had written: "I've given birth to you, and I can kill you as well."

The Council of Ministers was a regular circus, everyone elbowing each other aside in their efforts to lobby officials. And so Yemtsov squeezed into an airplane with the vice premier, and while they were en route to a conference, he obtained permission to privatize Tezar and break it up into smaller segments.

If you cut up a living body, the pieces will still wriggle about in search of one another. But we had no other option.

And so now my principle will be this: No more of these inflated government contracts! First the money, then the order. You pay your money, then you get your goods—isn't that the way it's normally done? They had left us no choice: now it was money in advance. Tezar's military manufacturing was reduced to only five percent—just spare parts for anti-missile defense and a few bits and pieces. He divided Tezar into sixty subsidiaries, but he remained general manager of all of them. Part of their authorized capital came from the former Tezar; the rest would come from wealthy backers they had to seek out on their own. The aim of each of these individual cells was to survive, and so they were left to "wriggle." Each of these sixty firms had the same legal rights; the office of the general manager—now given the new designation of "holding company"—had its own legal basis.

There was one principle for all of them: Henceforth, *we don't care how you earn your money!* You want to use UHF for processing buckwheat? Fine. Microwave ovens (something we hadn't seen before) for the domestic market? Start turning them out! Someone wants to manufacture VCRs? Excellent. Plastic window frames, children's toys. As for those who have nothing going and can't pay wages, then don't pay them. You'll have to let your workers go.

The whole city was abuzz: "The electronics plant has switched to making garden rakes!" (That wasn't far from the truth.) Those who knew more about what was happening—the electronics engineers or managers of defense plants all over the country—said: "Yemtsov is tearing the Tezar empire apart!" Those workers who had not yet been laid off but were on their second or third month with no wages, and those who had already been laid off, were seething with rage. They gathered in raucous crowds at the factory office, cursing the manager. Yemtsov set up a meeting with them in the factory recreation center.

Still agile in his old age, thin as a rail and with the same bright eyes and face of his youth, he went to face the storm. He felt the same devil-may-care boldness that had served him so well at other times in his life. He knew he had not lost his ability to think on his feet and knew he would now take them utterly by surprise.

The hall was filled with loud, angry voices. Yemtsov raised his hand with its long fingers as a schoolteacher might when demanding silence. Speaking with all the volume and clarity he could still muster, he said: "Who is responsible for all this? Is it the Supreme Soviet we have today? But who elected the Supreme Soviet? Is it the managers who are responsible? Or is it the workers? *Whom* did you vote for? Did you elect managers, organizers, and businessmen who knew what they were doing? No! You rushed off to elect some self-styled democrats, most of them former instructors of Marxism-Leninism, some economists, ivory-tower professors, and journalists . . . Khasbulatov, Burbulis, Gaidar, Chubais—and I can list thirty more. Who elected them? So now you can take your red banners and march off to these wise gentlemen and look for justice. But I can see farther than they can, and I'm *saving* you! I may be leaving you unemployed, but remember: it's only for 1992 and no longer than that.

Coming from Tezar, you'll still manage to find work or adapt yourself to a new job. But anyone who goes marching off with a red banner to look for his wages will be left high and dry."

IT'S NOT DIFFICULT for a young man to rebuild his career and change his views and his plans. But a man of sixty-five?

You're confident that you're right. Yet you feel the bile rising in your throat when you think of how everything collapsed.

You have to have a mind that never loses its remarkable agility; you have to change, immediately, all those things that have guided you until now, as if none of them meant anything, and then set off marching briskly along some new path.

And you stumble at every step. A steady flow of microwave ovens and VCRs—better and cheaper than those Tezar produced—came from Japan. Well then, there's no point wallowing about, we have to shut down our own amateurish production. (And lay off even more workers. In fact, many engineers, office staff, and workers did not wait for layoffs and left. But who were the ones who walked away? At first, the very best of them, then the second best. What remained was a gray mass, the ballast. Out of a workforce of eighteen thousand, only six thousand were left.)

A year passed, and one quarter of the fragments of Tezar had gone bankrupt, failed, or were dissolved. Some, though, had found a way to make a profit. It meant looking very closely, seeking out areas where no one had ventured, no one had anticipated, no one had explored; it meant digging up the earth itself and searching beneath it and even looking into outer space. Here was something new that had popped up: portable hand telephones working through satellites. Let's look at that! We'll build base stations for them and electronic switching systems and sell numbers to subscribers—there's profit to be made! Even simple gas meters that Gazprom doesn't have but that everyone needs—there's profit!

Yes, gentlemen-comrades, we have nothing to be ashamed of; any sort of business suits us! Even garden rakes, even hats, even renting out our luxurious accommodations, our palaces and our kindergartens, even housing a store selling Scandinavian furniture! Even a supermarket! A casino or even a regular brothel! (Selling things is a way of life, but who will buy our old factory shops? And the state that's refused to give us help is still eager to take from us—for debts, for electrical power.)

The most promising idea, though, was to create our own bank jointly with those elements of Tezar that were successful. Given his quickness and acuity he didn't let pass that brief time when new banks were springing up by the dozens. Those who waited too long could sit and chew their nails. A bank is a sensory system for everything that lives and creates! And (something they never expected) three years later, the Tezar Bank was awarded the American Torch of Birmingham Prize. (Years before, recovery from the Great Depression began in the city of Birmingham, Alabama; hence the prize.)

Those managers of defense plants who had waited for state contracts for a year or two, or who had built up debt by continuing production, were now floundering pitiably like frogs cast up on a sandy shore. Yemtsov, however, had not only managed to do what was necessary in time but had not even been weakened by the sudden fracture in the continuity of his life and in the life of his country. He would still walk about his former holdings looking even more proud and authoritative than before, when he was a famous Red manager. Sometimes he would frown as he passed the casino and think: "I'd be happy to pay those half-baked impotents not to listen to their music." Once again he was a conqueror, though he kept all his old orders and gold "Hero" stars in the lower drawer of his desk. If your mind is agile and you keep your youthful passion for activity, you'll never fail. He would say: "My view is that making money is an interesting occupation. No less interesting than being the beating pulse of the military-industrial complex or, say, understanding cybernetics."

And when my son grows up, he should get some of his education abroad.

2

AN ATTEMPT HAD been made on the life of a banker in the building at 15 Karl Marx Street. There was an explosion in the building's lobby, but the banker was unharmed; he and his wife left immediately by car.

The call about the incident came to the oblast Organized Crime Division late in the evening. The duty lieutenant should have gone out to investigate immediately, but he knew how dangerous something like that could be at night, even with a backup of two policemen armed with submachine guns: where there had been one explosion there could well be a second and a third. And so the lieutenant waited until dawn—a late February dawn—and then set off.

The building was a co-op, and the tenants themselves had installed a steel exterior door to the lobby. The magnetized support for one of the two bombs that had been set off was still attached to the door. The interior wooden door had been blown through at the height of a man's chest, and the whole lobby was lacerated by fragments that lay scattered across the floor. The lieutenant had warned the building staff not to touch anything during the night, and the tenants who returned the previous evening had passed through the lobby with great caution. The lieutenant took all the measurements and compiled a description of the incident. The banker himself (his name was Tolkovyanov; he was a younger man) was not at home. No one answered the door to his apartment, which turned out to be quite an ordinary one with just two rooms—something that surprised the lieutenant. The banker and his wife had not returned after the explosion; their two-year-old child, the building staff explained, was probably with his grandmother.

With that, the investigation was complete for the moment, and the lieutenant hurried back to his office in the Division to arrive before his two coworkers and the major came to work. He made it back in time. But for some reason the major did not come in, and at ten o'clock Lieutenant Colonel Kosargin himself arrived. The lieutenant ventured to report directly to him.

The lieutenant colonel was about forty and was now in civilian clothes; he was fit and neat with a distinct military bearing. He had spent fifteen years in the "Organs" and had left the state security service a year and a half ago. He had been here for the last year.

The lieutenant gave his full report and displayed the schematic drawing he had made. Kosargin's eyebrows also rose as he wondered about the banker's modest apartment.

"What would you like me to do now, Vsevold Valeryanych?"

Kosargin had a lean, energetic face, and his constant expression was one of immediate readiness for the task at hand.

"What was Tolkovyanov's first name, did you find out?"

"Aleksei Ivanych."

"How old is he?"

"Twenty-eight."

A crease appeared across Kosargin's smooth forehead. What was he thinking about? Was he trying to recall something?

"I think I'll take this on myself. Call the bank and get hold of Tolkovyanov."

The lieutenant readily turned to leave, relieved that he had not been blamed for his delay over the past night, and went off to carry out his instructions.

Kosargin remained seated. He had a very sharp professional memory. In '89 he had happened to question an Aleksei Tolkovyanov during the time the local university students were creating some disturbances, clashing with the cadets of the border guards' school across the street. The cadets had taken it upon themselves to use their fists to put the students in their place. The information on Tolkovyanov was that if he was not the ringleader of the students, then he was at least one of their main instigators. In those days, interrogations were tough: Don't lose your head over all this *glasnost* nonsense; don't be taken in by the disgusting stuff they're allowed to print in the newspapers these days; if you keep this up, we'll find a nice little camp for people like you, the kind of place you won't come out of alive.

Yes, in those days . . . Kosargin still could not comprehend *how* all this had come about. And the direction it had taken. And the speed with which it had happened, and the things that had been destroyed! The Organs themselves were thoroughly shaken, and one by one the cleverest and most energetic people within them had begun looking for something new and even resigning. Where could they go? Into these new private businesses and management boards. Some of them became nearly as wealthy as bankers and thus provoked the understandable resentment of their colleagues, who had stayed at their jobs and missed such opportunities. And now, it seems, even this ex-student has been able to move without a hitch into that world, unlike you.

This made him even more eager to take on the case and investigate, if only to satisfy his curiosity.

Tolkovyanov turned out to be at his job in the bank and was expecting visitors from the Organized Crime Division.

Kosargin went to see him. He left his driver on a quiet street near a new, seven-story bank building with a vast expanse of glass and one of the enigmatic names they were now inventing. He went inside. The reception area on the second floor had a Western-style counter, not glassed in. Despite his civilian clothes, the receptionist immediately knew who he was; then another young man greeted him and took him at once to the bank president; the president had come to the outer office to meet him.

Yes! Though that interrogation had taken place almost six years ago, Kosargin recognized him at first sight: it was he. That same tall fellow with a face that seemed a bit simple. He might have been a village cowherd dressed in city clothes. He was not, however, in a business suit, as one would expect from a bank president. He wore a loose, casual, olive green sweater, though his shirt collar—a lighter shade of the same color—was carefully arranged on the outside. He had a narrow gold ring on his finger, the sort they were now wearing as wedding bands.

The banker gave no sign that he remembered their past encounter.

They went into the president's office. The furniture within was a mixture: there were some contemporary pieces—low, plump leather armchairs grouped around a small table covered with magazines, but also a few antique, or at least reproductions of antique, chairs with high, straight, carved backs and bare wooden seats; these were arranged around a table covered with a green cloth. On the wall hung an antique clock with a bronze pendulum and, when it now struck, a soft, ingratiating chime.

Kosargin declined an armchair and sat on one of the wooden chairs, placing his slender portfolio on the green cloth of the table; the banker sat at his desk, which was placed crosswise to the table.

He was in full possession of himself: he appeared entirely unshaken by his experience and his face showed no trace of fear, only his undivided attention. And, even on such a morning, he had not neglected to shave. His long ears, set high on his head, accentuated the length of his face.

Kosargin mentioned only where he was from and did not give his name. Tolkovyanov did not ask to see his identity card, and it was only this that betrayed his preoccupation or uncertainty.

The circumstances? Well, this was how it happened. He had opened the steel door and was about to enter; his wife was following. Suddenly he realized that he had forgotten to take one of her bags and—did it take a second or half a second?—he stepped back instead of entering the lobby; the steel door had almost swung shut again when the explosion burst inside. Whoever had sent the signal had acted a fraction of a second prematurely, thinking that his victim would now be inside the lobby.

He gave a crooked smile, as if apologizing.

His very simple hairstyle—combed to one side, like a child's—added to the simplicity of his face.

"Do you have any idea who would want to kill you? Who might have ordered the murder? Who set off the bomb?"

Tolkovyanov looked right into his eyes. Attentively. Thoughtfully. He seemed to be taking Kosargin's measure.

And then—he recognized him! Kosargin could immediately tell from his expression.

Yet Kosargin did not respond and said nothing to prompt him.

Tolkovyanov had no names to give him.

He was still pondering.

Folding the five arched fingers of one hand into the fingers of his other hand and then, with apparent effort, unfolding and folding them again, he replied: "I'm not certain that your department can provide any effective assistance in this matter."

ALYOSHA HAD NEITHER imagined nor anticipated an attempt on his life, and yet one had just taken place. Still, when he had set off on the rocky road through this twilight world, he should have expected it and been prepared for it.

As for the person who had *ordered* it, Alyosha suspected, though he had no proof, that it was the head of the Ellomas Company. His bank had a turbulent relationship with them, one that demanded great caution, and now Alyosha thought he understood where and how he had erred. Sometimes a single careless remark was enough to create a bitter enemy. Anyone who enters the world of finance must never give vent to his feelings or lose his self-control.

And as for the one who had carried it out, he would be much more difficult to find. Alyosha could not even speculate, although it was only through that person that he could begin to untangle it all.

Should he rely on the police investigation? Or, perhaps, simply wait things out?

What is it that pushes us into these vague and pointless speculations, such as: What if he had picked up Tanya's second bag earlier and had not chosen to step back precisely at that instant? Both of them could well have fallen into the trap . . . Alyosha's daily schedule was so regular that a murderer would have no difficulty finding the right moment. But why something so complex? Why not simply use a pistol, at point-blank range? Probably the plan had been to leave a false trail, not here in this provincial city but leading back to B—, from which Alyosha had once come, to study at the local university. Recently there had been two murders in B—, both committed in the same way—an explosion set off remotely. Their idea was quite clever. But how could he convince anyone that he had no debts or scores to settle in B—, only fond memories of his childhood and youth?

Among his fond memories were the well still being used in the yard of his little provincial house; the grass here and there in the yard that had not yet been trampled down; the whole residential district of little single-story houses with their gray, decrepit, carved gables; and the boys of this district. (And what he and these boys didn't get up to! They pasted up posters all over the town with the slogan "Attack the priests!" They put together a plan for blowing up the last church in B—. And when there was some talk of going to war against China, they decided that if the battle came as far as the Urals, they would create groups of partisans in the forests right here, along the Volga.) Then there was his school—and what a fascinating place he found it, ever since he first stepped through the door. Five years later—physics! Later still—chemistry! What marvelous subjects, revealing things he had never seen or even guessed at, yet all the while they were right there in the world around him. The woman who taught chemistry was amazing, and so beautiful as well! All the kids were full of enthusiasm for chemistry, but Alyosha left the others behind: from grade nine he was working well beyond the school program and was ahead of the grade tens. But then there was physics. The teacher was quite useless. He was dull and he simply did not understand his own subject or realize what an amazingly iridescent treasure had been entrusted to his uncaring hands. He had no idea how to set up an experiment, so Alyosha prepared everything for him. At first, when he arrived at school well before classes and stepped behind the mysterious partition of the physics room, he would wander about and lose himself in dreams among the objects there: the rotating rings, the sparks that would fly from the contacts on the black cover of the coil, the blued-steel indicators behind the glass on the instruments, the inscribed measuring glasses and tubes, springs of all sorts . . . A mysterious, invisible current seemed to flow through all these things, and even the movies with their galloping horsemen seemed scarcely on the same level as this bewitching world.

But soon, when Alyosha was a little older and had found his bearings, he realized that these were all childish, outmoded things: the real current of physics was moving much faster, and it was not moving here. His elders advised him to read magazines—*Science and Life, Knowledge Is Strength, Nature*—and he began haunting the town library, where he could read his fill. The things that were going on in the world! Imagine what was being achieved or was on the threshold of being achieved: Computers that could perform millions of operations in a second, that could direct entire industrial processes with no interference from humans! Computers that were capable of manufacturing more computers just like themselves! Computers in radio navigation! The transformation of heat into electricity with no mechanical operations! Solar batteries! The meteoric rise of quantum electronics! Lasers! The ability to see and take photographs in total darkness! It was as if the different branches of physics were a pack of hounds that had torn themselves from their leashes and were racing off in all directions. The molecular clock. The "frontier sciences," the physical-chemical synthesis of substances with predetermined qualities. We were already on the threshold of a managed thermonuclear synthesis. Biotics. Bionics: technological devices that copied biological systems. And then, astronomy: the Big Bang Theory! The universe was by no means eternal; it had been created—all at once? And Black Holes that swallowed up matter utterly and without a trace—into nothingness!

Meanwhile, young Alyosha was wasting his time in this lackluster school lab, memorizing some old rubbish paragraph by paragraph!

The whole thinking world was rushing ahead, flying, circling about, being transformed in a breakneck rush. He could not stay here any longer; he could not be held down in this backward town of B—, even if it did now have some factories. Would other people discover it all, invent everything, reach the very limit of what could be done and leave nothing for Alyosha?

He rushed to the university in the city, excellent student record in hand. He entered the Faculty of Physics, and for his first two years, he was delighted by all the subject areas that were waiting for him. He had to grab everything he could—more than just one area of specialization—not only because they were utterly fascinating but also because the more areas he covered, the greater his chances for success.

These were the two happiest years of his life. Alyosha threw all his energy into his studies, trying to learn and investigate everything he possibly could.

He was always confident of one thing: Whatever I take up, whatever job I set out to do, I will always succeed! (He also found time to be a Komsomol activist, never resting and always consumed by one task or another. He even restored an old car, a regular boneshaker, from what was no more than a pile of scrap someone had discarded, and every evening he would carry the battery up to the third floor of the student residence to be charged and then carry it down in the morning. The other kids laughed and jeered, but they were the ones who would ask him for a lift when they were late.)

Then in '86, after his first two years at the university (just at a time when new hopes for society were stirring!), something happened that seemed to break his life in two: he was drafted into the army for two years.

Couldn't they have done this earlier? Or waited until he graduated? Why did it have to happen right in the middle of his studies?

It was as if his air supply had been obstructed.

Never to be restored, perhaps.

Life had never been easy in the army, but this was the very height of the practice of hazing—*dedovshchina*. You could expect no mercy from anyone senior to you. Still, in those years Alyosha was not skinny as he was now; he was heavy and strong, knew how to throw a punch, and could hold his own.

The army assigned him to communications. Even there he tried keeping up by reading books on physics. But there wasn't much chance for that. He gave up trying.

Then he turned to reading the newspapers and watching television: he had to try to keep up with the life that was changing at such dizzying speed during his two years in the army. All sorts of "informal" organizations were springing up; people were spontaneously getting involved in unauthorized activities—something unheard of!

He came back from the army to his third year at the university—"his" university, though perhaps it was no longer his. Was it the right place for him? Yet it no longer seemed to be so. (He realized, though, that among the multitude of self-styled colleges, universities, and even research institutes that were now springing up, their university still maintained its tradition-ally exalted place.) It seemed as if the army had pulled out the pivot point of his soul—his love of science. He still earned only the highest grades, but what was missing was the constant sense of the *beauty* of science, a beauty that at times even sent shivers down his spine. What remained was not beauty but merely the opportunity for practical application. Or was it just the pursuit of whatever was profitable, as in all areas of our life now?

At this same time, the students were caught up in the rush to organize these now permitted societies and movements, and many were drawn into them. Alyosha was as well: If it's possible to seek justice for people, then how could he remain on the sidelines? This was a sacred dream he had cherished since childhood: to live not just for himself but for everyone! What he saw around him were only ramshackle structures groaning under their own weight and simply waiting to be torn down by a new generation with a new vision. The meetings! The associations! Some were permitted, others not; protest marches with banners would be allowed one day and forbidden the next. Much of the energy of protest went to these things and even to brawls with the neighboring cadets. Then came the interrogations by the state security organs. (Not long before he would have simply been packed off to prison, and no one would have said a word.)

Yes, indeed, life was now moving along many different courses. Then came a law permitting the creation of cooperatives. But to get permission to set up a cooperative, you needed a bit of influence somewhere higher up. At this point, right in the midst of these student disturbances and just after Tolkovyanov had been dragged off to the KGB, the first secretary of the party Oblast Committee came to speak at the university. He allowed questions, and Tolkovyanov stood up: The university is being remodeled, but it's not being done economically. There are cost overruns and wasted materials. Authorize us to form a student cooperative, and we'll make the repairs—better and more cheaply. And permission was granted! The kids rushed to their work. This was his first chance to test his business acumen, doing work he believed in, that could realize an actual profit. But then a wave rolled across the country from the opposite direction: Shut down all the cooperatives! And they were shut down.

In fact these were not real cooperatives, begun with no resources and no starting capital. A "cooperative" succeeded when its owners were backed by ready cash of undisclosed origins. Some of them produced intricate locks for metal doors or doorbells that rang with various melodies, or even dish antennas for satellite TV. These things were ready and waiting, but the consumers didn't rush to buy them: they didn't fully trust "Soviet" goods and wanted foreign products.

In the meantime, the news from Alyosha's former classmates now completing their studies was depressing. Graduation from the prestigious Faculty of Physics had always guaranteed a move into at least a corner of our triumphant world of science; it meant a place under the majestic arches of its thought, an entry into the separate regime of its leading scientific research institutes. But now these young folks had to look for work, trying for certain jobs and failing to get them. Something had happened to Higher Science; it was as if the air had been let out of it (the most severe blow came when funding was cut). Graduate students were in an even greater state of shock. You mean there are vacancies? Even more of them? That was because scientists were leaving the university and going away. Something enormous had come crashing down; the collapse had blocked the roads and left the students unable to breathe. Institute hallways stood empty; there were spiderwebs in the corners of the laboratories; dust built up on the desks.

Could you believe it? The whole of life had suffered a great fracture. It was an outrage! For what?

Alyosha, who had endured the break caused by his army service, was now better prepared to endure this one.

Yes, it was clear enough: he would have to find an entirely new way to live.

The buy-and-sell era had already begun. There were all sorts of new, unheard-of "business firms." Some had contrived ways to deal in state property, but within the framework of laws not yet equipped to deal with such things; and such firms immediately became hugely profitable. How could he stand apart from this era? He had to live on something, after all, and buy an apartment so he could get married (to Tanya, who was in her final year in the Faculty of Literature).

Alyosha tried to find a way to join one of these firms, then another—to find a place on their margins, as a helper. But he felt only disgust at the waste of his time and effort. How could he possibly devote his life to such rubbish, just farting around with no hope of doing anything creative?

But given the times, there seemed no other way. He could only marvel at how some of the party brass who had formerly been unapproachable, stonily standing guard over "the people's property," had suddenly been reincarnated as resourceful and rash entrepreneurs, eyes peeled for any chance to make a profit and any opportunity to scoop something up.

And what of these stock markets popping up everywhere like mushrooms? When he first visited them, Alyosha was stunned and deafened by it all so that his brain seemed to pulsate: the brokers, the middlemen, the speculating buyers and sellers of vouchers, stock certificates, foreign currency, the blinking indicator board, the rapidly changing legends on them—and everyone rushing here and there (guarding their attaché cases, afraid that someone might follow anyone who'd had a stroke of luck and knock him off). How could anyone live like that?

Yet you'd have to get used to it. Their company was formed of three clever friends, one also a physicist, the other a mathematician. They were all almost the same age; they thought alike and had similar views and hopes. They had many ideas, but ideas aren't money. They saw commercial banks springing up around them, some of them quite small. This business was totally foreign to them, though it appeared tremendously promising and ripe with possibilities because the former stringent regulation of state credit had made development all but impossible. But it was very difficult for a small bank to establish itself, since it was shaken by every tiny shift in the economic or political wind. Even before starting, one needed a good deal of bribe money to get a license to open a bank. And once it opened, one had to have some start-up capital. Fortunately, someone (a "sponsor" in the current parlance, and one with his own aims in mind) appeared to help them get started. They chose an impressive name: the Transcontinental Bank. They found themselves a spot in two basement rooms, and they explained to their first, startled clients: "This is just temporary. Our main office is being renovated at the moment."

No one could have predicted how it might have ended had not Alyosha met one of his old classmates, Rashid, who had dropped out of the university but had not gone into the army. They had been good pals in the past. Now they met, had a drink together, then another drink, and Rashid became a partner in the Transcontinental Bank. His own countrymen were behind him, and here, in this city, the links among these countrymen were stronger than elsewhere. His countrymen were also able to put them into contact with sources of money and help them work hand in hand with the oblast administration, which was also seeking out new ways of doing things. Before long they built themselves an impressive seven-story building, rented out the upper floors, and established their bank in the two lower ones.

Rashid was well connected, Alyosha had a clear head, and they complemented one another; the four partners lived in harmony, though they each held different equity in the bank. Tolkovyanov, like the first astronaut on the moon, was treading on unknown ground. But here too he figured out a new approach: how to manage clean and speedy clearing so that the rapidly disappearing Soviet trade links could continue to work for him. What helped more than anything, of course, was pure chance. With the constantly jumping foreign exchange rates, an accurate sense of the trends in the money markets could bring in amazing profits. Here again, Alyosha turned out to have a gift for correct guesswork.

Once the wave of success had begun to roll in, there was nothing to do but hang on as the wave rose higher and higher. (He had to concoct some explanation for his friends, who couldn't understand who had helped him rise this high.)

Still, he felt disgusted with himself. He could clearly see he was being drawn into one slightly shady deal after another, and into some that were far worse than shady. Yet there was no way to get by without that. And he wasn't alone, he had three partners. But perhaps this would only last to a point when he could put the bank on solid, honest money and shake off all this filth. Then, let's hope, there would be only reputable business. Would he ever be able to achieve full freedom of action? If he did, he would begin doing good deeds. The first one would be to support the schools; perhaps he could support striking workers to help them get what they wanted or, conversely, support some useful factory and keep it from bankruptcy—like the one that was using UHF waves to dry vegetables. We don't live only for the day; we give up something in one place and earn something in another.

But would he ever be able to break free from this world of fast-buck artists? He had already had dealings with some of these money-hungry swine, and they gave him the shivers.

He and Tanya had talked this over more than once. She was not just a good adviser, she was often a few steps ahead of him and not always in full agreement. She was even more anxious to have everything clean and aboveboard. But she also realized that this was impossible, that there was no way to get around it. They could drop the whole thing and squeamishly wash their hands of it, but then what? Sink into poverty?

Another thing was their relationship with the government. After losing its grip on everything in the country, the state bureaucracy maintained only the tenacity to smother businesses with incredible, absurd taxes, the likes of which were seen nowhere else in the world, and to crush them under a burden of regulations and heaps of paperwork, thus pushing everyone to do the same thing: to get around the law and to deceive. Apart from a few fools, everyone took this devious route. (But even this had its positive side: once the bank got fully on its feet, it would be able to pay the state honestly: we live in this state, after all, and we rely on what it provides. But one doesn't expect outright robbery from the state either.)

Then came the explosion.

Alyosha discussed it with his partners, but he was the one to make the final decision.

If they had already made one attempt to murder him, then would they not make another? Apart from his own pistols and, of course, the fellow with the submachine gun in the hallway of the bank, he had no cover, no one to defend him. And least of all, it seemed, the people from the Organized Crime Division . . . The Ellomas plant, now, as Tolkovyanov knew, had its own security, using some of its own people along with police from the Division and some outright criminals as well. All those strands had now become thoroughly intertwined and interrelated.

Was it really possible to keep them entirely out of our circle?

Was there any way to keep absolutely secure? Only if Alyosha immediately turned tail and headed straight out of the country. He had enough money to do that. That was precisely what everyone expected him to do. The whole city, at least everyone who knew, was expecting that. No one would have been surprised.

But how could he leave his organization, now three years old? News of the flight of the chief banker would immediately spread, the investors would rush in to take back their investments, and the whole enterprise would fly into tiny, useless fragments. The strength of a bank is the sum of the resources it can attract.

He and Tanya spent a few difficult evenings together.

They would talk, and they would fall silent.

So, are you prepared to let our little boy be killed by a bomb?

Another long silence.

Suddenly, as if just in passing, Tanya said:

"My grandmother used to say, 'A needle will serve when it's got an eye, a person will serve when he's got a soul.'"

That seemed to sum it all up. And even more: How could he get by, living abroad, unless he turned to the business of robbing or smuggling? Russian scientists? Yes, they are in demand over there, but not young, half-educated ones like me.

On the surface, life went on as before. But no one knew the struggle going on within him, and no one knew the decision he made: I'll stay here, as if nothing had ever happened.

Meanwhile, the housing cooperative decreed that Tolkovyanov was to pay for repairs to both entrance doors and the lobby. The damage, after all, had happened because of him . . .

Now that was painful: What business was it of theirs? And why should he strive if that was the only thanks?

During these same weeks, there was also a whole series of murders in Moscow, murders of some very prominent people. Some were shot, others killed by bombs.

He spent every day expecting something. It was terrifying.

He began wearing a bulletproof vest and traveling with an armed guard.

A new practice had taken root at the time: "A reward is offered for information leading to . . ." Why not try that?

He placed an ad in the newspapers: ten thousand dollars for anyone providing information about those involved in the attempted murder. He did it without much hope, just to try something. But, amazingly, only a day later, a letter mysteriously appeared: I have the information you need. I want eleven thousand.

This demand for such a tiny increase in the reward was surprising. It seemed to be a joke or an attempt to draw him into a trap. But the letter did propose a meeting during the day, in a crowded square in the city center.

But you're not going yourself! His partner Vitya, his friend since school days, took on the task. (Another person would be watching the meeting from a distance.)

The meeting went off, and there was no trickery. The man was prepared to give names. But now he wanted not eleven thousand but twenty-five.

Now that seemed more realistic. Vitya scoffed at the man, though: No, we won't give more than twelve and a half. You have to tell us who ordered it and who carried it out. And bring photos of them. (That seemed a more reliable way.)

The man faltered in some confusion. He thought for a time and then agreed. In the meantime, as a "deposit" on the information still to come, he said that the person who had ordered the murder worked in the Ellomas firm. He didn't know who had carried it out, but he would provide the name of the man who had ordered it.

The reward was paid.

Ellomas! Just as Alyosha had suspected. It must have been one of the senior people there, a manager.

So now what? When the partners met, they decided unanimously that they should go no further without help from the police.

Was that unethical?

But whose ethics were being violated?

Tolkovyanov phoned Kosargin.

YES, THERE WAS something to that young man. Kosargin had been deeply impressed by his meeting with him today. How could you ever expect it? Once he was just a lanky student playing at being a dissident. We should have packed him off somewhere deep in Yakutia and been rid of him. But now he has this lavish, seven-story glass palace and he's making these huge business deals. Businessmen line up at his bank when they need help to cover a temporary shortfall in their budgets. And he's staked out a place in this grim and foul age of ours as if he'd been born into it.

You, on the other hand, are over forty and used to law and order, and no matter how you twist and turn, you still can't fit yourself into this new world.

The Organs! Was there anything as eternal and unshakeable as they? Was there anything in the last days of the USSR that was more dynamic, more vigilant, more resourceful? What a group of select young people with higher education had poured in during the Andropov years! Kosargin himself had only a law degree, but alongside him worked physicists, mathematicians, and psychologists. A career in the KGB offered tangible personal benefits, interesting work, and a sense that you were having a genuine influence on the future of your country. These were the bright young lads who worked with the aging, ossifying veterans. (Though what a wealth of experience those veterans had.)

And suddenly this whole structure, more elegant and beautiful than the Moscow skyscrapers, did not collapse, to be sure, but was punched full of holes, and cold winds blew through the cracks that had developed from the misunderstandings, doubts, and the manpower drain of those who were frightened. Some left voluntarily, some through staff reductions, some moved to the management of the Union of Veterans. There were still others who were drawn into these same new businesses. The latter were first seen as traitors to the Cause; then they were envied as smooth operators who had struck it lucky; many wondered if there was still time to follow their example.

If only, through some miracle, the Organs could regain their former power, their significance. But could that ever happen? They'd let the opportunities slip past them. And where was it all leading? He did not have the mind to foresee it.

Kosargin despised the defectors from the KGB and would not allow himself to follow their example. But the cracks in the old structure, which had once been so solid, were opening ever wider, and the winds that blew through it carried away things that would never return. The most serious weakening had been in their self-consciousness, the loss of their Higher Purpose. And so Kosargin left—not as a traitor to the cause, but to take a position that was still of prime importance in this new and insane age: he joined the struggle against organized crime. (Should he have completely turned his back on what the new age could offer? That meant staying on and fossilizing in a job that, perhaps, would never be of use to anyone.)

And so, what about this young fellow? What surprised Kosargin was that he never asked for help. Was he still offended because of the incident a few years ago? Or was he planning to run off somewhere and hide? That didn't seem likely either.

He didn't refuse help for very long, however. He called within a few days.

Kosargin's staff had, of course, opened an investigation, if only formally and listlessly. Kosargin himself went to that same office again. Now, though, lying on the green table were three or four enlarged copies of American hundred-dollar bills taped together—was that a joke of some kind?

His favorable impression from the last meeting with Tolkovyanov was confirmed: there was something simple and countrified in his features; he looked you right in the eye, attentive and frowning slightly, though without fidgeting. All the while his voice remained calm and steady; he did not change his tone or grow flushed. This was not a pose; it was not put on and was entirely effortless. It must be his usual manner. Another attempt on his life could be made at any time, yet he betrayed not a sign of fear.

They discussed the arrest. A pair of plainclothes policemen had come to the square, near the spot where the last meeting had taken place. Had the man really become so careless? Had he never anticipated that this might happen? Tolkovyanov's friend gave a signal, and the man was easily arrested.

But indeed, he was so confused and out of his depth that he had brought no one to back him up. An even greater surprise was that he quickly confessed: he himself had attempted the murder!

What he disclosed was something quite trivial and almost comic. He, too, was a physicist, a product of the age in which he was living. Nothing had turned out for him, and he had already served two prison terms but been given early release both times. He looked absolutely wretched, someone you could push over with a feather. He had been unsuccessful at everything he had tried and become burdened with debt. His wife cursed him and then brought a proposition from her brother: he could earn ten thousand dollars by killing someone, but the murder weapon had to be a bomb. With no money, and suffering the constant nagging of his wife, he at last took up the offer, getting five thousand in advance. And then the attempt failed. Those who had ordered the murder were furious at getting mixed up with such a chicken-hearted fellow and meanly demanded that because he had failed, he must return not just the five thousand he had taken but double that sum. Then he saw the newspaper ad for the ten-thousand-dollar reward. His head in a fog, he first demanded eleven thousand but then came to his senses and asked for twenty-five. Then he showed them the photo of his brother-in-law.

Kosargin's men rushed off to arrest the brother-in-law, but he had disappeared. He had left some traces, however: he did work for Ellomas, though not in any senior position. There the trail ended, and no one else could be implicated. What they did have was the accused, alive and in their hands; his statements; a photo of the man closest to the person ultimately responsible; the speculations of the intended victim; and the observations of the investigators. Such was the case that was sent to trial.

While these things were taking place, Tolkovyanov had twice come to the Organized Crime Division to meet with Kosargin. Kosargin had a policeman's hunch that he had hit upon a vein of ore here, one that might well lead him much farther upwards toward the mother lode.

The mother lode? It was here that Kosargin ran into a stone wall: his bosses would not allow him to go searching for any mother lode.

He and Tolkovyanov discussed the case and then went on to speak about other things. Now that he had lost his own certain and clear path through life, Kosargin thought that coming to understand this young man who was obviously on the rise might help him regain his own sense of direction. Even now he wondered if he might not be letting some opportunity slip past him.

"Why don't we have a drink?" he suddenly suggested to the young man, even while reaching into the cabinet in the wall. Tolkovyanov nodded his agreement.

They began with the topic of honest business dealings. There were hidden forces with serious sums of foreign currency at work in their city, and they had become intertwined with ambitious, unscrupulous profiteers and outright criminals. How could they be eliminated? In fact, could they ever be eliminated? Would we ever be able to foster honest enterprise when, it seemed, the state was doing its best to suppress just such a thing?

Then the conversation turned to the state itself. And then—like pouring a liquid into connected vessels—it moved on to the Organs. What was their purpose at the moment, and how should they develop in the future? Were they simply self-serving or could they perhaps serve Russia as well?

When deep in conversation, Tolkovyanov had a particular habit: he would rest his elbows on the table and put his ten fingers together, moving them slightly to create various shapes. Was he putting together some sort of framework? Did this help him resolve the problem he was considering? His brows and forehead revealed a certain tension. Then he would shift his intelligent, calm gaze to Kosargin. Clearly, he found this conversation interesting.

All through these past days, he had never shown any sign that he was harried, overburdened, or frightened.

Their conversation imperceptibly changed direction until Kosargin found himself revealing to this person (a person he had dismissed as a young puppy not long before) his deepest concerns, not merely about his job but on much more cerebral issues: What was to be done? Would Russia be robbed blind? Think of the billions that are being sent out of the country! (This must have sounded rather droll, coming from one who was virtually the supreme crusader against organized crime in the oblast.)

Tolkovyanov was well aware of all this, but he stated his opinion calmly: The funds that were flowing out of Russia would flow back in a few years, in the next decades, at the latest; they would come of their own accord, and they would help turn the wheels of our Russian industry.

How could that be? The logged-out forests would not come back. And the treasures that had been dug from the earth would not come back.

"So you mean that the thieves will keep what they've stolen?" Kosargin objected, with genuine indignation. He had a fierce hatred for these money-grubbers. (Deep inside, though, wasn't he a bit envious of them . . . ?)

"Suppose they do keep their booty," Tolkovyanov said. "The money will still come back and form part of our gross revenue. Of course we can't get rid of all our criminals. But their money will be laundered in the same tub with their foreign investments."

No! Kosargin could not believe the outcome could be that neat and happy.

Tolkovyanov, trying to soothe him, continued: "And the brainpower that's been draining away will also come back—not the very best of it, perhaps, but still, not everyone we've lost will be able to find a place out there." It was obvious how painfully he felt the continuing flight of people looking for some warmer spot. And here in Russia, graduate students were now receiving ten-dollar stipends.

And on our streets? A couple of these well-fed mugs each stop their Mercedes at an intersection and hold up all the traffic while they have a conversation! The traffic cop timidly turns the other way. How is a career policeman supposed to watch that?

After a few glasses, when they had come to a better understanding of one another, Kosargin even ventured to say, casually: "Aleksey Ivanych. You're a man with a scientific and technical background . . . What do you think? What are *we* supposed to do in this damned society we're now living in? I mean, *us* . . ." He tried to make himself clear without venturing to use *that* word, *those* letters, but had in mind his former colleagues still stuck in the service. But also, what were we to do generally?

Tolkovyanov did not allow himself to smile, and with great tact and discretion tried to present some reasoned and sensible options.

On his way home, Kosargin passed the famous monument to the Warriors of the Revolution. It depicted some steep cliffs from which three heads projected—a worker, a soldier, and a peasant. The whole city, following the quip of some street comedian, called it "Zmei-Gorynych," after the three-headed dragon of Russian folktales. (And truly, there was a certain resemblance.)

He had to smile. How the times do change!

YES, INDEED, THINGS moved in the most unimaginable ways. Kosargin's job was an example. There were always some thugs with shaven heads and submachine guns guarding the Organized Crime Office, but the office was a lot more sophisticated than that. Kosargin wasn't stupid, by any means, but what wisdom did he have to impart to his onetime arrestee? Any smart person could not fail to realize that the system could solve nothing by itself: You might have the best cabin on the ship, but what did it matter if your ship was sinking?

The point is, are *they* capable of changing? Remember what Tolkovyanov was like at the interrogation. Still, there was no way a person could avoid thinking about the overall situation in Russia; that was true of today's KGB people as well. It wasn't always about oneself. Though these company men from Ellomas weren't without brains either, and if they managed to gain some political power, they would soon quadruple their capital.

. . . And so they went on. Two months had passed since the attempt on his life, and all was well. The investors had confidence in their Transcontinental and were not about to pull out their investments; they even increased them. Large-scale farmers began coming in from the surrounding areas; they came to them for money, not to the state sources and not to the Financial Division.

Then, at the end of April, Easter came. Tanya was busy baking Easter cakes and coloring eggs, something she had not done before.

"Please," Alyosha implored her, "this is all fine, but don't color any eggs. I don't want to touch any colored eggs. Easter cakes are fine, but don't even think of having them blessed by a priest. I won't eat them."

"Why on earth not?" A stray curl was hanging on her forehead. "Granny always colored eggs and had the cakes blessed. What's the matter, don't you follow our religion?"

"Our religion?" She had never said anything like that before, but perhaps she was right. What other religion would I follow? And it might well be that religion can pull a person out of depression and despondency. Still, what did the blessing of Easter cakes have to do with it?

Tanya came to him and placed her cheek against his: "Don't you realize that we were doomed? That we were saved by some Higher Power? What do you think was keeping us safe these past months, if not that Power?"

All right, one might say that. But there's also the theory of probability. And theoretical variants in any experiment.

There was, however, a different kind of explosion, the Big Bang.

There were also Black Holes.

And there was the incomprehensible foresight of the DNA molecule.

A FEW DAYS later, the attempted murderer went on trial. Even Kosargin was astonished: given that the accused had made a full confession and provided all the material evidence, he was sentenced not for attempted murder but for "illegal possession of a weapon" and given four years in a labor camp, and not even a strict regime camp.

Obviously, someone had given the wheels of justice a good bit of grease.

At this point, Tolkovyanov grew very alarmed.

He asked Kosargin to get him a copy of the photo of the accused's brother-in-law from the police files. But it—that particular piece of evidence—had disappeared from the trial documents without a trace. It was still listed in the file index, however . . .

None of the names of the principal managers who had ordered the murder were mentioned in court, but they could not but be aware that

Tolkovyanov *knew*. Then he ran across one of them on the street—ironically, near the university where he was going to sit in on a scientific conference as he sometimes still did. He forced himself to give him only a passing glance and to say nothing.

Should he flee somewhere abroad? This would be a way to save his wife, his son, and himself, of course. But Alyosha could not run away.

He would protect Tanya like some fragile piece of glassware. But he could not run away.

He was amazed at himself, walking around every day in this heavy bulletproof vest, a man with a submachine gun at his heels. He had taken a second apartment to give himself some room to maneuver . . . Who wasn't getting killed these days? Lenders were being killed for one reason, borrowers for another. His head was whirling: deposits, investments, deductions, balances, taxes, propping up businesses. But within all this intense whirl, even when he was utterly worn-out, he maintained one indestructible and unmoving point within himself: that was to follow—by chance, by what he heard from someone else, by some scientific article he managed to glance at—the latest developments in physics. He heard rumors of successful experiments by a group of our scientists who were able to raise the octane level of gasoline through irradiation. A monumental discovery! It would reduce world demand for oil. The Arabs learned of it and rushed here to buy the invention and then stifle it. Our side did nothing to support them; the scientists didn't care so long as they could line their own pockets. So they sold it.

But still, it was *our* people, Russians, who made the discovery! No, Russian science isn't finished yet, nor is Russian know-how.

"Just wait!" he imagined himself saying to someone. But saying to whom? The image of the person was blurred, but it was someone vile and hateful. "We'll get back on our feet once again!"

Still, it seemed that it was not the banker Tolkovyanov who was to restore Russian science. The government had established a foreign currency "corridor" to channel exchange rates, cutting down the furious gambling and huge profits. The state allowed banks to multiply but had no thought of supporting them. New regulations were coming to govern the banks' capitalization, liquidity, and stability. The weaker banks were now on their last gasp. The market for securities partially guaranteed by the state was still holding up, however. Those who had very distinguished clients were managing, but Tolkovyanov did not fawn upon these change-lings from the former party bureaucracy who barely deigned to give him a nod. And then the most serious thing: his partner-friends, forced into a tight corner, began having disagreements and then even split. What had happened to the enthusiasm they had all felt just so recently, when they were expanding on the leaven of their own success, when they chatted like old friends, happily placing their beer mugs on those silly mats made of enlarged hundred-dollar bills? Now there was one disagreement after another: No, that's not the way to build up capital; no, that's not where we should be spending. First Rashid, then the others asked to withdraw their shares, which represented most of the bank's resources. Money had brought them together, and money had driven them apart.

These quarrels were more unsettling than the decline of their business. Gloom settled over him.

When money is involved, there's no limit to the passion and the thirst for vengeance.

The circle of Alyosha's friends grew smaller. The whole situation in the world of finance had become a dark forest; you never knew when a pit might open beneath your feet or a dagger be thrust in your back. He carried on by guesswork: He bought a building in the city market; he set up two stores; he set up a dozen money exchange booths. But he was short of working capital and needed more credit. Where should he turn? He went to ask Yemtsov, one of his backers in the past and a man who knew he had to encourage a new generation.

Yemtsov had always supported him, but with a jolly familiarity.

"So, the greenhorn's here. Tell me, how's your little half-assed moneymaker doing?"

He was now almost seventy, yet he still had the same vitality, the same eye for the ladies, and the same agile body and mind. And how had he been able to survive all this? To fall from such heights . . .

Yemtsov recognized no obstacles: We've charted our course and off we go, no room for the gutless! We've hit a wall? So we'll find a way around it.

"You're stuck, are you? Need some help? Well, that's possible."

But what if you're not yet thirty? And they can kill you any day? And your friends are deserting you? And how many more mental convolutions will it take to find your way through this ever-changing labyrinth? Will you ever be able to get out of it?

And so he went on, lamenting the passing of the hope-filled years of his youth, his two years in the Physics Faculty before the army. Perhaps he should have stood his ground then and not changed direction. Perhaps he shouldn't have given in to temptation. He could see a light, far off in the distance, and it was growing dimmer.

Yet a faint light persisted.

1996

NO MATTER WHAT

I

SUPPER FOR THE reserve regiment was served at six in the evening, even though lights-out did not come until ten. Someone had correctly figured that the men would get by without any more food that way, and would sleep through until morning.

Lights-out may have been at ten, but no amount of political reading could match up against the long, dark November evenings, and the lights in the barracks were dim besides. So the soldiers were allowed to hit the sack earlier, and night inspection was done earlier, too.

Lieutenant Pozushan was company commander, a straight arrow not so much from service (they had been hurried through military school), but from his internal sense of duty, and the present dread moment for the Soviet Union. Bitterly he swallowed the radio news accounts from Stalingrad. We were barely holding them back, it seemed, and the lieutenant even wished their regiment had been sent there. He could find no peace on these dull evenings, could not even sleep. And tonight, as the hours dragged on to midnight, he up and went to inspect company quarters.

All quiet with the first and second platoon—only the dim blue light of the tinted bulbs. The stoves were already dark and had cooled. (The rooms were heated with tin stoves, with makeshift ducts leading out the windows. The old basement furnace had long stood dormant.)

At the third platoon, not only was the stove still hot, but five of the men sat huddled around it, bundled in their dark, padded jackets and pants, butts right on the floor.

The lieutenant entered—they flinched. And jumped up.

The lieutenant attached no meaning to this at first, but let them sit, just scolded them quietly, so as not to wake the others: Why weren't they asleep? And where did they get the firewood?

Private Harlashin answered right away: "Woodchips, comrade lieutenant. Picked them up over at the target range."

Well, all right.

"And why aren't you sleeping? Got too much strength? You better save it for the front."

They hemmed and hawed; nothing clear.

Ah, it's their business, after all. Probably telling each other stories about girls or the like.

He was already turning to leave, but suspected something. Up *this* late? And they certainly hadn't been expecting him. And the fire in the stove was weak—it could hardly warm them.

"Oderkov, open the door."

Oderkov sat right by the door of the stove, but gave a blank look: What door?

"Oderkov!"

Among them the lieutenant discerned junior sergeant Timonov, their section commander.

The soldiers froze. No one moved.

"What is this? Open it, I said."

Oderkov lifted his arm as though it were made of lead. Took the turn-handle, strained to lift it.

All the way to the end.

And with no less strain he pulled on the door, and pulled some more.

Inside the stove, amidst the glowing coals, was a round, soot-stained, standard-issue mess pot. A steam odor poured into the room, cutting through the foul air of drying stockings.

"What are you boiling?" asked lieutenant Pozushan, still just as quietly, not to wake the platoon, but very strictly.

It became clear to the five of them that he would not drop it. No avoiding an answer.

Timonov got up. Not very firmly. Arms at his side, but squirming. One step closer to the lieutenant, to be all the quieter: "Sorry, comrade lieutenant. We were on mess hall duty today. Grabbed us a few raw potatoes."

Of course! Pozushan only now realized it: Their battalion was on duty today and tomorrow. He had forgotten that the supply sergeant ordered a team to work the mess hall. And so they went.

A darkness slid, not over the lieutenant's eyes, but into his breast. Like silt muddying the water. Like dirt.

Not swearing at them outright but with a pained voice, he let out a plea to the fighting men, all of them now on their feet: "Are you nuts? Do you have any idea what you are doing? The Germans are in Stalingrad. The country is starving. Every grain gets counted! And you?"

What else to say to them, so mindless, ignorant, and unconscientious? What else to infuse into their backward heads?

"Timonov, take out the pot."

With the mitten that lay nearby, Timonov took the red-hot handle and, trying not to nick the coals, carefully lifted and pulled out the pot.

The bottom of the black pot was still covered with spots of glowing ember.

The embers burned out. Timonov held on.

The other four awaited their demise.

"An offense like this, why, this is grounds for court-martial!" said the lieutenant. "Very simple and easy: Just hand your names to the Political Department."

Something else unpleasant now tugged at him. Oh yes, that's it: Timonov was the one who had come to the lieutenant to ask if the regiment would write to his collective farm in Kazakhstan in defense of his family; they were being hounded for something. Pozushan couldn't remember what for, but it was clear he couldn't help; the regiment commanders would never sign a paper like that.

It came together oddly somehow. Either it made Timonov all the guiltier, or maybe less so.

The potatoes were boiling in their skins. Looked like about twenty of them, small ones.

And they gave off a teasing smell.

"Go pour out the water in the sink and bring the pot back. Quickly."

Timonov went, but not quickly.

In the dim light, the lieutenant scanned the faces of his silent fighting men. Their expressions were gloomy, complex. Biting their lips. Eyes down, or to the side. But outright repentance—no, he couldn't read it on any of their faces.

Heavens, what is this coming to?

"If we go off stealing government property, how are we going to win the war? Just think about it!"

Dull and impenetrable they stood.

Yet this is with whom we march. To victory. Or to defeat.

Timonov returned with the pot. One could not even tell if all the potatoes were still in it.

Those undercooked potatoes.

"Tomorrow we sort this out with the commissar," said the lieutenant to the other four. "To bed." But to Timonov: "Come with me."

In the hallway he ordered him: "Wake the supply sergeant, and put the pot in his custody."

He himself could hardly get to sleep afterward: a horrible episode, and in his own company! And he had almost missed it. Maybe this had occurred before? Lawlessness and theft are all around, and he didn't even suspect it, just learned of it by chance.

In the morning he closely interrogated supply sergeant Guskov. The latter swore that he knew nothing. Why, nothing even remotely similar had ever happened in the company.

Looking into Guskov's perceptive countenance, his little mobile eyes, Pozushan for the first time wondered: That trait, which he so liked in Guskov—his organizational capacity, prudence, and quick resolution of any difficulties that arose, all of which greatly eased the job of a company commander—could cheating also be a part of that trait?

Still early, before breakfast, the lieutenant went to battalion commissar Fatianov. This was a crystal soul, remarkably pleasant, straightforward, with big clear eyes. He conducted excellent political instruction with the men, not by rote, not in a mechanical voice.

Their battalion staff were assigned to two little rooms in a small house, across the wide square, which was used to place the entire reserve regiment in general formation, when necessary, or for marching drills.

It was a cold, dank November morning, foggy with drizzle. (And what is it like today in Stalingrad? The morning reports gave no clear picture.)

In the first room sat two middle-aged clerks, who hardly noticed the lieutenant's entry. Is the commissar in? They nodded toward the second room.

Knocked on the door. And opened it.

"Permission to enter." He crisply brought his hand to his temple (he was getting good at saluting). "Permission to address you, comrade major."

Major Fatianov sat at the battalion commander's table, but along the side. The commander was not in. At a second larger table by the window, all covered in papers, sat the quiet, mild-mannered captain Krayegorsky, the chief of staff. The major was without his overcoat, but in a cap. The captain was dressed for indoors, his carefully trimmed graying hair exposed neatly on his head.

"What's new, lieutenant?" asked the major, as ever both kindly and with a hint of a laugh, while leaning back in his chair.

Pozushan, with trepidation, reported everything. Four or five pounds of potatoes carried off from the kitchen and pocketed. There is suspicion that this could have occurred other times when his company was on kitchen duty. It is possible that this occurred in other companies, as well. The episode is directly suited for court-martial, but how can we go that far? (Not only out of pity for them, the fools, but heading for the front, it is also unwise to thin one's own ranks.) What measures, then? What punishment? Should the episode be made public within the company? Or within the battalion? Or not public at all?

The major narrowed his wide, clear eyes. He gazed attentively at the lieutenant. He was thinking it over.

Or was he?

He took his time with an answer. First he sighed. Clutched the back of his head—and here his cap shifted forward, its peak toward his forehead. Sighed once more.

"An exemplary case," he uttered with great strictness.

And sat silent.

Was the next step forming inside him? Some punishment?

"You know, lieutenant, you weren't with us the summer of '41. You didn't see what huge warehouses were burned. And what looting went on as it happened. Both in the cities and in the army itself. Good heavens, what a hauling-off!"

"True, I did not see that, comrade major. But even from military school I know: People steal. From the quartermasters to the kitchen-hands to the supply sergeants. We students were always like hungry dogs, always getting the short end. It's all the more reason to fight it! If everyone is going to steal, we will collapse the army's own supports."

The major yawned slightly.

"Ye-e-s. You have the right perspective on it. Educate your men that way; your company has a weak political officer as it is."

The lieutenant stood, a bit disheartened. He expected a firm and immediate decision from the commissar—and instead all was adrift. This was nothing like the commissar's own words during their political instruction.

The door now opened wide, and the battalion supply sergeant entered with dispatch, wearing a brand new padded jacket. In his left hand he carried by the handle an identical round mess pot, without a lid, except that it was a pure, clean olive green.

"Comrade commissar!" with a swing of his right hand to touch his ear-flapped hat. "The sample! Be so good as to taste it."

Taking the *sample* was indeed the job of the commissar of the battalion on duty. But this sample was over half a pot of creamy hot millet, enough to serve four, and heavily buttered, too, like nothing ever seen in the regiment's mess hall.

"Ye-e-s," prolonged the commissar once more, took off his cap, and laid it on the table. This revealed his wavy, slightly curled dirty blond hair, which always kept his appearance agreeable and well-disposed.

The supply sergeant carefully placed the pot on an unoccupied corner of the table. Next to it he set out three wooden spoons, still freshly painted.

"Have a seat, captain," the commissar invited the chief of staff. And Krayegorsky started shifting over, together with his chair.

The sergeant saluted and left.

The pot was steaming and giving off a delicious smell.

"The battalion commander is not here, why don't you join us, lieutenant," kindly offered the commissar, with a glint in his bright eyes, as if he was having a laugh. But not at lieutenant Pozushan's expense, no . . .

No!!

"Thank . . . you," Pozushan struggled to pronounce. His throat seized, as if choking.

Hand to cap in salute, with bitterness like never before:

"Permission to leave."

But major Fatianov looked on—open, approving, friendly, understanding.

"Life marches on," he said quietly. "You cannot turn it on a dime anyway, no matter what. You cannot change human nature even under socialism."

And with a playful squint: "Let them finish cooking those potatoes. No sense letting them rot."

The lieutenant saluted crisply one more time, turned himself to the left, and pushed open the door.

2

HARD TO BELIEVE, but just before the war, men were still hauling barge-loads of salt from the mouth of the Angara up to the mouth of the Ilim. They did it in teams, harnessed to a tow-rope. In places they would take horses along for a boost, and waited on some stretched until help came from a tailwind. They managed all right, three runs a season.

In time, a fleet of small motorboats plied up and down the Angara, and for another twelve years after technical school Anatoly piloted different craft down to the Tenisey. But in '74 they started impounding the river near Boguchany, and motorboats were finished. No hydro station, either: just a mess. Further upstream, the Bratsk and Ust-Ilim dams had already been put up, leaving fewer than three hundred navigable miles, and little more than a hundred of them, up to Kezhma, that weren't dead, that still had any life. On this remnant, the boy who once went by Tolik—himself now fifty—would pilot what turned up.

So it was today. Both captain and steersman, he sat in the cabin behind the wheel, dressed in a heavily worn blue jacket, and guided a jet-propelled cutter, with a salon full of guests below deck. His soul was all in knots. He ached for this last reach of the river—in her true, undefiled banks—as though the pain were his own: Can we convince them? Could it work?

The side window was slid open, and the familiar fresh breath of river air flowed in.

Over on the River Lena, lit buoys and markers were still intact. You could make as many runs as you can manage, and soon you would earn enough for an apartment. But here all the buoys had disappeared over the past twenty years, despite a guaranteed depth of just two feet. So you guide by memory, by wit, by a sharp eye. You must see every whirlpool ahead of time and note where it spins. Forward, and you read the river: all fifteen of the rocky shallows until Kezhma, with their slight elevation drops. But then no bankside slope, no rock, no cliff face, no little cape, no estuary could be confused with any other. It is only to the untrained eye that it appears all the same, like sheep in a herd, or like moose.

Moose and bears, for their part, had stopped swimming across the Angara: The water had grown much colder because of the Ilim hydro station. The waters of the Lena are so much warmer.

But the captain loved the Angara like his wife, and he would not trade her in for another.

Over the stately river, a sunny day was slowly breaking out. A glitter evenly covered the surface.

A line of white clouds stretched far beyond the right bank. But it would melt away.

The waters of the Angara are always quiet in June. From mid-August, the northerly wind will churn up hefty waves. August is also when the Sayan Mountains thaw and the big waters come rolling.

The low, narrow door from the interior stairs opened. The mechanic Khripkin squeezed through—head like a ball, body like a ball—and sat on the side bench. You couldn't fit a third into the cabin without blocking the door.

"What's going on down there, Semyon?"

Semyon may have been an unkempt fellow, with black, ungroomed hair and a face as if it was poured cast iron, but he had quick and perceptive eyes.

"Who wants anything to do with work, Anatol Dmitrich? Valentina Filippovna barely got started, but Scepura is already serving up drinks, right from early morning. The minister has his eyes on the appetizers, too, I think."

The captain took a course to the right bank, with a barren gradual slope in the distance.

It hadn't always been barren. Time was—an evergreen taiga stood here. Then a timbering camp was thrown up. The land was not part of the flooding zone, but adjacent, and the timber was valuable. So they clear-cut it. But once pine is cleared, it does not grow back; only aspen does, eventually.

Since pine logs do not sink, they were floated downriver. "All the local pine," he sighed, "just got jammed up senselessly near Boguchany, while in other places, look what great larch they took down! What birch! Except those logs sink, and there were no barges to carry them, so the trees still lie up there, rotting." He fell silent. "You try lying around like that."

"When was this?" asked Khripkin in his impatient tone.

"Ten years ago. Then seven."

"During perestroika, already?"

"Then too. One shipment after another. They threw up twenty-seven camps along this stretch, down to Boguchany."

Yet how much healthy forest stood even now, higher up in the hills.

He made his way to the left bank, since he could see a swirl gathering over the rocky shallows to the right.

Going with the current, the bow does not stir up the water.

A water not yet entirely robbed of its blues.

The repetitive rumbles of the motor could be felt all the way up in the cabin.

"If only he asked me," Khripkin figured aloud, "I would give him my piece."

The captain thought about it, without turning.

"Well, maybe go, liven things up a bit; just don't ruin it. We all know you have a . . ."

"I don't believe any of those bosses, whether the old ones or the new ones."

The captain turned around, by no means agreeing, but answering softly still.

"No, how come? You can talk sense with the new ones."

The mechanic sat a bit longer, glancing at the water.

He thumped his way down the stairs.

And came out into the front of the hall. Facing him were a few people on leather chairs that were bolted to the floor. Next to the minister— a hale and hearty fellow in a bright-colored summer suit—sat Valentina Filippovna. She kept a stack of papers on her knees, but carried on without looking down, without pause, with conviction. Behind them sat two from the entourage: one an athletic, broad-shouldered bull of a man; the other—with a big open notebook. Across the aisle was regional head Zdeshnev and a dried-up-looking fellow from Irkutsk, wearing a black suit.

Back yet farther, behind the seats, was a similarly bolted table, already fitted with a white tablecloth, two servers in white aprons carrying and setting down on it plates, bottles, glasses. Here too was the fat man Scepura, his graying hair in a crew cut, in a bright multicolor American sweatshirt underneath an unbuttoned sportcoat. He gave orders quietly, but with quick, sure motions of his hands.

The mechanic would have been happy to stand by and listen, but he was not endowed with a mug that belonged here. And he would have been even happier to have his say, but there was no butting in.

So he went—slowly, one steep step after another—down to the motor room.

Valentina Filippovna was chairman of the regional committee for environmental protection and rational use of natural resources. Although she was still very young, no one called her by the diminutive "Valya." She had an open face, a head-on look without any flirting mannerism, and she was chiseling away at the high-placed guest that had flown in.

"They started building the Boguchan hydro station two years before the project was even ready, such was the hurry. But it has been twenty years now, and the whole project has become outdated. Even at the intermediate level to which the water has been raised, the entire sturgeon hatch is dying. Musquash are dying by the tens of thousands. Nearer the dam, algae blooms are turning the Angara into a swamp."

The minister listened on—not just attentively but sympathetically. He shook his head in disbelief. Once or twice he signaled his aide, a slender man with an elongated, intelligent face, and the latter took notes down quickly.

She spoke with such passion, fingers touching her throat, as if it were about her own fate.

"And now, if the latest decree of the government is acted upon, completing the station to its maximum project height, it would mean flooding another half-million square miles. Underneath that land are more than 120 million cubic feet of peat. And a magnesium ore deposit, several hundred million tons . . ."

"Ore, too!" tossed the minister over his shoulder to the aide.

He was in middle age, naturally vibrant, alert. His tie, according to some new fashion, was lowered; and the collar was unbuttoned at the top. Leg over leg, even swinging back and forth at times.

To either side, behind the wide clean windowpanes of the salon, the bluish-gray river water rushed by; while farther off the banks passed by, now hill, now meadow.

The waterjet motor did not impede their conversation.

Valentina Filippovna, herself an applied chemist, a graduate of the Forestry Academy and with work experience at her back, did not stumble and did not tire in explaining to the high-placed guest—with an increasing hope—what troubles had already piled up; how the treatment systems at Bratsk and Ust-Ilimsk and the Baikalsk pulp and paper plant were unwisely applying chemicals that killed nature's own capacity for biological treatment.

The minister, one could sense, was calm, firm in his accomplishment, sure of himself. If someone like that takes up an issue—how could he not succeed?

. . . But there is more: All the timber that was hastily felled is now decomposing at the bottom of the Angara—it is giving off phenols and turpentine, so that the once legendary pristine waters of the Angara have degraded down to Class V, now even Class VI, the worst level of ecological hazard. But if one were to stop the completion of the Boguchan hydro

station, more than a hundred miles of running river could be saved, and in
those miles reached the Angara can cleanse itself. Otherwise, the whole of
the Angara dies; all of it will be stagnant water . . .

Even in her rather short service, Valentina Filippovna had seen her fill of
bosses who were endlessly calm, even if matters were falling apart in front of
their eyes. They were groomed to be that way; and they were all large, too,
following some rule of selection different from the rest of us. But this one—
no, he is different. And his is so highly placed besides! If this one speaks . . .
His youthful, perhaps cheerful look also gave her comfort for some reason.

The resourceful Scepura, having arranged everything back at the table,
walked up and, to ease the possible fatigue of the guest, invited everyone,
if not to break off the conversation completely, then to continue it at the
table. (Once or twice he looked askance: What is this activist doing here,
meddling about, breaking the rhythm?)

But the minister wouldn't bite on the offer. He wanted to hear other
voices, too.

That dried-up fellow in the black suit, the governor's representative,
kept silent the whole time, but looked on a bit sardonically.

Then Ivan Ivanovich Zdeshnev hastened to speak up. He was the
manager of the expansive district surrounding the river. He did not look
like much of an administrator. He had a simple snub-nosed face, a jacket
that wasn't formal and didn't match the color of his slacks. Still, he forced
himself too remember the importance of his own position, and the whole
confluence of troubles, and the high estate of his guest.

"You understand, I am sure, that I, as the *mayor* of these parts, am
under significant *pressing* from the population. We have all become hostages of the Boguchan hydro station here, of whether or not it will happen.
If it does, our livelihood will come to a poor end indeed."

He glanced at the minister's face to check if he had crossed the line
and spoken too boldly.

But the minister's eyes were filled with comprehension and a business-like significance. No, they exhibited no anger whatsoever.

What's more, the secretary in the back had written it all down in his notebook.

Ivan Ivanych knew well that there is a limit to permissible debate, that one must not argue too hotly. And yet . . .

"Look how Old Keul was relocated from the zone of flooding . . . It did not turn out overly well. The village is three hundred years old. The villagers wouldn't go, and that was that. So then they took to burning down the villagers' cottages. The villagers fought back with pitchforks and axes. All right, then, they left the cemetery alone for the time being. But they still resettled the villagers to New Keul. Turned out that place sat atop quick ground: no building cellars there."

No, even now the boss showed no displeasure. Why, he seems . . . like an understanding sort of person. So Ivan Ivanych came out with another example, having no shortage of them.

"In the hamlet of Kata—Kata stream is right opposite Iodorma, where we are headed—one old lady never did let them tear down her cottage: 'Kill me here, on the spot.' They left her alone . . . And so she catches burbot in wintertime, and piles it up frozen in the barn. They bring her bread by helicopter, in exchange for the fish."

He now caught himself, for he had gotten carried away, and laid out well too much.

"Be so kind as to pardon me, but the *imidzh* of a *mayor* does not permit me to be silent, either . . ."

In reality, the visiting boss was no minister, but only a deputy—the deputy, however, of a very highly placed minister indeed. He came here to sort out the privatization of the huge, clumsy local timber processing complex, which needed a rapid and sure exit out of the hands of the state—rapid, because privatization had not only many friends but likewise many opponents. A monster like that no one could buy, and no one would want it all anyway, so the solution was to break it up into forty-two enterprises. That had all been passed during the past few months, and the deputy minister came just to close the deal as soon as possible. This he had done successfully, and knew he would make his superiors happy. Now, these past few days, he kept being asked to take a ride down the Angara, so why not indeed? And today, in his last day here, they took off in the cutter. But who was this woman? Who got her in here? She is so hot and bothered about all this! Must be she's not married. He hadn't ever heard of this problem of a downstream power station, so now what? . . .

The cutter went onward, but they had not reached Iodorma as yet, and Scepura, in full frontal assault, persuaded the company to sit down at the table. He bustled about warmly, all cheerful, as if on a big holiday, even though the day was as common as they come. Shall we start off with some champagne?

Corks popped from two bottles, glasses filled with foam. Valentina Filippovna wouldn't even take a seat at the table, somberly refusing for a long time.

The whole of Ust-Ilim had known Scepura—the round-headed little fat man, energetic despite being on the wrong side of fifty, and quick with words—even as far back as twenty years ago, when he was an electrician hanging on ropes above the Angara, erecting the dam. Here they assembled the best from the whole Union, and he made the cut. After that, he took law classes by correspondence course, then was promoted to the prosecutor's office, then returned to the pulp plant. Here he managed worker life, then made personnel decisions, then headed up the administration, signing permission slips for people to return back to Russia, and was even nominated for deputy director of the whole timber processing complex. When everything turned upside down, he became merely a hotel manager, and here he was: catering, pouring champagne, entertaining, his assistants at the ready.

Before the good cheer settled in, the taciturn representative of the governor had occasion to tell the visiting leadership of a few more gloomy items, leaving it to the guests how to report the issue further. So many power stations were built in Irkutsk province that up to fifty percent of the electric capacity has stood idle for the past three years. It was planned that aluminum smelters would consume it, but those wouldn't be built even in another twenty years. So if one were to complete the Boguchan project now, where would one send the electricity? China seems like the only option, but a high-voltage line halfway across the Siberian taiga is a more expensive proposition than completing Boguchan station itself.

The minister was amazed. It was all hard to believe, yet a real government official was reporting it. The situation was only getting more complex.

"Yes, to be sure," he resonated in a weighty bass. "These solid arguments need to be taken into account."

Then the governor's representative added that the Boguchan completion was being egged on by the Krasnoyarsk authorities. They settled over twenty-five thousand people down by Boguchan to build the dam, and now they have no jobs.

The minister raised his brow. "Egged on" sure did not sound like a government term, but then, but then even this breaks through sometimes, it's only human . . .

The promontories receded, first on the right bank, now also on the left.

What breadth!

The men had started on the vodka.

The minister's cheeks acquired a bit of rose.

He glanced toward the windows on the right, glanced toward the left, then pronounced thoughtfully: "Didn't Pushkin make some mention of the Angara?"

But no one offered to take him up on it.

In the meantime, the cutter approached the left bank.

The whole company left the table and went ashore to stretch their legs.

The shy captain descended from the cabin, too. And the mechanic popped out of the motor room. Scepura's assistants, in their white aprons, scurried and scurried to set up right onshore, next to the water, to prepare a barbecue and soup from the fish they had brought.

In single file, they ascended the pockmarked bankside hillock.

. . . There, a village street ran parallel to the river with houses on one side, and deep behind it, another—much shorter—set of houses. The street was comprised of something like a road—but no wagon could make it through here; its axle would break in the ruts and potholes formed of dried mud.

Besides, it wouldn't have anywhere to go, in any direction.

Nor was it much of a place to walk or stretch: You could break your legs here.

With the motor off, silence stood over the entire Angara, on both shores, and for several miles beyond. Only the ring of mosquitoes by one's ears.

The houses, still undestroyed, stood in a row. One of them even had freshly painted light blue decorations at the roof-end. In front of it, the sides of a turned-over flat-bottom boat were painted with the same blue color. Along the row of cottages, not a single door, not a single window was open. On one house was a sign: "Everyday wares." The bolt on the door had rusted, but not yet the sign.

No one. No chickens to peck at the ground here, no cat to sneak by. Only the grass grows on, oblivious to tragedy. And the peaceful green treetops in the front yards.

Life had been here . . .

Then again, here was a tall pile of freshly cut thick branches, just the size for splitting into firewood. So people live here even now.

It grew warm; the day had heated up.

Suddenly a cuckoo. From across the Angara—how far that must be, yet how audible.

That is breadth. That is stillness . . .

All stood around in silence.

Then Zdeshnev called out lustily: "Za-bo-lot-nov! Niki-forych! Zabolotnov!"

Meanwhile, he explained to the leadership. This was the hamlet of Iodorma, twenty-two households in all. It had a clinic once, and a school through fourth grade, but now it has all been cleared out for flooding. Here, too, Irkutsk province ends, and Krasnoyarsk lies beyond. But Zabolotnov, sixty-three himself and with an old sick wife, wouldn't go anywhere. "Here lie my father and mother," he said, "and I am not leaving." Well, they let him alone for now. And so, in the new times, with collective farms disbanded, he has taken up farming on his own. What you see on the other side of the Angara isn't the bank, but two islands, with a sleeve of the river behind them. On the rocky island he keeps his calves, and on the fertile grassy one—the dairy cows. The milk is transported downriver by cutter. His wife cannot move about anymore, so he rows across the river at dawn and does the milking himself. He has plowed and planted there, too.

"He does all this alone?"

"No, he has his two sons with him. One of them painted these roof decorations. Their wives live in New Keul. They will be coming in summertime, bringing his seven grandchildren. Why, there he is."

He was walking from somewhere, a long rein hanging in his hand. Wearing sackcloth pants, a cheap color-drawn jersey and a black short-wool cap, he made a so-so impression, a nondescript, ragged little man, yet with a firm step. He looked over the whole scene from afar and understood it was the leadership.

He approached.

"Good health and greetings!"—his voice was not that of an old man.

No beard, and keeps up with his shaving. Face and neck look brown, with a wart on his cheek.

Only Ivan Ivanych extended him a hand, and shook it.

"So tell us, Nikiforych, how many head do you have?"

"Oh, used to raise three hundred. Nowadays, if we're not counting the leased-out cattle, seventy are left. And a score of horses."

Hard to believe he could run all this.

"So how do you manage?"

"Oh, I'd be managing a lot better if not for the scoundrel speculators. The regional co-ops fell apart. The meat plant cheats you. The milk plant cheats you. An honest buyer is what we need, but where do you get one? We can't get to market without our own engines, either."

Ivan Ivanych put his questions to Nikiforych, but set his eyes on the visiting boss.

"So how do you get your bread?"

"I can get up to twelve hundred pounds off an acre sometimes, after it's been fallow; that's enough for us. We grind it, and we bake it."

"Where are your sons?"

"Over on those islands."

"Two sons?"

"There were three. One drowned. Age sixteen," he sighed. "His boat capsized," he sighed again. His eyes, not wide to begin with, compressed further. "God gave him. God took him away."

He fell silent—and everyone stayed silent out of politeness.

Nikiforych, as if none of these arrivals was present, as if not seeing anything, faded out and quietly concluded, persuading himself: "I do love God."

Everyone became uncomfortable and awkward. They stayed silent again.

And now hobbled over his old lady, in a dark skirt and warm, brown knit sweater. She was carrying a clay pitcher, careful not to trip, and two mugs. These she placed on a wide log.

She bowed: "Fresh hot milk. Care to sample it?"

Valentina Filippovna: "Do I ever, missus. Thank you."

She poured, and began to drink, even closing her eyes: "Can't get this in the city anymore."

No one seemed to be drawn to the second cup, and so the quiet captain walked up from the back row, with an innocent look.

Yet he exchanged a conspiratorial glance with Valentina Filippovna.

He poured in silence, and began to drink.

Ivan Ivanych, meanwhile, had found a way to continue: "So, say, Vasily Nikiforych: How do you view the new life?"

Eyes alive again, he answered: "Seems it's taken a turn for the better. They never dispossessed my father, but they sent him, age seventy-five, to work under some kid. 'I am a landholder,' my father would say, 'and they stuck me under that pipsqueak.' He died of the bitterness."

Even while answering, Zabolotnov realized that these guests had not come to listen to his stories. In that case, it was obvious what brought them. So he continued: "Such a merry folk we had here, a working village. Fields were sown on every bank. A place full of life. Rye stood two meters tall. Every island in green. Hayfields. Cropfields. Potatoes sprout here—thirteen-fold. Now, all have quit. Hopeless. You break your back not knowing what comes next."

This boss seemed to be a listening one; he understands it all, nodding his head. What's not to understand here? Such a land of plenty—and to abandon it, put it under shallow standing water . . . But he answered cautiously:

"The government in Moscow has its reasons. One can't see them from here."

Zabolotnov didn't lose his nerve.

"So what about Moscow? I've been to Moscow once. The sky there is low. And people walk about in a herd."

Thus they stood, in a cluster on a random slope, some higher, some lower, beside two pits. The odor of smoke beckoned from the bank below, where the barbecue and fish soup were coming along well.

Zabolotnov finished his thought: "What course has been set—for river or for man—is the one to follow."

The untidy mechanic reared up from behind, walked around the others and fired off, looking straight at the minister: "And do we have any say?"

The boss readily turned with a receptive look: "Of course you have a say. We have democracy now. That is what campaigns are for."

It seemed the mosquitoes avoided the cast-iron figure of the mechanic—was it because of his smell? But then they flew past Nikiforych, too, like one of their own.

"And when there's no campaign? When a bear tears a cow to death, he doesn't just eat it; he lets it lie around, so it has an aroma."

The minister didn't understand, and crossed his brows: "What question are you talking about?"

The unkempt portly mechanic stared familiarly at the equally portly, albeit taller and carefully coiffed, minister.

"We have questions piled up taller than that rye, which used to grow here. You want a question: How about the timber complex, why did they rip it into forty enterprises? Now they have all stopped. For every man there are three foremen, and all are out of work. Meanwhile, those who broke it up lined their pockets with millions. And not in rubles, either. They steal in a big way, not like us—and they know how to hide it and not get caught."

The modest captain looked at the mechanic with reproach, but the latter didn't see him. He had been afraid of his getting wound up and rabid, ruining everything. All was coming together, and the boss seemed amenable: So speak gently to him. And not about everything all in one go.

The minister's lips grew willfully curled. And for the first time he said in a scolding voice: "Without direct proof, you have no right to make such statements."

But Khripkin was not a bit fazed: "Make statements or not, no one will hear us. Now then—all that is left of the Angara is this middle stretch, so let it go to rot, too? Whoever had a brain could produce electricity just by turning wheels in the current, without any dams. Instead they put up a whole series of them. And now we're going to finish it off? The water is not even warm enough for the fish any longer."

Valentina Filippovna fixed her gaze on the minister. No, he wouldn't just ignore this, would he? Hadn't it touched him? How could he not be inspired by the doomed breadth of this proud river, standing here over this reach? He must be feeling something.

He was sure to be feeling the bites of the mosquitoes, because he kept slapping at them, but even then his arm didn't twitch nervously, as if sure that it would reach and crush its target.

As for this greasy troublemaker, you cannot explain everything to him—and why talk specifically to him, anyway?

The mosquitoes were getting the better of the others too, just when the ever-present Scepura quietly reported that the food was ready. But—with the mosquitoes, and not to invite extra people—why not repair to the salon?

They descended to the bank.

Nikiforych stood as he had stood, legs apart. No motion. No surprise.

Zdeshnev found a moment to say to him: "Maybe, old man, we will get somewhere with this."

The mechanic walked alongside the captain. They had not been invited to the salon.

"This tourist? No-o, Anatol Dmitrich, you need to know their type. They are not going to reverse anything, no matter what."

But the melancholy captain kept hope.

Valentina Filippovna walked uncertainly, head bent down, trying also not to trip on her heels.

Down by the bank the boss caught up with her and said quietly, with sympathy: "Don't be downcast. All your arguments have been noted. They are going to be taken into account."

She threw up her head toward the minister joyfully: "Thank you!"

The cutter reversed course and started upstream.

The bluffs along the bank reappeared in the distance, then drew closer. Later, a crag passed by.

Back in the salon, the men boisterously savored their fish soup, with vodka.

Scepura held court the loudest: "Oh yes, I was, you might say, a manager with a future. But now, they broke me under."

Who doesn't let loose a bit with vodka, served with soup and a barbecue? The minister's face grew softer, redder, even more youthful. In a high position, you simply have to comport yourself with dignity. But here, we're all people; and there is a hot meal, too.

"I had more troubles at work than you'd expect, for my age," roared Scepura, "but I don't skulk about it. And I hate to hear how people say now that *all that* was unnecessary, the wrong path. What do you mean, wrong path? What about all our victories? What about Bratsk and Ust-Ilimsk?!"

It made for a good riverboat tour, all in all. That evening, board the plane and fly to Moscow. Then, in a couple days, a trip abroad. All these arguments, these doubts—they make sense, too, of course. But he remembered, quite suddenly he recalled, the words of that woman: "the *latest* decree of the government." . . .

"When was that?" he asked of the Irkutsk fellow.

"Three months ago, in confirmation of the previous one."

We-e-l-l, what was the purpose, then, of lunging toward the top, contesting the point: You would only harm yourself.

After all, he knew the lay of the land in the halls of power. If a decision is adopted, and even reconfirmed, there is no changing it anyway, no matter what. All will proceed according to plan.

glossary

Akhmatova, Anna (1889–1966): major Russian poet. Her apolitical poems of the post-revolutionary years were harshly criticized by Marxists, and she was forced into silence for some years.

Antonov, Aleksandr (1888–1922): member of the **SR** Party who headed the peasant uprising in Tambov Province in 1920–1921. He was killed in battle.

Bagramyan, Ivan (1897–1982): marshal, participant in most of the major Soviet battles in World War II. He served for a time under Georgi Zhukov.

Bedny, Demyan (pseudonym of Yefim Pridvorov, 1883-1945): poet, satirist, and propagandist for the Communist Party.

Belinsky, Vissarion (1811–1948): influential nineteenth-century critic. His approach to literature was later adapted to form one of the central components of the official Marxist-Leninist socialist realist aesthetic.

Beria, Lavrenty (1899–1953): from 1938 to 1946, the powerful minister of the interior, who controlled the security forces and administered the labor camps. After Stalin's death he was appointed as first deputy prime minister and reappointed to head the **MVD**. He was arrested on June 26, 1953 by Khrushchev and others within the leadership and, after a secret trial, was executed on December 23 of the same year.

Beskin, Osip (1892–1969): art critic and journalist.

Bezymensky, Aleksandr (1898–1973): poet and early proponent of proletarian literature, active in **RAPP** and **Litfront**.

Blyukher (Blücher), Vasily (1889–1938): Civil War hero and military commander arrested in 1938 during Stalin's purge of Red Army commanders. He died in prison.

Bruski: novel by Fyodor Panfyorov (1896–1960), which tells of peasant life during the time of collectivization.

Budyonny, Semyon (1883–1973): commander of the 1st Cavalry Army during the Civil War. As commander-in-chief of the southern and southwestern fronts in World War II, he was blamed for the Battle of Kiev, the worst disaster ever suffered by the Red Army. Nevertheless, he continued to enjoy Stalin's favor.

Bulganin, Nikolai (1895–1975): political officer and, with Khrushchev, member of the collective leadership after Stalin's death.

Cement (*Tsement*): 1925 novel by Fyodor Gladkov (1883–1958). The novel deals with the restoration of a cement plant by a communist activist and set the pattern for later "production novels."

Cheka: an abbreviation from the Russian Extraordinary Commission (*Chrezvychainaia komissiia*), formed in December 1917 as the military and security agency of the Bolshevik government. In 1922 it was replaced by the GPU (State Political Administration), a department of the NKVD (People's Commissariat for Internal Affairs of the Russian Republic), but in 1923 it became subordinate to the Council of People's Commissars of the USSR as the OGPU (All-Union State Political Administration). Subsequent administrative reorganizations brought new names for the security services: the NKGB, the MGB, the MVD and, from 1954 to 1991, the KGB. Despite the name changes, those who served in the "organs" often referred to themselves as Chekists.

Chernyshevsky, Nikolai (1828–1889): literary critic, novelist, revolutionary, and nineteenth-century Russia's most prominent radical journalist. His ideas helped shape Soviet approaches to literature and art.

Chubar, Vlas (1891–1939): Soviet politician and party official. From 1923 to 1934 he was prime minister of the Soviet Ukrainian Republic.

Chuykov (Chuikov), Vasily (1900–1982): commander of the 62nd Army that defended Stalingrad; he later commanded Soviet occupation forces in Germany.

Czechoslovak Legions: After the Russian Revolution and Russia's abandonment of the war in 1917, a force of 40,000 to 50,000 Czechs and Slovaks, former prisoners of war, were to be evacuated via the Trans-Siberian Railway to fight with the Allies on the western front. As they traveled eastward, they became involved in the Russian Civil War, often fighting against the Bolsheviks and taking control of large sections of the railway.

The Death of Ivan the Terrible (*Smert' Ivana Groznogo*): 1866 play by Aleksei Konstantinovich Tolstoy (1817–1875); with *Tsar Fyodor* (*Tsar' Fedor Ioannovich*, 1868), it forms part of his historical trilogy.

Denikin, Anton (1872–1947): former tsarist general; from 1918 to 1920 he commanded the White Army forces in southern Russia.

desyatina: a traditional unit of land measure, 2.7 acres, used until Russia adopted the metric system in 1924.

Dobroliubov, Nikolai (1836–1861): influential radical journalist and literary critic. His 1859 article "The Dark Kingdom" viewed the plays of **Aleksandr Ostrovsky** as social documents revealing the oppressive nature of the world of Moscow merchants and, by implication, of Russia itself. In his "Ray of Light in the Dark Kingdom" (1860), he claimed to find a symbol of revolution in another Ostrovsky play.

Extraordinary Commission: see **Cheka**.

Fellow Travelers (*poputchiki*): Soviet writers of non-proletarian origin who accepted the 1917 Revolution while practicing an art largely independent of Marxist ideas.

Forward, Time!: 1932 novel by Valentin Kataev (1897–1986). The novel deals with the construction of a metallurgical plant during the first five-year plan and has become a classic of socialist realism.

Friche, Vladimir (1870–1929): literary scholar and theoretician of the sociological method. His books of the 1920s set forth an uncompromisingly materialist view of the history of literature and art.

Frunze, Mikhail (1885–1925): outstanding commander of Bolshevik forces during the Civil War. He died on the operating table under mysterious circumstances.

Futurists: a diverse group of poets and artists who rebelled against the art of the past and found inspiration in urban and technological themes. In the years before World War I, they practiced experimental, avant-garde art. Many futurists tried to adapt themselves to the new Soviet order (see **Lef**), but by 1930 futurism had ended.

Golikov, Filipp (1900–1980): political officer, later marshal. After some successes in high military commands, he suffered a significant defeat near Voronezh and lost control of his troops. General Zhukov was called in to repair the situation.

GPU: see **Cheka**.

Grechko, Andrei (1903–1976): marshal, minister of defense from 1967 to 1976.

How the Steel Was Tempered (*Kak zakalialas' stal'*, 1932–34): fictionalized autobiography by Nikolai Ostrovsky (1904–36); regarded as a classic of socialist realism.

Industrial Party: a group of prominent engineers and industrial planners accused of "wrecking" and counterrevolutionary activity. Their trial, in November–December 1930, was one of the first of the show trials of the 1930s.

The Iron Flood (*Zheleznyi potok*): 1924 novel by Aleksandr Serafimovich (1863–1949) depicting the transformation of a disorganized mass into an effective fighting force by a Bolshevik leader.

Kaganovich, Lazar (1893–1991): Soviet political figure and Communist Party official; a close associate of Stalin. In 1957, he, **Molotov**, and **Bulganin** participated in a failed coup against Khrushchev. He was forced to resign his posts and in 1961 was expelled from the party.

Kerensky, Alexander (1881–1970): Russian political leader, active before and during the 1917 Revolution. He headed Russia's Provisional Government from July to November 1917.

Khalkhin Gol: river in Outer Mongolia on which Soviet and Mongol troops fought off fierce attacks by the Japanese between June and September 1939.

Kikvidze, Vasily (1895–1919): commander of a Red Army unit active in suppressing the Tambov uprising; killed in battle.

Kirponos, Mikhail (1892–1941): colonel general who succeeded Zhukov in commanding the Kiev Military District. He attempted to repulse the German advance on Kiev but found himself surrounded. Stalin refused him permission to withdraw his forces, and Kirponos was either killed or committed suicide.

Kirshon, Vladimir (1902–1938): dramatist. His play *The Rails Are Humming* (*Rel'sy gudyat*, 1925) deals with industrialization. His best-known play, *Bread* (*Khleb*, 1930) looks at collectivization and the liquidation of the **kulaks**.

Kogan, Pyotr (1872–1932): Marxist critic and literary historian; proponent of a rigidly sociological view of art.

Kolesnikov, Ivan (1860–1920): former tsarist officer who commanded a Cossack force against the Reds in the Civil War.

Koltsov, Aleksei (1809–1842): poet best known for his lyrical verse on peasant life and the Russian countryside.

Komsomol: abbreviation for the Communist Union of Youth (*Kommunisticheskii soiuz molodezhi*), the youth division of the Communist Party. Young people between the ages of fourteen and twenty-eight were eligible for membership.

Konev, Ivan (1897–1973): marshal; he led Soviet troops in the liberation of much of Eastern Europe.

Kotovsky, Grigory (1881–1925): noted Red Army cavalry commander in the Civil War.

Kovtyukh, Yepifan (1890–1938): Civil War hero and victim of Stalin's purges.

Krylov, Ivan (1769–1844): journalist, dramatist, and writer of satirical fables.

Kulak: strictly speaking, a peasant with enough means to own a farm and hire labor. The Bolsheviks used the term to describe peasants who were only marginally better off than their fellow villagers or those who resisted Stalin's forced collectivization of agriculture. In 1930 Stalin called for "the elimination of kulaks as a class," and millions were arrested, exiled, or killed.

Lef: The Left Front of the Arts, a literary group formed in 1922, whose members came largely from the pre-war **Futurist** movement. The movement aimed to solidify an alliance between the former Futurist avant-garde and the new Soviet regime.

Litfront: a short-lived literary group that emerged from **RAPP** in 1930.

Lyubov Yarovaya: 1925 drama by Konstantin Trenyov (1876–1945).

Malenkov, Georgi (1902–1988): one of Stalin's closest associates. In September 1953, he and Nikita Khrushchev took power as a dual leadership, but Malenkov was forced to resign in 1955.

Mamontov, Konstantin (1869–1920): Cossack general who commanded the 4th Don Cavalry Corps with the White Army; noted for his daring raids behind Soviet lines in August and September 1919.

Mekhlis, Lev (1889–1953): political officer, colonel general, and close confidant of Stalin. He represented the Soviet GHQ in the Crimea from late December 1942 to May 1943 but was unable to hold the Kerch Peninsula and was relieved of his command, though he remained in Stalin's favor.

Meretskov, Kirill (1897–1968): marshal; he held important commands on the Leningrad front and from August 1940 to January 1941 served as chief of the general staff. In June 1941, he was arrested and confessed, after interrogation, to involvement in a military conspiracy. He was released a few months later, but his evidence was used against other officers.

Molotov, Vyacheslav (1890–1986): politician and diplomat, leading figure in the Soviet government from the 1920s. He formed a short-lived alliance with **Beria** and **Malenkov** after Stalin's death.

MVD: see **Cheka**.

Nekrasov, Nikolai (1821–1878): poet and publisher, known for his sympathetic portrayals of the tribulations of peasant life. In 1877 the painter Ivan Kramskoy (1837–87) depicted the fatally ill Nekrasov lying in bed.

NEP-men: From 1921 to 1928 the Soviet regime instituted the New Economic Policy (NEP), a period of limited private enterprise to help restore the economic life of the country after seven years of war, revolution, and civil war. Many small businessmen, who were known as "NEP-men," prospered during this period.

NKVD: see **Cheka**.

Novikov, Aleksandr (1900–1976): chief marshal of aviation in World War II. He was arrested in 1946, tortured, and forced to make a false confession implicating Georgi Zhukov in a conspiracy.

October (*Oktyabr'*): literary group and journal formed in 1922 by young Communist writers who wished to create a new proletarian culture. They fiercely opposed all non-proletarian literary groups, and particularly targeted **Voronsky's Pereval**.

OnGuardists: writers and critics grouped around the journal *On Guard* (*Na postu*). The journal was uncompromisingly opposed to non-communist and non-proletarian writers.

Ostrovsky, Aleksandr (1823–1886): prominent nineteenth-century dramatist, best known for his plays set in the milieu of conservative business people.

Pereval (The Mountain Pass): literary grouping that developed around the journal *Red Virgin Soil* and the ideas of **Aleksandr Voronsky**. Though nominally Marxist, the group rejected the emphasis on ideology and party guidance advocated by **RAPP**.

Pereverzev, Valeryan (1882–1968): literary scholar and theoretician of the sociological method. He attempted to apply Marxist ideas to literature and called for the rigid application of economic determinism to the study of literature, an approach for which he was charged with "vulgar sociologism" and arrested in 1938.

Pieck, Wilhelm (1876–1960): first president of the German Democratic Republic, 1949–1960.

Pilnyak, Boris (pseudonym of Boris Vogau, 1894–1938): major Soviet novelist and short story writer of the 1920s. His early works in particular were written in a mannered, "ornamental" prose and were severely attacked by "proletarian" critics.

RAPP: acronym for the Russian Association of Proletarian Writers. It was the most influential proletarian literary organization from 1928 to 1932 and called for literary realism informed by Marxist-Leninist values. Although it claimed to represent the official line in literature, it was liquidated in 1932 along with all separate literary groups.

Rokossovsky, Konstantin (1896–1968): cavalry commander. He was arrested, imprisoned, and tortured in 1937 but released in 1940. He served under General Zhukov during the battle to defend Moscow. After the war Stalin appointed him Poland's minister of defense.

The Rout (*Razgrom*): short novel (1927) by Aleksandr Fadeev (1901–1956), considered a classic of socialist realism.

Rybalko, Pavel (1894–1948): marshal, noted specialist in armored warfare.

Scorpio (*Skorpion*): publishing house that existed from 1900 to 1916 to promote the symbolist movement.

Shakhty Affair: In 1928, fifty-three engineers and technicians were accused of sabotage in the coal mining industry. Their widely publicized trial took place from May to July of that year.

SMERSH: Russian acronym for "Death to Spies" (*Smert' shpionam*), the wartime counterintelligence directorate of the Soviet Army.

Smithy (*Kuznitsa*): group of proletarian writers, most of them poets, formed in 1920.

Shaposhnikov, Boris (1882–1945): marshal, talented military administrator. He served as chief of the general staff in 1940–1941.

Shcherbakov, Aleksandr (1901–1945): colonel general; close associate of Stalin; held many important posts in the party and government, including that of head of the Red Army's political administration.**SR (Socialist Revolutionary):** a member of the Socialist Revolutionaries, an important political party in early twentieth-century Russia. Its roots were in the earlier populist movement, and it enjoyed broad support among the peasantry. The party was essentially destroyed by the Bolsheviks during and after the Civil War. A "Combat Organization" within the party subscribed to terror as a political weapon and was responsible for assassinations of a number of high-ranking officials. This organization supported itself by "expropriations" in the form of bank robberies and blackmail.

Suslov, Mikhail (1902–1982): major Soviet political figure during the Cold War. He led the conservative resistance to Khrushchev's reforms.

Telegin, Konstantin (1899–1981): lieutenant general, political officer; Zhukov's deputy during his term as commander of Soviet occupation forces in Germany. In 1948 he was arrested for alleged corruption and sentenced to twenty-five years in prison but was rehabilitated after Stalin's death.

Timoshenko, Semyon (1895–1970): marshal, close associate of Stalin. Although a competent commander, he suffered a serious defeat at the Second Battle of Kharkov and was removed from front-line command by Stalin.

Tukhachevsky, Mikhail (1893–1937): marshal and head of the Red Army from 1925 to 1928. He played a key role in the modernization of the Red Army in the 1930s but was arrested in May 1937 on charges of treason and espionage and executed in June of the same year.

Uborevich, Yeronim (1896–1937): former tsarist officer; held important commands during and after the Civil War. He fell victim to Stalin's purges and was executed along with **Tukhachevsky** in June 1937.

Ulagai, Sergei (1875–1945): commander of a Kuban Cossack division that fought the Bolsheviks during the Civil War. In August 1920 he landed a large body of troops from the Crimea in the Kuban area in hopes of rallying the Kuban Cossacks against the Reds.

Ulbricht, Walter (1893–1973): first secretary of the East German Socialist Unity Party from 1950 to 1971.

Vagranka (The Cupola Furnace): short-lived group of proletarian writers.

Vasilevsky, Aleksandr (1895–1977): former tsarist officer; one of the most effective Soviet commanders during World War II. He was chief of the general staff from 1942 to 1945.

Vatutin, Nikolai (1901–1944): military commander; served in many staff positions and led troops in the defense of Leningrad, the defense of Moscow, and the Battle of Stalingrad. He was fatally wounded in a clash with Ukrainian nationalist partisans.

Vlasov, Andrei (1900–1946): commander of the Soviet 2nd Shock Army. He was captured by the Germans in July 1942 and with their encouragement formed the Russian Liberation Army of several hundred thousand Soviet war prisoners to fight against Stalin. After the war ended he was kidnapped from Europe by Soviet troops and executed in Moscow in 1946.

Voronov, Nikolai (1899–1968): artillery specialist and marshal of artillery (1944).

Voronsky, Aleksandr (1884–1937): Marxist literary critic and theorist. Skeptical about the possibilities for a separate proletarian literature, he supported the **Fellow Travelers**, for which he was severely attacked by Marxist literary groups.

Voroshilov, Kliment (1881–1969): military commander and politician, close associate of Stalin. His leadership of Soviet troops during the Winter War with Finland (1939–1940) was disastrous, and his failure to prevent the Germans from surrounding Leningrad led to his replacement by Georgi Zhukov.

verst: from Russian *versta*, a pre-revolutionary unit of length, about 0.66 mile. Although abandoned when Russia adopted the metric system in 1917, it remained in popular usage long thereafter.

Vrangel (Wrangel), Pyotr (1878–1928): former officer in the tsarist army who commanded anti-Bolshevik (White) forces in southern Russia in the later stages of the Civil War.

Vuchetich, Yevgeny (1908–1974): Soviet sculptor, major representative of the socialist realist style, and specialist in military monuments.

A Week (*Nedelya*): early proletarian novel (1925) by Yury Libedinsky (1898–1959).

Workers' Faculty (*Rabfak*): post-revolutionary institutions that prepared workers for study in institutes of higher education.

Yakir, Iona (1896–1937): Red Army commander. In the 1930s he worked closely with **Mikhail Frunze** to modernize the army. He was arrested in 1937 and executed along with **Tukhachevsky**.

Yeliseev: a luxurious food emporium, in operation in Moscow since 1898.

Yeryomenko, Andrei (1892–1970): general who held many important commands during World War II and who helped plan the defense of Stalingrad.

Young Pioneers: an organization for children ages ten to fifteen, formed in part to replace the scouting movement and instill Soviet values in its members. Virtually all children joined the movement.

Zinoviev, Grigory (1883–1936): Bolshevik revolutionary and Soviet politician. He broke with Stalin in 1925, was arrested in 1934 and tried in 1935 and again in 1936.